THE
WRONG
STUFF

THE WRONG STUFF

*The Adventures and Misadventures
of an 8th Air Force Aviator*

TRUMAN SMITH

University of Oklahoma Press
Norman

This book is dedicated to my wife
Margot H. Smith
and our children, Rex and Simone,
and grandchildren,
Heather, Kayla, Ryan, Ian and Rylee

Library of Congress Cataloging-in-Publication Data

Smith, Truman, 1924–
    The wrong stuff : the adventures and misadventures of an 8th Air
Force aviator / Truman Smith.
        p.   cm.
    Includes index.
    ISBN 978-0-8061-3422-2 (paper)
        1. Smith, Truman, 1924– 2. United States. Air Force. Air Force,
8th—Biography. 3. World War, 1939–1945—Personal narratives,
American. 4. World War, 1939–1945—Aerial operations, American.
5. World War, 1939–1945—Germany. I. Title.

D790.S588 2002
940.54'213'092—dc21
[B]
                                                            2001055699

The paper in this book meets the guidelines for permanence and durability
of the Committee on Production Guidelines for Book Longevity of the
Council on Library Resources, Inc. ∞

6   7   8   9   10

CONTENTS

FOREWORD

Truman Smith's war was in the skies of Europe. while mine was on the islands of the Pacific. Even so, a world apart, the contrast of our experiences has served as a bond to our half-century friendship.

We met as students on the G.I. Bill after the war at the Pasadena Playhouse. And while we both went into various roles as *Story Tellers* in Hollywood, we overlooked our personal stories. However, True has finally given us an exciting part of his life in *THE WRONG STUFF*.

If I were asked to direct a reader of this story, I would suggest it be read with the mind of a 1940's twenty year old; in some ways more naive than a twenty year old of today. For this a *period piece*, not contemporary, and should be regarded as a unique piece of history and given consideration a reading Steinbeck of the 1930's or Hemingway of the 1920's.

Unlike the postwar "ME" generation, the very real question of whether we would win or lose the war made us a "WE" generation. In transition from a Great Depression, *SURVIVAL*, not self-gratification, was crucial.

TRUE points out the basic instincts of survival and sex that drives us humans, but it is survival to which he gives the higher priority in telling it like it was. This is not to say that he ignores the cause of the postwar Baby Boom. God knows, fighting men, out of necessity, generate a lot of testosterone. Yet, in honesty, sex lacked the exuberance exploited in today's entertainment.

While certainly entertaining, the purpose of *THE WRONG STUFF* is in telling it like it was, because it is not a novel, but *THE REAL STUFF*.

BURT KENNEDY, screenwriter, producer, and director, is the author of BURT KENNEDY, HOLLYWOOD TRAIL BOSS, in which he recalls working with such notable Western actors as John Wayne, Kirk Douglas, James Garner, etc. . .

FOREWORD

As a longtime friend with a similar career, Truman Smith asked for my reaction to his story *THE WRONG STUFF*. My first response was that the title was wrong, because it suggested the flip side of the popular hero image.

However, into reading the book I realized the abundance of *THE WRONG STUFF* in the grim reality of flying combat in the hostile skies of Europe during World War Two and I recalled another dear friend of mine in cadet training, killed in a midair collision of two B-17 bombers. Not yet in combat, 20 young men snuffed out, because somebody did something "WRONG."

But would anyone really want to re-suffer the agonies dredged up by *THE WRONG STUFF?*

Yes. There was the then young bride whose husband, a ball turret gunner on a B-17 crew, did not return. Other wives, mothers, fathers, friends, children and now grandchildren yearned for information about their loved ones no longer alive. Maybe it was wrong for Truman to open the *Pandora's Box*. On the other hand, some incidents cannot be closed until they are better understood.

Truman Smith brings a unique insight into his Right of Passage, both terrifying as well as humorous, which he shared with others confronted by the ultimate test of combat in the persistent shadow of *THE WRONG STUFF*.

Being with Truman in the cockpit is to experience and to know the challenges. Being with him in London, rushing to live his fullest before *THE WRONG STUFF* ends his tomorrows, is to know the frustration of losing a "sure thing" in the blackout.

This is an exciting adventure for those who were and for those who were not there.

Carlton F. Weber
Lt. Colonel, U.S. Air Force, Retired

PREFACE

As the author of *The Wrong Stuff* I am grateful to the University of Oklahoma Press for their courage in breaking with the tradition of publishing scholarly works by printing my unscholarly effort to tell it like it was in the greatest air war in history.

This prologue is also an epilogue, in that it is both a beginning and an ending, a survey of the actions and reactions to the book. It might be called "foresight" and "hindsight," as I attempt to give the reader an in-sight into the experience of its production and reception.

I was both elated and disappointed when the first printing by Southern Heritage Press sold out, concluding our agreement, and leaving me a Successful Failure as an author – without books to sell. The book's popularity had exceeded my expectations by being accepted into the Air Force Museum; the American Air Museum at the Imperial War Museum, Duxford, England; the Smithsonian Institution's National Air and Space Museum in Washington D.C.; the Mighty 8th Air Force Museum in Savannah, GA; the Pima Air Museum in Tucson, AZ; the Commemorative Air Force in Midland, TX; the 385th Bomb Group Memorial and Museum in Perle, Luxembourg; Texas Military Forces Museum, Austin, TX; Flight of the Phoenix Aviation Museum, Gilmore, TX; Wisconsin Veterans Museum, Madison, WI; Grant County Museum, Ulysses, KS; Sam Houston Memorial Museum, Huntsville, TX; and by readers from around the world. It had even been required reading at the U.S. Air Force Academy in Colorado Springs, CO.

Okay, it was a good start, but I did not have any more books to fill outstanding orders. While Carlton F. Weber, a longtime friend and retired Air Force Lt. Colonel, had encouraged (and even pushed) me into writing the book, it was Nedwin C. Hockman, Emeritus Professor of Film and Video Studies at OU, also a retired Air Force Lt. Colonel and a very biased friend, who took his copy of *The Wrong Stuff* to the OU Press and recommended they get it back in print.

I couldn't help but think how ironic it was that, in the beginning, an agent in New York had judged the book unworthy, because it was about World War II, which had happened a long, long time ago, and, therefore, that nobody would be interested in it. But then, that was before Tom Brokaw brought forth *The Greatest Generation*.

So how did readers feel about *The Wrong Stuff*?

One of the first readers to contact me was a seventeen-year-old girl in England, who admired the B-17 Flying Fortress. She sent me a picture of a B-17 mural on the wall of her room. My response to her was, "Ohhh, to B-Seventeen . . . again." She wrote a review on Amazon.com: "Truman is a truly great person, and I love his style of writing. If this book was written in a conventional literary style, you would lose the fact that he was one of many thousands to have had similar experiences." I found it interesting that she later went to college and arranged to join the Royal Air Force as an airborne electronics specialist.

Not everyone was as forgiving of my style. A reader from South Africa objected to my "off-putting" style, because of my "capitalisation" and "italicisation" – spelled with "s's" in place of "z's." Even so, I think he did the *honourable* thing by saying that *The Wrong Stuff* was a "valuable addition" to his library.

As for the capitalization, I was merely trying to overcome the limitations of page size when it came to such things as describing the sound of two fifty-caliber machine guns firing with their muzzles only inches above my head. For when the fighters are coming in to kill you and you see their guns blazing, the reaction is more deserving of a "B-R-R-R-R-R-R-O-O-O-O-O-M-M-M!" instead of a "bangy-bangy" in print.

A reviewer from Tel Aviv, Israel, wrote: "This book takes you with the pilot to bombing flights over Europe thirty-five times. It's a good book, full of detail (how does the author remember all that small stuff, from fifty years ago?), and a casual, fun read. Why isn't there a movie??? There's a lot of good material here! The 'worst' part, the two hundred enemy planes battle, should not be left un-movied!"

This question of remembering and recall has come up several times. It has also amazed me, and I have given it much attention after the book came out, because, like the Dalai Lama answering an interviewer about recalling some of his former incarnations replied, "Sometimes I can't even remember what I did yesterday." And so it is with me.

The really important events in life just have more sticking power. But what about "all that small stuff"? Did some readers think I was just making things up?

As I mention in the book, all humans are programmed with the instincts of sex and survival. It's a great design concept, or we would not be here. Not mentioned in this book are the technical aspects of the survival process.

In the beginning it started with, and still remains, the amygdala, which is central to the primitive brain and is triggered by emotion, responding to anger, avoidance, defensiveness, and fear. In other words, if someone is shooing to kill you – you are likely to remember it. But what about the "small stuff"?

I went through my logbook and notes. My mother had saved all of my letters as well as newspaper articles (not clippings, but entire newspapers). I also referred to old histories and reference materials and to personal contacts. Like Moon Baumann, who had asked, "Do you remember the time Burnell had to shit in his helmet?" This might be considered "small stuff" now, but not for Burnell at the time – just before the fighters attacked.

So as I wrote down these things (at maybe three in the morning in a trance, or hypnotic state) a mental door opened and many details come forth. I feel that the book had written itself. I thought I had forgotten some things. It was like opening Pandora's box, and some things would have best been left forgotten.

I have so far received only one verbal objection to the use of profanity, which the lady retracted when someone, unknown to me, told her, "If you're going to tell it like it was, which Truman did in his book, then you have to TELL IT LIKE IT WAS!" Of course you do, because war itself is most profane. So now, if you too should become entranced through the magic of literature, join with me in doing "The Wrong Stuff."

Truman J. "Smitty" Smith
Lt. Colonel, Retired, United States Air Force
Member of the Distinguished Flying Cross Society

ACKNOWLEDGMENTS

Air Museum, Ponca City, Oklahoma and Aviation Boosters.

Ernest G. "Moon" Baumann, Lt. Colonel, US Air Force, Retired.

Baumann's Crew Members: Robert Moody, Robert P. Eutrecht,
        Henry J. Burnell, Samuel Rudolfsky, Robert Carmen,
        John E. Corscadden, Herbert L. Hill, Fred L. Dyer.

Ray Bowden, English Author, *Plane Names & Fancy Noses*.

Walter Coblenz, Motion Picture Producer.

George Collins, Major US Air Force, Retired (9th AF).

Members and Aims of the Confederate Air Force
        & Gulf Coast Wing.

Archie Di Fante, Historical Research Agency, Maxwell AFB.

John Furia, Screenplay Consultant.

Professor Nedwin Hockman, Lt. Colonel, US Air Force, Ret.

David Johnson, Author, *V-1/V-2, Hitler's Vengeance Weapons*.

Burt Kennedy, Motion Picture Writer, Producer, Director.

Scott Klososky, Author, *The Haldeman Diaries*.

Richard Norris, Aviation-Motion Picture Consultant.

Mike Pappas, Gunner-Togglier, 385th Bomb Group, 8th AF.

John & Joyce Rasco, Technical Assistance.

Andrew Ryan, Surviving brother of Steve Ryan, (Billet-mate).

Bill Shannon, Navigator, 385th Bomb Group, 8th AF.

Ed Stern, Editor, *Hardlife Herald*, 385th Bomb Group Association.

Members, United States Army Air Force, US Air Force & 8th AF.

Bob Westmoreland, Author and Professional Photographer.

Cecil Williams, Lead Bombardier, 91st Bomb Group, 8th AF.

Geoffrey Williams, English Author, *Flying Through Fire*.

Carl Weber, Lt. Colonel, US Air Force, Retired.

THE
WRONG
STUFF

1st Lt. Truman J. Smith, July 1944

INTRODUCTION

T HE RIGHT STUFF is an eloquent book written by Tom
Wolfe, about the creme de la creme of American pilots who
were selected for the U.S. space program, because they had
THE RIGHT STUFF.

Nature's Law of Equal and Opposite balances the Good with the
Evil and the Right with the Wrong. Therefore, to arrive at THE
RIGHT STUFF there had to have been THE WRONG STUFF. For
without the mistakes of yesterday, today's technology could not have
evolved; which makes our Today, in which we live, a product of
Yesterday.

Thus, the Yesterdays, with the Wrong Stuff, are essential for our
Todays and Tomorrows, because it is the mistakes and not the successes
that give us wisdom to cope with the complexities of life.

Unlike lower forms of life, that are guided mainly by instincts,
which are correct 90% of the time, we humans, who are guided by
logic, are fortunate if we are correct 50% of the time.

So it is that we parents – by instinct – attempt to instruct our
progeny from the wisdom of our experiences.

However, not yet having acquired wisdom, our offsprings prefer to
make their own mistakes by ignoring our good intentions and advice.

Even so, directed by some sort of futile instinct to bequeath my
hard-earned wisdom to my children, Rex and Simone, I've said to
them, "Did I ever tell you about the time I – ."

"Yes, dad, I think you did."

Well, if they wouldn't listen to my experiences, I would write them
down for the future when, much wiser, they could read and appreciate
my achievements. I even decided that the title for such
accomplishments, under the circumstances, would have to be WHO
CARES ?

Had my life really been that boring; having been born into the
Great Depression; surviving the Great War; having lived on four
continents; explored the Great Andes and the Great Amazonas,
crashing into the Amazon river; majoring in Drama at the then Great
Pasadena Playhouse and graduating BDH (Before Dustin Hoffman);

directing television in Hollywood, California? Had I really lived such a dull life?

At least *MY WAR OF '44* itself should be worthy of remembrance. Yet, I kept going back to the thought of my children and – *WHO CARES ?*

Then one afternoon my wife, Margot, and I were taking care of our granddaughters, Heather and Kayla, who were five and four years old, when Heather was attracted to the television on which was featured the Japanese attack on Pearl Harbor.

Contrary to the notion of TV executives, that violence attracts an audience, such oversaturation of brutality has actually immunized our society.

Therefore, Heather and Kayla generally ignore the ugly stuff on TV. On the other hand, television has educated them beyond their years. They can discern the real from the make-believe rather well and are quite aware of the suffering produced by warfare around the world.

Heather, being older at five, is also mindful of the past and present, gaining assurance that President Lincoln's and President Washington's wars were long ago and not for her to worry about.

So when television brought the Japanese attacking Pearl Harbor to her, she somehow sensed it was different than the current wars of her time and asked me, "Grandpa, is that your war?"

I answered her that it was my war and reached for the world globe we often refer to in helping them learn where they are and I explained that it had been a World War and that I had actually fought my war on the other side of the world in Europe; hoping to give her a sense of security by a separation of time and place.

She put her finger next to mine on the globe and asked, "Then we don't have *that war* anymore, do we?"

I assured her that we didn't have "*that war*" any more.

Heather then looked at me with a smile and blew me away by saying, "Thank you, grandpa."

Wow!

Somebody *did* care.

Then others expressed an interest; mainly young men who had been boys, too young to have participated in Vietnam.

Vietnam was fought nobly by American troops, but disgraced by Presidents and Congressmen with their *Wrong Stuff.*

Vietnam...Hard to believe that it had happened so long ago. Korea? Even longer. And World War Two?

"Now, *that* was a glamorous and romantic war."

Well, that's what I've been told – by those who weren't there.

"Back then *we* did it *RIGHT*."

"*We* did it RIGHT?"

"Well, we didn't have the disgrace of the MIAs, because all of those missing in action back then were accounted for."

Well, let's try to set the record straight.

Over 20,000 American servicemen, captured by the Germans, and recaptured by the Soviets during World War Two, were and are still missing. Not 2,000, but over 20,000 Americans captured in Europe have never been accounted for. There was also a like number in the Pacific, where the Japanese preferred killing them rather than taking prisoners.

President, former General, Eisenhower was forced to abandon them and their plight when it became necessary to stop the Communists in Korea. Such a decision had to have broken his heart.

So what was *WRONG* and what was RIGHT?

Any sane concept of right and wrong in warfare is flawed, because war is insane – and the rules are quite different.

Good Guys don't win wars. Victory goes to the Bad guys. Even a domestic war against crime will never succeed unless criminals are made to suffer *more* than their victims.

The "Japs," as they were called, who attacked Pearl Harbor and committed gross war crimes, and the Nazis, who killed their own citizens, as well as the Soviets, who killed even millions more of their own citizens, were the Bad Guys in our own Good Guy viewpoint. But as *bad* as they were, they were finally defeated by the "Good Guys," because we were better at being *bad* than they were.

No?

We're the only sonsabitches in the history of the world to have dropped atomic bombs on civilians. And as bad as that was, we created more destruction and killed even more women, children and elderly with the conventional bombing of Dresden, Hamburg, Berlin and countless other targets.

"When in doubt, aim for the church in the middle of town where most of them live."

Was it wrong or right?

Since we had convinced our enemies that we had the means and the will to be – not only the Bad Guys, but the worst in the history of the world – we avoided World War Three. So most would have to agree that doing the *wrong stuff* actually turned out to be right.

"Glamorous?" "Romantic?"

"Well, at least it had the support of the people and as a result it didn't last as long as Vietnam."

However, the length of a war is not the only criteria. The Vietnam War lasted five times longer than the war of the Eighth Air Force in Europe. Yet, the Eighth Air Force lost 8,314 bombers and 60,376 air crewmen with 79,265 casualties in less than 36 months. Just try to imagine it.

The Eighth Air Force suffered higher losses than any other U.S. Force in War Two. And what a force it was!

How many airplanes have you ever seen in the sky at one time? Maybe ten? Have you ever seen a hundred planes in the air at the same time? Two hundred? Five hundred? Can you even imagine the sight of a *thousand airplanes*?

How then can you possibly comprehend an air armada of *TWO THOUSAND AIRPLANES*? – as far as the eye can see in any direction...AIRPLANES!!! It was truly – AWESOME!!!

Yet, more than four times as many that had flown away from England on a single mission in such an armada would never return from the aerial battleground above enemy-occupied Europe.

General James Dolittle said, "The world had never seen combat like this and I pray they never will (again)."

The danger is in not knowing. And in knowing, not remembering the way it was.

"But can you remember enough of the *Wrong Stuff* to write it down?" a young writer asked me. "Can you recall such things as the weather with any clarity?"

"Oh, YES!" I told him, "I can recall it vividly. It was a dark and stormy night..."

And so it is that I begin.

Put on some background music of the Big Bands of the forties; mix in some Wagner and Von Suppe's *LIGHT CAVALRY OVERTURE*. Turn the thermostat way down cold. Try to forget the comforts of home and family. Get real depressed and let's DO IT!

Col. E. Vandevanter, Jr.(center) first commanding officer of the 385th Bomb Group (Heavy) winds down with other officers of the group after a mission. Col. Vandevanter was CO from the group's formation until August 1944.

WHO, WHERE, WHEN
CHAPTER 1

It was a dark and stormy night when the ten of us arrived in the back of a 6x6 Army truck at the 550th "Werewolf" Squadron Headquarters at Great Ashfield, East Anglia, England, where the 385th Bomb Group (Heavies) was stationed. It seemed appropriate, if not prophetic, that it was *April Fool's Day* in 1944.

The six enlisted men of our crew were taken care of first and escorted to their Quonset hut "billet," as the British call the barracks. Then we four officers were guided to our billet: 2nd Lt. Ernest "Moon" Baumann (Pilot); 2nd Lt. Robert "Ears" Moody (Navigator); Flight Officer Robert "Eut" Eutrecht (Bombardier) and me, 2nd Lt. Truman "Smitty" Smith, their twenty-year-old copilot. Everyone on the crew was senior to me in age by an average of three years.

For the sake of simplicity each crew was identified by the name of the pilot. Thus, we were Baumann's Crew; although it might have been more appropriate to call us Baumann's Dog and Pony Show – without the pony, because each of us had been trained to perform our individual tricks or specialties.

Up in the nose and on the point was our bombardier, "Eut" Eutrecht, who was much like an English Pointer; long and lean, always on the lookout and ready to point. After all, he was the "Bomb-Aimer"– point the target and bomb it. He was focused and high strung. Some might say nervous, but I think it was mainly his immaturity, since he was only twenty-one and even physically he had not yet filled out his six-feet-two frame.

By contrast our navigator, "Ears," was mellow, much like a patient golden retriever. He reminded me greatly of the actor Van Heflin in his Academy Award winning performance as an alcoholic intellectual in *"JOHNNY EAGER"* (1942). At twenty-four, and even with thinning

Top Row: Robert "Ears" Moody, Ernest "Moon" Baumann, Truman "Smitty" Smith, Robert P. "Eut" Eutrecht. Bottom Row: Henry J. Burnell, Samuel Rudolfsky, Robert Carmen, John E. Corscadden, Herbert L. Hill, Fred L. Dyer.

blonde hair, "Ears" had not yet reached the peak as an alcoholic-intellectual, but he seemed to have the potential. And when he applied himself, he could even navigate us from A to Z. However, he was not always motivated to do it in proper sequence, which often added suspense to our flights.

"Moon" Baumann, our pilot, was of German lineage. By canine comparison, he was more like a German shepherd, although a bit on the small side. Even so, his manner conveyed the meaning of the saying:"It's not the size of the dog in the fight, but the size of the fight in the dog." So with a B-17 and its crew of ten, "Moon" was very much larger and more lethal than his 145 pounds.

And as Moon's copilot, I was his right-hand-man, or *boy*. Four years younger, I did outweigh him by at least thirty pounds; more muscular than mental, because I still had a lot to learn about flying and living. Even my temperament had not yet developed, because I suppose I was more like a mongrel pup with a hint of coyote ancestry—chasing butterflies and mystified by everything, including my own tail.

Burnell was our flight engineer. Whatever airplane we flew turned out to belong to him; the same as any car belongs to the little bulldog that has been left inside of it. Most of the time he rode standing between Moon and me making note of the plane's performance, except when he was needed to operate the twin fifty-caliber machine guns in the top turret just behind us.

Aft of the top turret was the bomb-bay and aft of that was the radio room, guarded by "Rudy" Rudolfsky, a quiet yet nervous little *terrier*. Rudy was probably the smallest and the oldest on the crew who, to me, seemed totally out of place. I had the feeling that he should be in some high school teaching Radio or Shop, but of all places, not flying combat in a Flying Fortress.

Aft of the radio room was the waist of the ship with two gunners: Dyer, left waist and Carmen, right waist and armorer. Dyer was a likable Dachshund, while Carmen, with his black hair and chiseled facial features resembled a stealth-like Doberman.

Midship in the ball turret on the belly of the plane, with the temperament of an Irish Setter, was red-headed "Corky" Corscaddin.

Finally, managing the twin-50's in the tail was the classic bloodhound from Appalachia, Herby Hill.

T his was Baumann's Dog Show; an eclectic, yet homogeneous, *pack*, where hopefully the whole would be more than the sum of its parts in contributing to the war effort.

The "WAR" was in its making in the spring of 1944 and, as a nation, we had not yet really begun to fight, because we couldn't. We had truly become, as the Japanese characterized us, a "Sleeping Giant."

Hitler had taken the whole of Europe for the Third Reich, offering the sale of Jews to the world. But there were no takers; not even the Land of the Free and the Home of the Brave, because we had lived in isolation, suffering our own problems of the Great Depression.

However, not wanting a war, the Japanese in the Pacific brought the war to us in 1941 when the U.S. Army numbered only 175,000 men; ranked 16th in size, behind Rumania. Having forgotten that the primary purpose of a federal government is national defense, we proved that a small military force is an invitation for attack.

So if we got lucky and worked hard enough, there might be a very questionable chance that the United States would survive, even though the odds were against it.

No, there was no foregone conclusion that the U.S. even had a future in 1941. It would simply cease to exist without the *will* and means to defend itself. But with what? It took a total effort just to put bread on the table during the Great Depression.

It was in the 1930's that Japan and Europe faced the same problem, except they had decided to do something about it. Japan, an island, needed expansion to acquire raw materials and resources. Germany also needed resources and room for living, *Lebensraum*, which it had lost as a result of World War One. So Hitler was indeed welcomed as a national hero by putting everyone to work and promising that he could feed the world by controlling the fertile Ukraine of the Union of Soviet Socialist Republics.

Why not? The Communists could not get the job done. They were not even able to feed themselves. Stalin had starved over 300,000 people in his home state of Georgia by shipping the food to Moscow to empower himself as leader of the U.S.S.R.; executing another *twenty million people* to maintain his authority!

Socialism was simply not workable and would destroy civilization.

According to whom? The United States? No.

It was Hitler who was the enemy of Communism.

Charles Lindbergh, the *LONE EAGLE* and American folk hero, along with Truman Smith (no relation to the author of *THE WRONG STUFF*), an Army major who had been appointed as the U.S. Air Attaché in Berlin in 1935, agreed with Hitler that Communism had to be stopped.

However, this is not what President Roosevelt needed to save the U.S. from the Japanese, who had been backed into a corner by U.S. trade sanctions.

What the U.S. needed was all the help and time it could get and why it had already allied itself with the USSR and Britain against the Japanese and therefore – against Germany.

But what about America's hero, Charles Lindbergh, who was apparently allied with the Nazis?

The fact that Germany's Air Marshall Goering presented a medal to both Lindbergh and Smith made them "Nazi sympathizers."

At least that was the opinion of President Roosevelt and his administration. So the charge was then publicized by the press and noted broadcasters like Walter Winchell and Drew Pearson that Lindbergh was unpatriotic.

Thus, Lindbergh was silenced and Roosevelt went on with the preparation for war against Japan and Germany in alliance with Churchill and Stalin.

Even so, it was not a "done-deal" that the Allies would win the upcoming war. In fact, it was most unrealistic that the Allies could even hope to defeat the Axis powers on a world scale.

By 1940 London had suffered the Nazi "Blitzkrieg" and Britain was on its knees, threatened with an invasion of German forces.

The U.S. finally enacted compulsory military service to try to build an Army, even though the Axis – Japan, Italy and Germany – already had the largest military force in history.

No, the survival of the Allies at the beginning of the 1940's did not even appear to be a possibility. Yet, they did not give up and the "Sleeping Giant" finally started to awaken.

Within 48 months, while the British, Soviets and Americans sacrificed their lives in a delaying action, the United States was miraculously able to build a military force, as well as support the British and Soviets.

And while it was still far short of what was required to defeat the Axis – and the Eighth Air Force had nearly been decimated in England; 1944 was destined to be a memorable year in world history.

So on April Fools Day 1944, Baumann's Dog Show took the stage. Our billet was not a Quonset hut, but the equivalent of a rather standard wooden barracks equipped with two rows of twelve, single iron beds spaced perpendicularly to the two long walls for a total of twenty-four bunks. There were windows in the long walls that were covered with blackout curtains. The mattresses consisted of square "biscuits," placed end-to-end for the length of the bed.

The inside of the roof doubled as the ceiling. Which is to say, the building was uninsulated and any heat generated by the two small stoves, less than three feet high, rose upward and away from the living space into the open attic.

Thus, the first six feet or so above the concrete floor were uncomfortably cold. It would have been totally unacceptable to prison inmates and good cause for a riot by their prison standards. Yet, this was to be our home. The question was, for how long?

While our hope to escape the wet and cold English springtime weather was quickly dashed, our reception was even more chilling.

The four individuals who were grouped at the far end of the open billet hardly acknowledged our entrance. And while we gave a cheery greeting and asked if we could move in, the response was depressing.

"Sure" one of them said, "Take any of those bunks at that end. They're still *warm*."

Then the group went back to its own.

One of them wore a leather A-2 jacket with Captain's insignia and pilot's wings. What the others were could not be guessed, but we assumed they, like us, were the flying officers of two other crews.

It turned out that the dandy wearing a red satin robe with a white scarf around his neck and smoking a pipe, as if he were to the manor born, was the Captain's navigator. The other six were dressed in an assortment of flight suits, long underwear and one wore a faded orange letterman sweater with a big blue "B" on it.

We tried to ignore their cynical un-welcome to us as we unpacked and put our bunks in order, accepting the fact that we, as replacements, were at the bottom of the pecking order and were naturally the intruders into their privileged and obviously very selective "club" of aerial combatants, who literally made their living by killing intruders into their midst over enemy occupied Europe.

Perhaps it would have helped to have had some sort of a briefing about the world of combat prior to being dropped into the middle of it. Except, there weren't any experts yet, because it was all part of a desperate "EXPERIMENT" to prove daylight bombing in the hope of winning the war.

Winning? There were no guarantees and we had already damned near lost it before getting started. The prospects were definitely not good.

So the question at the time was not really so much about winning as it was in just surviving. It was to be a marathon and not a quick sprint.

The only bragging right of the 385th was that it had led the entire Eighth Air Force on three attacks against Berlin at the beginning of March 1944, but nobody had been able to bomb the target visually due to bad weather – until the third try.

However, the Eighth Air Force, led by the 385th Bomb Group, did *finally* hit BIG "B," and that was certainly worth bragging about. It was an accomplishment that, in time, I would learn to appreciate.

It was not to Berlin, but it was to Germany that I began with my FIRST mission on Saturday the 8th of April, 1944, just a week after our arrival.

MISSION #1
Quakenbruck, Germany, 8 April 1944
Saturday: 30 ships up   (5:30 Flying Time)

The Standard Operating Procedure was to break up a new crew and assign individuals to more experienced crews for the first few missions in order to help them adjust to the environment of combat.

I was assigned to fly copilot for First Lieutenant Mullins, whom I didn't know and who made it clear that he was not interested in getting to know me. Later I would realize it was best not to get to know anyone too well. Strangers die easier.

The ship we were assigned was the older model B-17 F, which weighed 32,000 pounds empty. However, it grossed twenty-seven tons when loaded with 2,700 gallons of gasoline for fuel, which amounted to 22,000 pounds, and a bomb load of 6,000 pounds of high explosives, plus the weight of ten crew members, equipment and heavy . 50 caliber ammunition for a dozen machine guns. This meant it weighed five tons more than the popular German Mark IV tank, without the armor, and it was *expected to fly*.

Our position in our Group formation was "Purple Heart Corner," better known as "Coffin Corner," which is the bottom ship in the bottom flight of the Low Squadron.

The main disadvantage in this position, unlike the High Squadron, was the inability to climb up and into the Group for protection in case of lost power. Also in the game of "crack the whip," the slightest increase of power by the leader meant that we had to firewall it at the tail-end to try and keep up.

Thus, the position we were to fly deserved its identification as "COFFIN CORNER," sometimes called "PURPLE HEART CORNER."

The Group formation usually consisted of twenty-seven aircraft, stacked in three Squadrons of nine aircraft each to form a "Box." Spare aircraft were sometimes attached to the High Squadron to fill in for aborting aircraft in case of early malfunctions.

While the plan view of a Bomb Group looks like an arrowhead, so does the profile view, with the Lead Squadron as the point and the High and Low Squadrons forming the barbs. No two aircraft fly at the same altitude, nor directly behind, nor ahead of each other. This gives room for individual maneuvering and reduces the chances of colliding.

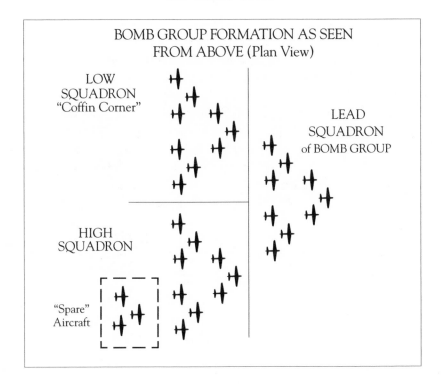

BOMB GROUP FORMATION AS SEEN
FROM ABOVE (Plan View)

LOW
SQUADRON
"Coffin Corner"

LEAD
SQUADRON
of BOMB GROUP

HIGH
SQUADRON

"Spare"
Aircraft

According to the *book*, ships were *supposed* to maintain a 50 foot separation.

The B-17 "F" model has twelve .50 Caliber machine guns. The B-17 "G" model has thirteen .50 Caliber machine guns. The way the aircraft are staggered in formation reduces, but does not eliminate, the chances of shooting into each other. So with 30 aircraft put up for the Quackenbruck mission, we had almost 400 machine guns for protection – as long as we maintained "Group integrity"; which meant keeping the "herd" packed together in tight formation.

The key word was "together." But having been given twenty-seven tons of an old war-weary "bucket of bolts," I doubted we could even get her up to our assigned altitude of 27,000 feet and keep "together" with the others.

And if that wasn't enough, we were also expected to ride this slow and heavy "flying bomb" just five miles above Germany for most of the day in order to drop our three tons of bombs onto a well-defended target before they could blow us up.

It didn't take a lot of experience to figure out just whose side the odds favored. At the time, I didn't know whether three tons of bombs made a bigger bang than ten tons of 100-octane fuel. But then, it really didn't make much difference since I was riding right in the middle of it all!

Another worry on my mind was that we were going to try to do this tricky job at only a-hundred-and-fifty miles an hour. I wondered, "Do these people really know what they're doing?"

Of course they didn't. It was all an "EXPERIMENT"! The British had already proved to their satisfaction that daylight bombing could not be done. So, it was no wonder that the Eighth Air Force had the highest casualty rate of all U.S. Forces.

Even so, it is noteworthy that no bomb group of the Eighth Air Force had ever been forced to abort a mission by enemy action.

The best evaluation of U.S. strategic bombing was given by Albert Speer, the Minister of Munitions for the Third Reich. He believed that if strategic bombing had started earlier and had continued a bit longer, it would not even have been necessary to invade Germany, because it would have been defeated by the inability to fight a war for a lack of resources. And that, of course, was the theory of strategic bombing.

But such a conclusion was after the fact and the fact we faced at the time was that the theory had not yet been proved. And an even more important fact on the 8th of April, 1944 was that I was betting my life on the success of this unproven theory.

Well, maybe not "its" success, but "my" success in surviving 25 combat missions. It was a question constantly with me that would deprive me of sleep and food and any pleasures I might consider. But, why had the goal been set at 25 combat missions?

William J. Bell

A P-47 Thunderbolt like "My Fran."

It really didn't matter just how many missions we had to fly. We were in the military and would try to do what we were ordered to do. However, curiosity begged an answer as to why the particular number of 25 missions had been selected.

The High Command of the Eighth Air Force was responsible for the overall requirements of Plans and Operations for the accomplishment of the Air Force's Mission. They reviewed the objective and the results in projecting the requirements: food, fuel, logistics, personnel, aircraft – down to every nut and bolt. In fact, the air offensive had been delayed in the beginning due to a lack of proper clothing for fighting the war in the sub-zero temperatures of high altitude flying.

Therefore, the number of missions to get the job done was not simply a number picked out of a hat, but it was based on what could be expected to meet the requirements. And quite simply, the Air Force could not count on flying personnel to survive beyond 25 missions. Thus, a tour of combat was set at 25 missions.

So, in the predawn hours of 8 April, 1944, as we were hauled in the back of a 6x6 truck to the mess hall, the briefing, the aircraft revetment and the wait to start engines, I thought about how I had gotten into this mess in the first place.

W hile it had been exciting to have soloed an airplane on my sixteenth birthday in 1940, it was a small accomplishment compared to James Cagney in "CAPTAIN OF THE CLOUDS," a movie about a dashing Canadian bush-pilot who volunteered for the Royal Air Force and was eventually given a bomber to fly.

Nobody had given *me* an airplane to fly back in 1938 when I was fourteen years old. I had saved up four dollars for my first half-hour flying lesson.

My flight instructor had been Johnny Erickson before he'd gone to Canada to join the RAF. They gave *him* an airplane. Unfortunately, he was killed shortly after his arrival in England.

Two insurance agents, Ralph Cooley and C.E. Barr, had their own airplane at the airport in Ponca City, Oklahoma, where I tried to learn aviation by osmosis – being there, soaking it up, cleaning airplanes, bumming rides, listening to air stories, learning the ground stuff and on rare occasions getting to learn the air stuff. Ralph and C. E. were sympathetic to my ambition.

Ralph became the Commander of the new local Civil Air Patrol that was started in 1941 and he took me along as his observer, letting me fly.

Since I had spent a summer at Fort Sill in the Field Artillery with the Civilian Military Training Camp (having said I was 16 when I was actually 15 in 1939), I was appointed the local CAP's only Sergeant, instructing a wide assortment of civilians in such things as close order drill.

My greatest problem, as Drill Sergeant, was keeping everyone in "goose-step" with a former World War One German submarine sailor who had immigrated to the U.S. and – he even had *his own airplane*.

In 1941 Ralph left Oklahoma and joined the RAF in Canada, where they gave him PBY Catalina Flying Boats to ferry across the North Atlantic. It seemed that everyone except me had an airplane to fly, even C.E. Barr who was left in Ponca City with the Luscombe that he and Ralph owned.

Thus, C.E. became my mentor and I became his "experimental" student. It was a good deal for the both of us, because C.E. needed the practice the same as I, but for a different reason.

The Battle of Britain started the 10th of July 1940 when the German Luftwaffe began bombing Britain in earnest. The Royal Air Force had only 704 serviceable aircraft, while the Germans possessed 1,392 bombers and 1,290 fighters. And by September the 7th, 1940 almost one fourth of the R.A.F's pilots had been lost.

The Luftwaffe gave England hell. Through July and August the radar sites and airfields were attacked along the south and eastern coasts. On the 24th of August, 1940, the first German bombs struck London, but it was a tactical mistake, because they had not yet destroyed the R.A.F.

The Royal Air Force consisted of volunteers from many nations, including the Americans in the Eagle Squadron. It was to the R.A.F that Winston Churchill paid tribute, saying that never had so many owed so much to so few, since their brave actions did, in fact, convince Hitler to give up his intentions to invade England.

However, the aerial attacks on England continued to the point that it was unsafe to train pilots there and flying schools were established in the United States. One such school was the #6 British Flying Training School secured by the efforts of the community and aviation experts, such as Tommy Smyer, in Ponca City, Oklahoma.

I had gotten a job as a laborer, digging ditches and pouring concrete, during the summer school break in 1941, in the construction of the #6

B.F.T.S. Darr School. And since it was before Pearl Harbor and the Declaration of War by the U.S., the Royal Air Force training in the U.S. was done under civilian contracts.

Thus, my mentor, C.E. Barr wanted to be an instructor at Darr School. So he practiced his instructing on me in order to qualify for his Instructor's Rating and we both taught each other about what should and should not be done. Like the time he knocked the wind out of me by jabbing his fist into my stomach to teach me to "RELAX!"; proving his point that the plane would still fly without my intense piloting.

As C.E.'s "professional" student, I told him that punching students in the gut, while very effective, was a teaching technique that I was sure the British would not approve.

By the next summer, having graduated high school and joined the Air Corps, I worked as an aircraft dispatcher at Darr, assigning students to aircraft in the Primary Flying School.

So it was that airplanes and warfare belonged together and I had signed my fate by wanting to fly airplanes.

At least that was what I *thought* I wanted at the time. It was simply my destiny. But how would it play out?

Well, that's what I was going to find out.

O n the darkest of nights, at three-thousand feet up, it is possible to see the striking of a match at ground level. So to witness the explosion of two bombers, loaded with fuel and bombs, colliding in the dark is, at first-experience, overwhelming.

Even though it must have been five miles away, I didn't hear it above the sound of engines, nor feel the impact of the blast. But twenty lives were snuffed out and, except for the grace of God, it could have been us. And this wasn't even the main event.

Even so, I sensed that the natural paralysis of such a shock had to be overcome in order to function properly.

We were just starting out and over *friendly* territory with nobody shooting at us. And if flying itself wasn't enough challenge, it was compounded by an unproven *theory* (Somebody's *guess*) that we might stop the Third Reich with airplanes.

Well, it was admittedly an act of desperation, because nothing else had stopped the Nazis. I mean NOTHING had been able to halt the Third Reich in its progress toward total domination of Europe.

There was no longer even any standing room left on the Continent from which to fight. Britain's foot soldiers had been pushed into the sea at Dunkirk. This meant that the only fighting force left was the U.S. Air Force for daylight bombing and the Royal Air Force for nighttime raids.

Yes, it was truly an act of desperation; the outcome of which would determine the future of civilization itself.

It didn't do me any good to think about our disadvantage and the real possibility of our losing what was turning into the largest war in history. But as true as it was, we had not yet won anything. Our enemy was ahead of us in preparation and performance. So I preferred to ignore the consequences and to focus on doing my duty for whatever good it would do for my country somewhere down the line.

The whole experience of taking off at night and climbing up through the darkness to form up into the Group, plus the rarefied atmosphere at 10,000 feet, was literally breathtaking.

The sunrise was beautiful. Twenty-nine other B-17's circling our assigned radio "Buncher" beacon, jockeying for respective positions to fit into the formation, was quite an air-show. And while I had flown practice formations, I had never seen so many Flying Fortresses in a single group.

And beyond our Group, other groups were forming up. I had never beheld so many airplanes in the sky at one time. It was the most awesome experience of my life. Somehow I knew that it was an historical phenomenon and felt that, if only in eternity, it was probably worth whatever it would cost me to be a part of it.

Mullins reminded me that I was more than just a spectator to the event when he hit my arm and pointed to the engine gauges, the booster pump switches and the supercharger levers.

Getting into the rarefied air at 10,000 feet meant we needed more power, especially to hold our place in formation; and it was obvious that our old war-weary bird was not feeling very well. In truth, she was really one sick old bird.

The Group was formed and we set course for Germany, climbing for the designated altitude of 27,000 feet as we went. But, damn it, it took everything we had to keep up at only 150 miles an hour. All of which suggested that it was going to be one long day.

Ahhh!!! That's why the Group's formation speed was only 150 miles per hour; so that we could keep up. That was a great idea! Fastest was not necessarily the best, because it was better to keep the herd together instead of stretched out along the Bomber Stream where we could be picked off individually by the Luftwaffe.

God help anyone who was unfortunate enough to get left behind, because Air Marshall Hermann Goering had ordered the Luftwaffe to take advantage of such odds and to knock down the stragglers.

GREAT! We hadn't even gotten to Germany yet and, despite our desire and efforts down in *Coffin Corner*, we were struggling and – *straggling!*

Our old tired reluctant "dragon" was draggin'. She groaned and argued all the way. The throttles were locked at full open and extra power was added with the superchargers.

Even 150 miles an hour seemed too much for her. I couldn't recall Jimmy Cagney having such power problems. All he had to worry about was somebody shooting at him.

Our battle was not with the Germans, but with the goddamned equipment! The throttles were locked wide open and the power required to keep us in formation had to be adjusted constantly with the supercharger levers for each of the four engines.

Somebody before us had recognized the problem and had attempted to solve it with some jury-rigged, jill-farted extension levers that stuck up out of the control console like four random sticks jammed into a puddle of mud.

Since there was a separate "stick" for each of the four engines, it was not possible to control them all with one hand.

So, with his hands full with the control wheel in one hand and grabbing at the power "sticks" with the other, I tried to assist Mullins with my two hands. The whole procedure was as awkward and frustrating as a "slip-out" during the critical moment in intercourse when all hands get in the way of each other.

And this is the way to go to war? It was ridiculous!

We were so occupied in trying to get our act together that I was unaware that we had reached our operating altitude of five miles above the earth.

This meant we were into the sub-stratosphere, which is a lethal environment. For without oxygen, you are unconscious within ninety seconds! A few more seconds and you are *dead!*

One of my duties was to call for a "Crew Check" on the intercom every fifteen minutes, and everyone else was supposed to check on each other for the effects of the treacherous anoxia, because it could sneak up and kill you while you were in a state of euphoria.

As we climbed higher the outside ambient temperature lowered to fifty degrees below zero. The temperature inside was a bit warmer in the nose, the cockpit and the radio room, but it was actually colder in the waist and the tail than outside, because the slipstream from our four propellers drove the super-cold wind into the open waist windows of the older "F" Model Fortress.

Thus, the chill factor on our two waist gunners must have been *two-hundred degrees below zero*!

Waist gunners on the B-17 "F" Model could be identified by what might appear as ugly "saber scars" on their cheeks; scarred by frostbite from wind getting to their bare skin between helmet, goggles and oxygen mask. As for touching any metal parts with bare hands it was to leave your skin on the metal.

Even in the relatively warmer cockpit I discovered that the condensation of my breath coming out of my oxygen mask had frozen into icicles on my silk neck scarf. This caused me to consider my mask. I squeezed on it and found that the insidious ice was cutting down my oxygen flow. So I crunched it loose.

While the thin and super cold air was a grim hardship on the human body, it also worked against the performance of equipment and machinery. Guns could jam, bombs hang up and – .

DAMN! The #2 engine went wild!!!

It was a "*runaway*" and Mullins called for me to, "Feather Number Two!"

Like the different gear ratios in a car, aircraft get different ratios of power and thrust from the propeller pitch which can take greater or lesser bites from the air. A coarse pitch takes a larger bite than a thin or flatter pitch. A coarse pitch, however, puts a greater load on the engine and is reserved for cruising at slower rpm's.

Since reciprocal engines develop higher horsepower at higher revolutions per minute, High RPM is used for taking off and also emergency power with the propeller taking smaller bites in a flatter pitch.

So besides the thin air making it necessary to use superchargers, the colder air caused the hydraulic valves on the controls to malfunction and the super-cold air also caused the propeller governor, that controls the pitch of the prop, to change the propeller into flat pitch! Not a thin or fine pitch, but into a NO-pitch mode.

No pitch, no bite. No bite, no pull. No pull, no drag on the engine. And with no drag on the engine, it's a "runaway," beating itself to death – until the feather-button I'd pushed started to reconfigure the angle of pitch toward the other extreme of its range, taking larger bites of air until it would stop in the full-feathered position.

This limitation is called the "feathered" position, because the prop, like a feather, is held in line with the flow of air across the airplane, which is the designed purpose for feathering a prop, because it reduces the drag from the flat side of a prop being pushed through the air when an engine fails.

I knew that, but Mullins had just taught me the un-designed use for the feathering button, which can be used to control a runaway engine and still get some power from it, instead of shutting it down.

All I had to do was to pull the button out and unfeather the prop before it went into full feather and stopped. And when the engine started to run away again, to push the feather-button in, and – so on and on with endless repetition – while also helping Mullins jack around with the power "sticks."

I looked at Mullins, his face covered by his oxygen mask, to see if the runaway engine would convince him to abort our flight.

We were somewhere over the North Sea and hadn't yet reached enemy territory, so we wouldn't get credit for a mission if we turned back now, despite our best intentions and hard work. But I was so pissed at the goddamned equipment that I was ready to settle for a non-mission and start all over the next day.

However, it wasn't my call. It was up to Mullins. I don't know what he saw in my eyes, but I could see in his that Mullins was not even considering turning back for England.

DAMN IT!!! This meant I was going to have to ride the goddamned feather-button all the way to Germany and back for the next eight hours. Already my fingers were cramping from snapping in and snapping out the feather-button. I was also going to have to keep working at adjusting the power to try to stay in formation.

The job at hand reminded me, how as kids, we tried to pat ourselves on the head with one hand and rub our stomachs at the same time with the other hand. Flying was certainly not a glamorous business at all. In fact, it was turning out to be pretty damned ludicrous.

What was going to happen when the fighting started? Well, I was going to die with a fuckin' feathering button in my hand was what was going to happen!

In the midst of the tornado in my brain flashed G-8 AND HIS BATTLE ACES. What? Why?

My mind was in a search-mode for some answers and, lacking actual experience, was trying to lock onto any reference to aerial combat.

But, G-8 AND HIS BATTLE ACES ?

As a kid between World Wars, like most kids, I read the World War One aerial adventures of G-8, wishing and daydreaming of such high adventure. However, such adventure was not for me.

Wrong! Those daydreams were now turning into a nightmare, because I was not down there at only 5,000 feet hammering slugs from my Vickers machine gun into a Fokker D-VII. However, I was up at 27 Angels busting my knuckles on a goddamned feathering button.

Things were certainly not going as I had expected, what with the malfunctioning equipment and the flak.

FLAK?

Well at least I had expected the flak and sure enough it was there: billowing black puffs of smoke announcing that we had finally arrived in German airspace over enemy occupied territory.

And although it was my first experience in combat, I didn't need any explanation about the meaning of flak.

Just as my emotions were about to change from anger into fear of the exploding flak, I was thrust back into anger, because the goddamned-monkey-fartin'-shit kickin' #1 *engine started losing its power!!!*

Well, what the hell? It was hardly unexpected, because "shit happens." And when it does, it usually compounds itself.

So it really didn't surprise me to see the Group slowly pulling away from us, leaving us quite alone over enemy occupied Europe as a straggler with the #2 engine insisting on running away and then the supercharger on #1 failing to provide power.

Still flipping my feather-button, I stopped jiggling the superchargers, because we didn't have to worry about flying formation any more. We had become all alone, a group of one, a *straggler!*

I looked to Mullins, wondering if he had any other good ideas. It was like he was hypnotized. He didn't even see me. His sight and mind were still with the Group as it disappeared ahead of us deeper into the flak. So we just sat there holding to the course, quite alone.

Since it was not Mullin's nature to say anything, and I had no combat experience until the flak started, I could only guess – and my guess was that we would just poop along until we got to the target – by *ourselves* – or – we got shot down.

At least I didn't have to make myself crazy with the "power sticks" any more. I would just play with the feathering button and wait.

While we were not able to catch up, we were able to hold our altitude; but at only 140 mph. There's a saying that, "You had to have been there to appreciate it," except that there could be no appreciation nor thankfulness to be stuck five miles above the middle of Germany, all alone, in a poopy old, worn out war wagon. And, there was even more.

Yep, if circumstances weren't bad enough, our #4 engine *also started losing power!*

That's right. When shit happens there's usually more on the way and this looked to be my first and last mission. With good fortune in not getting blown up or shot down, I might be spending the night in a prisoner of war camp.

So, with only one seemingly good engine out of four, the situation finally got Mullin's attention. He came out of his trance and gave me a brief glance.

Fate had resolved our dilemma. We had no choice in the matter. With major loss in power, we were definitely on our way down. The old bird simply couldn't maintain speed nor altitude. There were no other options. We – were – *going – DOWN!!!*

Mullins banked to the left, making a one-eighty degree turn for home, and we sacrificed altitude for a bit more speed in the descent.

By the time we reached Holland we had bled off 16,000 feet of altitude and were down to 11,000 feet. It was good and bad in that altitude is an ally, as long as it's *below* you. All the sky in the world above you won't help when the object is to keep from hitting the ground, and we had already sacrificed too much of it for the distance we had yet to cover to get back home.

On the other hand, the air is more dense at lower altitude and superchargers are not required. This meant that the #1 and #4 engines were regaining some of their strength and even the #2 runaway engine became happier and more cooperative in the warmer air. So, when we passed over the Zuider Zee in Holland we dropped our bombs into the water to lighten our load and to improve the planes performance.

"Hello Big Friend. This is your Little Friend at 3 o' clock. Are you happy?"

My eyes jumped to our right wingtip and a fighter pilot was waving at me from an American P-47 Thunderbolt with the name "MY FRAN" painted on the side of its nose.

Hot Damnnn! It could just as easily have been a German pilot and none of our gunners had even alerted us. But then, we wouldn't have known what had hit us anyway.

Mullins was tuned to the intercom and I had been monitoring the fighter channel, so I waved back and told our Little Friend that we were "happy" and asked if he could confirm our position.

"Roger, Big Friend, stand by" he said and jerked upward to gain altitude for a direct line-of-sight communications to his control in England, while I listened to his quasi-coded transmission.

"Hello Orange Grove, this is Orange Peel. I need some Orange Juice: Mares-Eat-Oats, Mares-Eat-Oats, Mares-Eat Oats…"

I could not hear Orange Grove, because we were too low and the curvature of the earth prevented line-of-sight reception from England. However, Orange Grove had immediately locked onto Orange Peel's transmission high above us; gave him the weather and location; which our Little Friend relayed to us from his "perch" up at 30 Angels, or 30,000 feet above sea level.

"Hello Big Friend, this is your Little Friend at Thirty Angels. Your feet are wet (Over the Channel), but you should have Chalky-Chalky-Chalky (White Cliffs of Dover) in about a half an hour on a QDM (compass heading home) of two-seven-zero…Are you happy Big Friend?"

I acknowledged that we were indeed "happy" and – as mysteriously as he had arrived – he was gone.

Five and a half hours after we had started engines that morning we shut them down on our hardstand at Great Ashfield. It felt great to be back home. But this was only the beginning – of what? The end?

FLAK: FLieger Abwehr Kannonen (Flyer Defense Cannons).

THE FLAK
CHAPTER 2

Mechanical-problems, people-problems, timing and plain
luck. Those are the main ingredients to life and certainly
to that pressure cooker of life: COMBAT; which can serve
as an excellent benchmark or reference to normal life experiences.
Think you've got a problem with losing your job or your home?
Think about it in relationship to losing your *life*.

Besides sex and survival there is another instinct with which we
are provided to help us through life. It is the mysterious and usually
unpredictable *SENSE OF HUMOR*. It can be thought of as the
lubricant that reduces friction and the salve that eases the pain of
outrageous fortune.

Baumersbach, a copilot in our billet, had ridden in the tail gunner's
position of our lead aircraft in order to watch the Group's formation as
"eyes" for the leader on the Quakenbruck raid. That evening he
complained of a strange feeling in his private parts. A visit to the Flight
Surgeon provided the answer to his mechanical problem.

Unlike the forward compartments of the ship, there is no heating
in the tail gunner's position. Sometimes tail gunners were even provided
a metal can with a concoction of powdered milk, flavoring and a stick
to stir the contents while on a long mission in order to make ice cream.
That's how cold it really got in the tail, where the air was even colder
than the inside of an ice cream freezer.

Tail gunners knew this, but not Baumersbach, nor any one else
who had never before been on a mission in the tail. So what had
happened was, when he relieved himself into the relief tube at minus-
fifty degrees, he frostbit his penis.

The fact he had been wearing an electric flying suit (the precursor
of electric blankets) did not change the law of Physics that states: *A
warm wienny exposed to minus fifty degrees – even briefly – will be bitten by
frost.*

It might be said that Baumersbach's misfortune was what broke the ice between the older crews and us newcomers. Again, it was just a part of the great EXPERIMENT where much was left to trial and, too often, error.

Everybody, even Baumersbach, had a good laugh; proving that comedy – usually based on tragedy – has healing properties.

It also helped to warm the relationship between all occupants of our billet when the whole Group had a "Stand Down" without a mission on Sunday. We got better acquainted, freshened up with a shower a quarter of mile away in the "Ablution," which the "Limeys" (nickname for the British) called the showers; then had lunch in the mess, which was another quarter mile hike for those who didn't have a bicycle – like me.

Yep, my bike had been a nuisance at times, but I was glad I'd taken the trouble to put it on board the brand new B-17G we had ferried to Nutts Corner, Ireland from Savannah, Georgia. After all, there didn't seem to be any regulation against it.

The saying "if you have time to spare, travel by air" could not have been more appropriate than for our flight across the Atlantic Ocean and to the war, because the idea of going to "war" did give us *pause*. Like in, "time to spare."

We felt justified in our reluctance, because it was customary to allow the troops at least a two weeks leave to see their loved ones, for possibly the last time, before going overseas. However, it was a privilege denied our crew.

We were ordered from Drew Field at Tampa, Florida to report directly to Savannah, Georgia, to pick up a new B-17 Flying Fortress and to fly it to Europe.

Corky, our ball turret gunner, assured us that we would have orders for leave awaiting us in Savannah. How did he know that?

Well, having had his schooling toward becoming a lawyer interrupted, he was the "Barracks Lawyer" for our crew and claimed he knew about such things. Besides, just to make sure, he'd sent a telegram to President Roosevelt to correct it.

"Ohh God," Moon exclaimed. "You aren't supposed to contact the PRESIDENT of the UNITED STATES! You're not even allowed to contact your Congressmen. There's a *war* going on! They might even send us to Leavenworth prison."

"And what?" Corky asked, "Shoot us *before* they send us off to combat to get shot?"

I had been the last to be assigned to Moon's pick-up crew at Drew Field in Tampa, Florida, in December 1943, shortly before my twentieth birthday in January. Prior to that, after graduating from pilot training in the Class of 43-I at Douglas, Arizona, I had been in Columbia, South Carolina, as a pick-up copilot on B-25's. The leaders were survivors of the *30 SECONDS OVER TOKYO* group and they certainly knew how to fly the B-25 Mitchell medium bomber.

By comparison, the B-17 heavy bomber seemed very large to me with its 104' wingspan. However, Moon put me at ease from the very beginning and was tolerant of my inexperience. In fact, the whole crew was very casual, had a great sense of humor and was the most non-military group I had encountered in service.

It didn't seem to bother anyone but me that Ears appeared unable to navigate us to the east or west coast of Florida. The reason he couldn't find Florida that first night I flew with them was simply because he couldn't stay awake. But then, since it kept me awake, he didn't see any reason for both of us to worry about it and he went back to sleep.

This is not to suggest that the crew was not dedicated. Why, there was the one night we completed a whole month's practice bombing requirements on a single flight.

After loading the bomb-bay with hundred pound practice bombs, we loaded some more into the radio room and put another load into the waist of the ship so we wouldn't have to return from the bombing range to the base to reload. That would have taken many more hours.

Burnell engineered some headphones into the bomb-bay where Ears and I hung onto the catwalk above the open bomb-bay doors and listened for Eut to yell, "BOMBS AWAY!" from his bombardier's position in the nose. The rest of the crew passed the bombs to us hanging in the bomb-bay and we dropped them through the open doors. Moon, alone in the cockpit, did all of the piloting himself.

It was a good thing it had been the darkest of nights so that I couldn't see the ground below us as Ears and I hung in the open bomb-bay wrestling the bombs into position and dropping them through our legs, because height frightened me.

When we had asked for the extra bombs from the Armament Officer, he protested until we explained how we planned to get the job done.

The assignment was to drop a single bomb on each Bomb Run and not to salvo the entire lot. Therefore, the arming-wires in the bomb-bay would not have to be used, since we could arm each bomb by hand just before we dropped it. It would be as easy as – what? Falling off a log.

"Just make sure you don't fall out of the damned bomb-bay," the Armament Officer cautioned when he gave us the bombs and complimented us on our dedication to duty.

Yes, sir, we were dedicated alright – when motivated.

The extra effort in getting rid of our month's required bombs in a single night earned us the luxury of – . Well, we all felt the nurses on the Base deserved to know how much fun it really was to fly at night. A couple of them agreed, or they wouldn't have been waiting for us in the dark at the end of the runway in the flight suits we had provided them.

It was a non-sexual affair shared by ten guys about to go overseas and two caring nurses. Everyone was on their best behavior.

Moon and I stayed in the cockpit while Carmen and Dyer put them aboard in the waist. They were shown how to crawl back into the tail where Hill gave them a view from his gun position. Rudy had Glenn Miller tuned in by the time they got to the radio room and Burnell went back from his top turret to escort them forward through the bomb-bay to the flight deck, crowded by the three of them and his top turret.

The B-17 is a machine whose only purpose is that of warfare. It was not built for comfort. It lacks the luxury of space in which to move about. It is even more crowded than a submarine, without padding, and with hard corners and "grabbers" to poke and to restrict your movement. But for one black-velvet night, there was at least one Flying Fortress that seemed to share, if only so briefly, in an experience of tenderness.

It was a bandage of comfort that the nurses brought aboard in their caring about what it was that we did. Everyone a gentleman, yet like a child, proudly showing off for recognition from a surrogate "mother."

Ears and Eut guided our guests down and forward into their shared "office" in the nose, which they had made more comfortable with lifesaving cushions. There were no refreshments to be offered, but they weren't needed. In a place between heaven and earth, with the heavy drone of the four Wright Cyclone engines in the background, Glenn Miller's orchestra personally serenading from the earphones and the dancing of lights below. The flight was one of pleasure, yet haunted by melancholy.

Too soon, it seemed, it was time to go overseas, so we gave our old "Crew-Car," which we had all chipped in to buy, along with more than enough gas ration coupons, to a girl who happened to work in the PX. We had overheard that her husband, a ball-turret gunner, had been shipped overseas, she had a child, and her commute to and from work was a long bus ride. So, we all decided to give her our car, with plenty of gas coupons. In return, she gave us her gratitude, along with the memory of the tears in her eyes. Then we left for Savannah, Georgia, to pick up our new airplane.

Corky was right. A direct order from our Commander-in-Chief, President Roosevelt, awaited our arrival in Savannah. And while leave orders for two weeks at home made us very happy, everyone else at Savannah was equally unhappy with us.

Fourteen days is not much time when commercial air transportation required a Priority, which we didn't have, and bus or rail travel would eat up a week's time for both ways. I opted for the train: three days and two nights in a chair car through assorted connections to Ponca City, Oklahoma, to see my mother, brother and not many friends, as everyone was off to the war.

The good news was that my dad arranged to catch a ride in a C-47 Troop Carrier transport, who favored him with an overnight stop in Ponca City, and we both flew back with them to Grenada, Mississippi. From there I caught a ride the next day in a cross-country AT-6 trainer to Augusta, Georgia, and then took a bus to Savannah, Georgia. Thus, my leave time was mainly spent in *travailing* half way across the United States and back. However, it was well worth the effort to be with family.

Based on the philosophy of smelling the roses along the way, we did our best to hook some "sniffies" as we slowly made our way to the European Theater of Operations from Savannah, Georgia.

Out of the ten of us, there was always one who qualified to be put into hospital so that the other nine could take the opportunity to see the sights.

When Moon discovered I had a temperature just before departure from Savannah, because I was trying to cut a wisdom tooth, he told me to report to Sick Call, but not to tell them about my inflamed gum. "Let 'em try and figure it out."

So while the rest of the crew enjoyed an extra five days of recreation, I had to have my hospital bed made and breakfast finished before six A.M. every morning in order to take batteries of medical tests. They never did find the cause for my temperature, which finally subsided on its own and they dismissed me.

Our first stop was in Maryland, where we were grounded, thanks to Rudy coming down with a cold. At least Moon *thought* he was about to have a cold. And as Aircraft Commander, Moon didn't want to chance anyone breaking their eardrums from changes in air pressure at altitude. And since we couldn't leave our radioman, as important as our mission was, we would just have to make the best of the unfortunate delay.

I don't know where the rest of the crew went, but I grabbed a train for New York City and, among many things, saw the musical "OKLAHOMA!" on Broadway. I had a fun time and went about as far as I could go – and even saw a dandy burlesque show.

Our next delay was Bangor, Maine, where Moon found an excuse to go to the hospital. But it wasn't much fun there, because transient crews were quarantined to base. The only social event was a dance for enlisted personnel. And since Carmen and I were the same size, he loaned me one of his a Tech/Sgt. uniforms so that I could get into the dance.

It was a fun time until Eutrech showed up in a Buck/Sgt. uniform and found out that I outranked him by two stripes. It seemed to be okay that I was a 2nd Lt. and he was a Flight Officer, which was the equivalent to a Warrant Officer. But when he found that I had beat him to the dance and outranked him as an enlisted man, he threw a fit and left. However, he reappeared an hour later wearing a Tech/Sgt. uniform the same as I.

After a week, we flew to Goose Bay, Labrador. It was March and we played in the snow, then jumped off one long night for Iceland. It was indeed a long night. Everyone on board was asleep, except for me, since it was my turn to fly.

With the autopilot on and the drone of the engines it would have been easy for me, too, to fall asleep, but my mind was whirling with a problem I had above the middle of the Atlantic Ocean.

We had been briefed in Goose Bay that we would be flying 500 miles south of Greenland on the way to Iceland, where we would stop to refuel. But up ahead of us, *the moon was coming up out of the ocean at an ungodly angle;* or so it seemed. Since I was fighting a problem of vertigo imbalance and didn't really know up from down, I *thought* I saw some mountains in the middle of the North Atlantic Ocean.

After arguing with myself until I finally convinced myself which way was up and which was down, I awakened Ears by yelling into the intercom and then got into an argument with him about what must have been "The Lost Mountains of Atlantis," because our course was

500 miles south of Greenland and I didn't know of any other hills in the middle of the Atlantic Ocean.

What upset me was that Ears wouldn't even raise himself up on an elbow and look out of the plexi-nose to confirm what I was seeing. All he did was argue with me that there weren't any mountains in the middle of the Atlantic Ocean. I told him that I *knew that* and asked him what it might be, but he didn't respond, because he'd gone back to sleep. So I went back to yelling into the intercom to wake him up.

"What in Hell am I seeing, Ears?"

No answer.

"Hello, Ears! Could I be looking at GREENLAND?"

"Don't be ridiculous" he barked back at me, "Greenland is *five-hundred miles* off to our left."

The longer we flew, the higher the moon climbed, the brighter it became and I could tell that what stood in front of us was more solid than any hallucination. There was no question that I was going to have to make some kind of a change before we started boring a hole into it.

Finally Ears called me over the intercom and casually said, "Alter course 15 degrees to the right."

I did so immediately and tried to call him back, but he must have gone back to sleep.

Such a major change in course was proof that we had flown *500 miles off course* – and the navigator went back to sleep! How laid back and unflappable could you get?

It took some getting accustomed to Ears' style of navigating, which was: don't worry about being in the wrong place at the wrong time, because the odds favor, on occasion, being in the right place at the wrong time, or being in the wrong place at the right time.

Now, while such a philosophy might appear illogical, it did actually save us more than once. For example:

German "U" Boats were mankillers. They had sunk megatons of shipping and killed thousands of sailors in the North Atlantic. Over 400 Nazi "U" Boats had been sunk along the Atlantic and Gulf coasts of the U.S.. They had even been sighted over a thousand miles up the Amazon River in South America.

But the single Nazi sub that could have had the greatest effect on us was the one between Iceland and Scotland, whose assignment was to shoot down Allied aircraft en route from America to Great Britain. However, and for whatever reason, we had not been told about it.

The scheme was for the submarine to surface, transmit the signal of the Stornoway, Scotland, radio beacon and wait. Since the submarine was closer to the approaching aircraft than Stornoway, the sub's signal was stronger. So anyone who let down on that signal would fly unsuspectingly into the muzzle of the submarine's waiting deck gun.

Even though it had been an oversight to have not told us about the enemy sub, it didn't really matter because we had Ears on our side.

That's right. When we picked up the false signal from the Nazi sub, Ears confirmed that his Estimated Time of Arrival was right on the nose and he navigated us into a landing approach to the location of the sub – *with waiting guns!*

But thanks to Ears' talent, we naturally missed the mark – and our demise. Thus, it was proven that there were advantages to being at the *wrong* place at the right time, or the right place at the *wrong* time.

At the time, not knowing there was a submarine waiting to knock us down or blow us up, I didn't appreciate Ears' talent and was rather upset with him. I was convinced we were *lost*, because we had broken out into the clear under the clouds at less than 200 feet above the whitecaps and *no land in sight!* We didn't even reach Scotland for over an hour longer. But did it bother Ears? No, he simply refused to waste his worries on anything that someone else would worry about.

The whitecaps seemed to almost spray over the top of our wing. The sea was angry, the weather dismal and – we weren't even wearing our life vests!

Where were the Mae Wests anyway?

Burnell had gone to sleep between Moon and me up at 9,000 feet before we had let down and he was still asleep. I woke him and asked about the Mae Wests. He looked out, saw the nearness of the big, ugly ocean and disappeared.

The life vests had been packed in the bomb-bay, along with our sheep-lined flying clothes, which we certainly could have used in Labrador and Iceland. So instead of sorting through everything – including my bicycle – to find something so seemingly unnecessary as Mae Wests (for what Ears had told us would be a "short flight" across the Atlantic ocean) we had bundled up with blankets and flown for fifteen hours!

It was rather obvious who Burnell was most interested in taking care of when he came forward with the Mae Wests for us – wearing two of them around his own neck.

So it was that we had fumbled our way to the 385th Bomb Group in England, taking time out for the community dance in Stornoway,

Scotland; AWOL at Nutts Corner, Ireland, where a hole in the fence led us to a grand time in Belfast, and then a few more pauses in England along the way.

I don't recall exactly where it was that I had set myself afire, not on purpose of course.

It had been at one of those community dances where I had offered a girl a cigarette, then asked her to dance. She flipped the fire from the cigarette and handed it back to me to save for later. I did likewise but, unskilled in such a custom, I evidently failed to extinguish all of my fire.

Twirling around in a vale of smoke during one of those '40's jitterbug numbers, some older man yelled at me, "Haiyh, Yank! You're on FIRE!"

Yelling "FIRE!" on a crowded dance floor caused a near panic and everyone joined in to beat on me until the smoke cleared.

It was a good thing that I had a sense of humor.

MISSION #2
Diest Shaffen, Germany, 10 April 1944
Monday: 31 ships up   (5:15 Flying Time)

Mullins and I were assigned to fly the same old worn out Model "F" Flying Fortress, but this time in the High Squadron as "TAIL END CHARLEY." What a joke. Maybe we wouldn't even be able to get it high enough to get into the High Squadron, because the old bird seemed allergic to high altitude.

However, the ground crew had worked some kind of magic and surprised us, because the old lady performed fairly well, although I was apprehensive, remembering how everything had turned out so badly the last time. But darned if the old *gal* didn't suck right up into the formation and perch us right up on top as Tail End Charley.

Over the Channel, the gunners cleared their guns with short bursts to make sure they were working and the engines rumbled happily, holding their r.p.m. and manifold pressure. The weather was good and soon – too soon – we were into the flak.

At five miles above the earth the air is so thin that it doesn't carry sound waves very well. When the flak exploded close enough to be heard, it was too close. It was also muffled. The "BOOMP-FFFF!" of an 88-millimeter shell at earth atmosphere could have broken an eardrum – at least. But the sound itself was not that frightening at this altitude. What the fragments of metal could do, however, was of more consequence. Then there was the unpredictable mystery of its performance.

Just a few feet in front of my windshield a shell exploded. To replay it in slow motion at such a close range would be to describe it as a black flower blossoming with a very red center, actually quite beautiful against the background of white clouds. Yet, there was no mistaking its intent and destructibility.

I grabbed my chest automatially, then looked at my hands in fear, expecting them to be covered with blood – wondering at the same instant what it would feel like to be hit, while at that moment feeling no physical pain.

Well, of course not. There was no sign of blood on my hands.

I doubted what I saw and looked down to my chest. Again, no blood.

I looked at Mullins. He was okay and hard at work holding us in formation.

As closely as the flak had exploded it made no sense to have not done a great deal of damage, but there wasn't even a nick or mark on the bulletproof (?) windshield. The only effect it had was on my mind, which was wholly devoted to trying to protect myself.

So I looked to the floor where I remembered the flight engineer putting my flak-vest and flak-helmet. But to my surprise, the first thing to catch my sight was a gapping hole in the side of the ship large enough to pass a basketball through it – RIGHT NEXT TO MY FOOT!

I had not seen the explosion that caused it, nor had I even heard it. Thank God, I was spared feeling it, because it could have taken my leg – and possibly my life. We were at least four hours away from base and any medical attention.

The best to be hoped for in case of a major wound would be for someone to stop the bleeding, give you a shot of morphine from the on-board packets – if some addict had not stolen the contents – put your hand on the "D" ring of your parachute and drop you overboard. If you didn't pass out from shock or lack of oxygen and were able to pull the rip-chord and pop your chute, then your only chance of survival was to be picked up in time by some "friendly" Germans who could and would get you proper medical treatment.

Now it might seem hopeless that some Germans, who had suffered unmercifully from American bombs, would care enough to save the life of a Yank airman, yet, they did it! Yes, they did!

However, any certainty of it was as unpredictable as the hot jagged fragments of a flak burst, because other Germans were not so merciful. Some even clubbed airmen to death.

An escapee had told me that he had watched as a German farmer killed his buddy with a pitchfork. Then the farmer broke down in tears, which had allowed him to escape.

Such were the contradictions of warfare.

I discovered another paradox when I tried putting on my flak vest, because the vest fits over the parachute harness. This meant the vest would have to be removed before I could snap the parachute onto the harness, which was necessary before I could use the parachute. All of which would have to be accomplished during a panic when disaster struck and the "G" forces inside a distressed airplane would throw everything out of kilter.

I no longer thought about the fate of flak. Why? I had no control over it and its destructibility was unpredictable. Oh, there was no doubt that it could tear things apart and I was convinced that eventually it would have to get me, but the evidence so far was that I wouldn't even see the one that got me. Therefore, there was no point in worrying about the ones that I could see.

However, I could do something about preparing myself for the eventual calamity, like solving the flak-vest parachute dilemma of which came first the chute or the vest, so that I would automatically do the proper thing by –. By the way, where was my parachute, anyway?

There it was, way down there under my seat and the stiff and heavy flak-vest prevented me from even reaching it. Ahhh me. I looked at Mullins, as if he could give me some advice.

Well, when did he get his vest and flak-helmet on anyway? God, what an unromantic knight in unshining armor he was with that gawdawful stupid looking un-American leather-covered flak-helmet that was probably a hand-me-down from the R.A.F.

Mullins looked like a Rugby player. At least my helmet had some class to it, because it was a regular G.I. helmet with cut-outs for earphones and some metal ear flaps riveted to it as an afterthought. His flak helmet looked like an unglamorous leather pot, albeit metal lined.

"BOOMPFFF - RATTLE - ZING!!!"

What sounded like a buzz saw going through a basket of tin cans came to me from somewhere deep inside our ship.

From deep inside of me a prayer invented itself. "GOD! I hope we don't come apart!"

Come apart? Were we coming apart? I didn't even know that much. How stupid could I be? I was confused and going a bit crazy. I didn't even know WHAT to be afraid of. Since I was worrying, I hoped I was worrying about the important stuff. There was no point wasting it on the *wrong stuff.*

I looked at Mullins and there he sat in his uncoordinated costume, like a grotesque character from a low budget science-fiction horror film. Actually I couldn't really see him.

What I saw was helmet, goggles, oxygen mask, all inanimate except for the flak bursts in the background.

I had hoped to learn some important facts from his experiences in combat, but Mullins told me nothing. At least not with words. By example he showed me that he had his emotions under control. But how do you get such control? It was as if he had icewater in his veins. It was as if he were an exceptional professional football coach, remaining calm in the midst of calamity.

"POP!"

I heard that one and jerked my head to the right of me where it had exploded, but it was history. It was gone.

"God, let it all be gone. Let this 'cup' pass from me."

It dawned on me that I was praying. Okay.

"Dear God…"

I drew a blank. What was I to pray for? Escape? Careful. Think about it.

The quickest exit from my present problem was death. But only God knows what that brings. "To be or not to be?" "Our Father who art in heaven…"

I seemed to be losing control. No icewater in my veins. Just hot red blood, and I didn't want to lose any of it. Yet, having certainly gotten the attention of the Supreme Intelligence, I didn't even have enough intelligence to know what to ask for.

"BOOOMPFFF-KRUMPF!"

"Okay, I'll tell you what let's do. I'll do my best to do what I've been trained to do and I'll leave all the rest of it up to YOU. I *mean* it! Okay?"

"KAABOOM-PHer!"

No damage.

"Amen. We've got a deal."

Somehow I felt better, despite the fact that the sky had darkened from thousands of flak bursts that left black puffs of smoke suspended in the thin air. There seemed to be some justification for the joke: "the flak was so thick that you could get out and walk on it."

Even so, nobody had been shot down or blown up, so there was evidence that, as bad as it looked and sounded, we *were* surviving. And there was Mullins. He had survived it many times. He was my justification for hope.

"BOOMPFFF-WOOMPF!!"

I could feel that one. It bounced us pretty badly. But look. All four fans were still turning. Great! Yeah, we could get through this one. But – what about twenty-five missions?

Don't think about it. This is the one we have to make. *RIGHT NOW* is the only moment that really counts. It didn't seem possible with all of the flak exploding in the sky, but we were doing it. We were still flying and so was every ship in the formation.

UP!

Every ship in the Group jumped upward from the release of the weight of our bombs when we dropped them over the target. Ninety-three tons of high explosives! A lot of destruction. But, not enough to end the war.

There was cause for celebration. The Captain in our billet and his crew had completed their 25th mission. Their tour of combat was finished. They would be going back to the States to be with family and friends – until their next assignment to fly another tour of combat in the Pacific Theater of Operation. It would surely take years before the war ended, with no certainty as to who would win it. So what was the hurry?

Yet, we were all happy for them and envious, because two missions were just the beginning of what was yet ahead. It looked like it would take months before anyone else in the billet would "graduate." But of course, the odds were against anyone of us seeing the end of the war. It was best to not think about it. But, how could one's upcoming death not be thought about?

A game of cards was seriously undertaken in an effort to put the thoughts of today and tomorrow out of mind. A non player had his own sense of diversion and secretly emptied the contents of a 50 Caliber shell into an ashtray.

The rest of us watched in anticipation.

"WHOOOSH!"

It finally happened. Baumersbach snubbed out his cigarette and ignited the powder, filling the air with smoke and ashes. Nobody was hurt. Laughter followed the shock of it and the game was over.

Everyone decided to go to the club for a "nightcap," except for me. I simply wasn't into drinking. Maybe I should write a letter home, but first the smoke needed to be cleared from the barracks.

I opened the doors at the ends of the billet to replace the gunsmoke with the penetrating damp, cold English air. It was a poor trade, because we had only two very small coal stoves for heating our quarters, but no coal. So it was a losing proposition.

The supply of coal had run out even before we had used up our ration of it. Thus, we had each scavenged combustibles. The inside blackout door, of which we had only one, was the first thing to be converted to heat, next were the board sidewalks to keep us out of the ever-present mud and even two toilet seats had shown up for fuel. However, circumstances had been made even worse after dinner.

The Captain and his "graduating" crew had suffered the shortage of heat all through the winter, so his bombardier had finally come up with a solution. It was a bit late for their full benefit, but the rest of us hailed his genius when after dinner he had staggered into the barracks with the answer to our common problem.

Now it is a fact that after the debriefing, after each mission and just before dinner, the air crew members were offered a ration of brandy, which was just the beginning for the bombardier. Since he had reason to celebrate his good fortune in "graduating," and there was a delay in serving dinner, he had decided to bypass dinner – having not had lunch or even breakfast – and had gone to the bar at the club.

Returning to billet after dinner we had all joined in the necessary and primitive ritual of breaking down our eclectic fuel source into pieces small enough to fit into the narrow throats of the two little stoves.

The bombardier staggered through the door with the final solution for heating the billet. Looking as Moses must have appeared with the sacred tablets, he stopped and straightened up to present his answer to the problem. For in his arms, like an ancient tablet of stone, he carried a single incendiary bomb, about thirty inches in length and weighing about thirty pounds.

We all cheered, each of us wondering why we hadn't thought of such a simple remedy. Nothing put out more heat than magnesium fire bombs and there had to be a large supply of them.

Well – we soon changed our minds when the bombardier unsafe-tied the bomb and slammed it down the throat of the little stove nearest my bed with a "THUMP"!

The fuse popped loudly and ignited the bomb, which sizzled and burned – and burned – and burned the magnesium – and burned the fire brick – and burned out the iron bottom of the stove – and burned the brick below it into ashes – and burned away the iron wall of the stove – and the chimney fell out of the ceiling, leaving a hole in the roof – and the stovepipe was also consumed when it fell into the pool of white heat.

Nobody did anything, except to stand motionless in awe.

When the fired eventually burned itself out, it then occurred to each of us that the solution had backfired, because we were left with only *one* little stove.

So alone in the billet, I hoped that everyone would get real drunk up at the club, or they were going to be mighty unhappy to find on their return that I had opened both doors to air out the place and that we were behind the power curve, so to speak, with no way to heat the barracks to any level of comfort.

I closed the doors, stuffed some sticks into the remaining little stove, around which everyone had huddled for the card game, then strolled down to my bunk feeling very tired from the days activities.

It had been necessary for us to cover our bunks with our sheep-lined flying gear of jacket and trousers in order to try to keep warm. I stripped down to my long underwear and snuggled myself down into my "fart sack."

Even though they were not a favorite of mine, I did find some reward for having had beans and brussel sprouts at dinner.

Sleep did not come. There were just too many thoughts in my head, like, would I ever get to be twenty-one years old? I tried to guess what that might be like. Would I even get to be a month older? A week? What about tomorrow? Where would I be tomorrow night?

Before I realized it the time passed and everyone returned from the club in good spirits, everyone except "Thumper," as they had christened the infamous bombardier.

Accompanied with much complaining about no heat in the barracks, the coldness motivated everyone to crawl into their sacks rather quickly. Their haste, however, was so great that nobody thought of turning out the lights.

The problem of who was to get out of bed and into the cold to turn out the lights became quite vocal. Orders were given and protested. Who outranked whom? It didn't make any difference. Nobody volunteered to leave what little comfort could be found in their bunks.

The solution, in the form of Thumper, finally staggered through the doorway. Great. We could soon go to sleep.

"Hey Thumper, turn out the lights!"

Thumper did not respond to the request. He just sat on his bunk giggling about some private amusement as he slowly undressed. He was so drunk that the cold did not bother him; not even when he took ALL of his clothes off. He only giggled more when everyone yelled at him, pleading for him to "*TURN OUT THE GODDAMNED LIGHT!*"

It was my fault. I made the mistake of yelling at him, "If you don't want to get out of bed, shoot 'em out!"

Yes, it was a real bad mistake!

But, it pleased Thumper and his giggles broke into wild laughter as he leaned out of his bunk toward his pistol in a shoulder holster hanging from a chair.

Since the light bulb he focused on was hanging between us, I would be in the line of fire, so I jumped straight up in bed and started running for the nearest door. SHIT! After what I'd been through, I was going to be killed by a damned drunken American bombardier.

I don't know if it was because it was the shortest distance or my dread of stepping barefoot onto the cold concrete floor, but I ran from atop one bunk to the next, stepping onto and into the occupants who groaned and yelled and also started for the door.

I hit the door just as Thumper fired his .45, hitting – believe it or not – a light bulb, which hung almost exactly between our positions. I heard the round buzz past me!

There couldn't have been one qualifying expert out of three hundred who could have hit that light bulb even if they were sober. Yet, Thumper had knocked it out with a single shot!

However, my amazement did not slow me, nor anyone else. Nor did it stop Thumper. He was determined to shoot out all of the lights and he kept blasting away – hitting nothing except the walls of the billet – which did not stop the rounds. They just whizzed on through.

The only safe place, I thought, was inside of a bomb shelter bunker, which I entered at full speed in the darkness of the blackout. I immediately discovered that the floor was covered with about five inches of very wet and cold mud, because my feet went out from under me and I hit the floor and slid on my back in the slime.

As soon as the shooting stopped, I left the shelter, determined to stomp a mud puddle into the middle of the damned drunken bombardier. But it didn't take long, under the circumstances, for me to cool down, because, covered with mud, I was *freezing*!

The only warm water – if there was any at all at midnight – was a quarter of a mile away in the Ablution, or the Cleansing Area. So I settled for stripping down to bare skin when I got back inside and wiped the mud off of me with a couple of towels. Quickly afterwards, I shivered myself into a perfectly clean uniform and shook myself down into my sack.

As I had gotten the worst of it, everyone else laughed at my misfortune and at the loss of my sense of humor. However, the war and our jeopardy had been forgotten, at least briefly, until each of us was eventually left with our private thoughts as we tried to rest in preparation for tomorrow, which was already – TODAY.

Messerschmitt Me 109, "The Enemy."

THE FIGHTERS
CHAPTER 3

I wondered if my eyes were open or closed and made an effort to blink. there was no change. because it was dark either way. The only difference was, I knew I wasn't asleep. It was quiet. Nobody snored. Combat crews did not snore, because you have to be sound asleep to snore. It was very quiet and dark in our billet.

I whispered, "Are you awake, Moon?"

"Yeah."

"Ears?"

"What?"

"Nothing."

The door at our end of the billet opened slowly. The silhouette in our doorway had to be Sergeant Gatt with flashlight in hand. He kept his "torch" pointed toward the floor so as not to disturb anyone as he stood there to arrange his cigarettes.

It was a ritual that might be regarded as a sacred ceremony. For Gatt, the "Priest of Appointment," was the one who anointed those who had been selected and dedicated to the battle for the day. He took his calling seriously and reverently, complete with the burning of incense.

Between his lips he would place four cigarettes at a time and light them all at once. Then devoutly, as if serving communion, he would go forth to those ordained for the day's battle and place between their lips the emblem of appointment: a lighted cigarette. The liturgy would be repeated until all who had been selected for the day's mission had been so alerted.

When he placed the cigarette between my lips I put my wrist in front of my face and inhaled so that the glow of it illuminated the dial of my watch. The time was 02:04.

I heard Moon ask him what he thought the mission might be and Gatt responded with what he had learned through his grapevine.

"It looks like it's going to be a very long one today. Twenty-seven hundred gallons and only eight five-hundred pound H.E. s"

Nothing unusual about the High Explosives, except the number of bombs was less in order to increase our range.

"Maybe Berlin?" Moon asked with some anticipation.

"The guess is," Gatt replied, "It'll be farther than Berlin."

"Farther than Berlin?" Nothing had ever been farther than Berlin. What in Hell did he mean?

Gatt didn't know. His job was in the Orderly Room. He only repeated what his informers from the flight line told him as a favor to the anxious air crew members.

As usual, the Enlisted Men of the air crews were the first to have been gotten up, driven to the mess hall, taken to Flight Equipment where they drew parachutes and flight gear, had their own briefing and were shuttled to the plane parked on the hardstand. There they inspected and installed the barrels into their guns, while we officers were given the privilege to sleep a bit longer.

Sleep? I hadn't gotten a good night's sleep since the first mission three days ago and I had 23 more missions to go. How long could you go without sleep anyway? Could you die from no sleep?

"It's time to go Lieutenant."

I awoke with Gatt standing over me with another cigarette. I checked my watch and saw that I had picked up about fifteen minutes of sleep. Even knowing that the mission was going to be a long one to Hell-and-gone – just *knowing* was enough to calm my anxiety and allow me to drop off into dead sleep.

Gatt knew this, bless his heart. And while he didn't know about the flying stuff and what it was like to be up there, he had a deep caring and respect for those he awoke to send off into the Wild Blue Yonder. And while he had the appearance of a tough-guy gangster, he treated us as gentle as if he were a loving mother; purposely starting to awaken us early enough to allow us to go to sleep, if only briefly.

Well, it was time to get up and to go and see what was farther away than Berlin.

PICTURED ABOVE RIGHT:
The Boeing B-17G "Flying Fortress." Note the "chin Turret" under the nose. The 385th Bomb Group flew B-17s with both the Square G and Red Checkered tail markings.

MISSION #3
Stettin, Poliz (Poland), 11 April 1944
Tuesday: 35 ships up, 3 down.
(11:00 Hours Flying Time)

Moans and low whistles filled the briefing hall when the curtain was drawn back to show the Operational Map with a courseline that stretched across the entire width of the map from England to near the northern coast of Poland, a Baltic seaport at the mouth of the Oder river – beyond and northeast of Berlin, which Germany had taken from Poland.

Stettin had a population of about 300,000. Its value as a target was that it was a main harbor for eastern Germany with ship building and repairs, and factories that produced iron, paper and textiles.

Not only would we have to fly over five hours to get to the target; but it was equally as far to get back home, depending on just how much opposition we encountered. The Germans would certainly have us in their back yard long enough to hurt us. Hell, it was shorter to Russia from the target than it was back home.

Moon and I exchanged glances for reassurance, because this would be our first combat mission together. No more flying with a veteran crew, although we had been assigned an experienced ball gunner who was filling in for our regular ball gunner, "Corky" Corscadden, who had reported in sick. Maybe Corky knew something we didn't know. If so, it appeared that we would know a lot more than he before the end of the day.

Not only was our regular crew flying together again, except for Corky, but we were assigned a newer B-17 G model with electronic controlled superchargers and a chin turret up front with twin 50 Caliber machine guns. Its name was *PRIDE OF THE YANKEES.*"

The Crew Chief met us as we unloaded at the revetment and he invited us into his tent where he had coffee warming on his own creation of a stove that was fueled by hydraulic fluid. It was much better than what we had.

The Chief was obviously quite proud of his brand new airplane and regarded us a bit like a father sizing up a first date for his daughter. It was made more believable by his appearance – a Technical Sergeant who looked old enough to be my dad.

I was the first into the tent and tried to see us through the eyes of the seasoned Crew Chief as Moon, Ears and Eut came in and laid their chutes on the ground around the warm stove.

Moon had been a salesman before the war. Not too many years before the war, because he was only twenty-four. However, he had sold many different things and, by his nature, he was a salesman.

"Hi Sarge," he said, reaching out to shake hands, "I'm Ernest G. Baumann. Some call me 'Dirty lil' Ernie.' I'll be piloting your fine airplane an' you'll probably call me even worse before I'm finished with it." He then introduced me, Ears and Eut.

The Sergeant accepted the aggressive and false bravado for what it was – an attempt at devil-may-care in the face of impending disaster.

He must have seen it many times before. Here this young second Lieutenant, with his cap pushed back on the top of his head so far there was wonder as to what kept it from falling off, was trying to establish himself as the confident leader of a bomber crew. And what a crew.

Both Ears and Eut were still hung over from just hours before and sort of folded down onto their parachutes as they contemplated the coffee pot on the little stove. None of us had eaten breakfast. Not so much from moving too slowly and not having enough time, but from a general loss of appetite prior to a mission.

Ears and Eut were like two zombies, just there. Ears was laid back anyway. Eut was only twenty-two, but looked oddly older, because he kept his hair cut so short it looked like he was bald. He also appeared to be a bit malnourished, and especially this morning, his complexion was ashen and sickly. The tallest on the crew, over six feet, Eut probably weighed the least of any of us.

Attempting to be hospitable, the Sarge offered to share some cans of sardines his wife had mailed him. He produced an open can with the explanation that it was sometimes difficult for him to get to the mess hall and the sardines were a great snack. When he made an offer to Eutrecht to partake of the little fish floating in oil, Eut almost lost what he didn't have and staggered to his feet on the way out of the tent.

Ears picked up both his and Eut's parachutes and left with the excuse that he'd best take care of our bombardier. Of course Moon and I knew, as I'm sure the Sarge did, that they were both headed for the inside of the nose of the ship where they would get on oxygen immediately to sober up.

I was almost surprised that Moon didn't join them, because he could match Ears drink for drink. But to his credit, I had never seen Moon crawl into a cockpit with any hint of inebriation. Exuberation, if there was such a word, was more fitting to Moon's attitude. It was as if he relished the chance to sally forth into combat. At least that was the impression he tried to give.

After listening to the Sarge expressing his pride in his new *PRIDE OF THE YANKEES*, Moon responded with an embarrassingly failed attempt to sound like an Englishman. "I say, that's smashing of you old man. Smithy and I shall endeavor to return safely without pranging your kite. Now, best we get cracking."

The Sarge and I exchanged glances of amusement and followed Moon out of the tent to *THE PRIDE OF THE YANKEES*. What a ham.

We tossed our chutes up and overhead into the forward hatch and joined the Sarge and Burnell in pulling the props through.

Oil tends to drain downward into the lower cylinders of radial engines. To start an engine with oil in the cylinder head is likely to "blow a jug" and tear up the engine. So the engines are turned over slowly by pulling the props through by hand.

Now, I had been a three year letterman as a running guard in highschool football. The Air Force had kept me in shape and modestly I could deliver above average power for my 175 pounds, but those three-bladed paddle props with a diameter of 13 feet, and held back by engine compression, was more than a match for me. That's why props were pulled through by at least two guys on one blade at a time.

Moon was my prop-pulling partner, but it was almost a joke, because he didn't weigh a hundred and fifty pounds. Nevertheless, he would lead the charge and tackle a prop like a miniature Schnauzer attacking a bull – being stopped in his tracks when the prop wouldn't budge. But like I said, it's at least a two-man task.

Even so, each time Moon tackled a prop it was as if this was the time he could make it work.

With the job finished and leaning against the blade to catch our breath, Moon said, "Kiss it."

"Whaaat?"

"Kiss the goddamned prop," he said and gave it a great big kiss.

I stared at him as if he'd lost his mind and he stared back.

"KISS THE GODDAMNED PROP!"

He'd never ordered me to do anything before, but this was a command. He was serious and I was dumbfounded. I guess he felt he owed me some kind of explanation, so he said, "It's for good luck. Kiss the goddamned prop." I did and he walked away.

After awhile I heard him calling for me in the dark, "Hey Smitty! Over here!"

He kept calling and I was able to find him behind the Crew Chief's tent and asked him what he wanted.

"Piss on the tent peg."

"What?"

"Piss on the goddamned tent peg."

I said, "You must've learned something on those last two missions we didn't fly together that I somehow missed."

"PISS ON THE GODDAMNED TENT PEG!"

"For good luck?" I asked.

There was disgust in his voice. "Now, why in Hell would anybody be stupid enough to want to piss on a goddamned tent peg if it wasn't for good luck?"

"Well, that sure as Hell makes good sense to me," I said, and joined him in pissing on the tent peg. I mean, you never really know about those things and there was no reason to invite any bad luck.

Having started in the dark we approached Denmark by early morning, but couldn't see it due to an undercast. However Ears, our "tour guide," informed us of our location over the intercom by stating that we were over the North Sea and approaching Denmark. I asked if he was positive and, before he could answer, we were greeted with bursts of flak.

"Ears," I asked, "If we're over the water, where is this fucking flak coming from?"

"Well" he answered, "It's got to be the island of Helgoland. Yeah, that's it. The map shows flak batteries on the island of Helgoland... So, we're right on course...Nothing to worry about."

Bullshit! Nothing to worry about? We no sooner got out of the flak than "Yeh, Yeh," as we called Carmen, reported from his right waist position, "Yeh, Yeh! Bogies!!!"

He was excited. "Yeh-Yeh. It looks like three bogies at three o'clock high – wayyy out there."

It was the calm reassuring voice of the veteran ball gunner that came over the intercom. "Just take it easy now. Nuthin's gonna happen – not just yet."

"Yeh-Yeh. There's three more joinin' up!! Can you see 'em?"

"Not from down here. Just take it easy. There's gonna be a bunch more before they decide to hit us...Just wait. You'll see."

Waiting can be the most difficult discipline there is; especially if you have to wait for somebody coming to kill you.

The undercast was building up and we were beginning to pick up clouds at our level. In fact, the clouds ahead of us extended above us at 27,000 feet up to perhaps 35,000 feet.

Unidentified aircaft were called "Bogies." Enemy airplanes were "Bandits." Friendly planes were "Friendlies."

I'd been watching the Bogies out to our right, but they were more difficult to see due to the increasing clouds.

Hopefully we would also be hard to see, if they were Bandits, but clouds meant moisture and moisture in below freezing conditions turned into telltale white contrails that marked the bomber stream.

We were 35 bombers with four engines each and soon each of the 140 engines was beating the latent moisture into ice crystals that streamed behind us like a great white highway. We were not hard to find or to identify. Just follow the white crystal road, because we were at the front of the parade.

I had gotten top grades in flying school for aircraft identification, but the real thing was different. Instead of a large silhouette flashed on the screen for a hundredth of a second and waiting for the image to reappear in your mind like a replay, the "Bogies" were too far away for me to identify. However, I was fairly certain of one thing. The "Bogies" would turn out to be "Bandits," because the only "friendly" fighter I'd seen had been that one single P-47 "Jug" and not six – DAMN!!!

A break in the clouds and I could see, not six, but – a dozen of those little rascals darting around. I switched communications over to tell Moon, who was monitoring the Command Channel, but he'd just heard that a dozen "Bandits" were queuing up at 3 o'clock High. Somebody in the lead ship must have had binoculars.

It was interesting to find that fighters also left contrails – even inside of the clouds. We flew through one that seconds before could have been a collision and a great big bang. Surely the Bandits could figure out that hunting bombers in the clouds was as high a risk for them as it was for us. It would be to their advantage to catch us when we came out of the clouds. I regretted the fact that there were no fox holes in the sky and that we couldn't just hide in the clouds until the danger passed.

By the time we finally came out of the clouds two hours later we were just northwest of Stettin – where about forty Bandits flying ME 109's waited for us!

There was a common philosophy among combatants that if you told three of them that two would be killed, each one of them would think to himself, I'm sure gonna miss you other guys. However, it was different with me, because I KNEW that I was the one who would be killed. The only questions were WHEN and HOW and this day looked like I'd be getting an answer to both.

As the Bandits queued up alongside to our right, less than two miles away at the 3 o'clock High position, in preparation for attacking us, I thought it would be a good idea to wear my parachute, but... *Where was the damned thing, anyway?* I hated to take my eyes off of the enemy as they pulled forward to get ahead of us, but I looked for my chute instead.

There, I found it, but I had to unbuckle my seat belt to retrieve it from under my seat and snap it on, thinking I would have had a helluva time trying to do it while in a spin or on fire.

I got it snapped onto my chest, but found that both the chute and I could not fit between the back of my seat and the wheel! I glanced forward and saw the fighters turning into us from 12 o'clock High – and I really wasn't ready for the shooting to start!

To hell with it! I unsnapped my chute, threw it to the floor, jumped into my seat and grabbed the wheel to assist Moon when needed.

The attacks were head on and, as the saying goes, "They sure tore us a new ass hole."

Our 150 mph plus their 400 mph made the rate of closure almost as fast as the speed of sound. Then there would be a brief time-out while they turned around to reassemble up on the "perch" off and above our right flank.

I was glad we were in the High Squadron, even though it was difficult to see much below us, because the bulk of the attacks were concentrated into the Lead and Low Squadrons.

"Yeh, Yeh!" Carmen called, "Get up here where I can get ya!"

"Get off the intercom!" I scolded, yet understanding his frustration of being a gunner and wanting to test himself.

Eut rumbled a few rounds out of the twin fifties in the chin turret, but it was ineffective and dangerous, because he was shooting down toward the Lead Squadron and could have hit one of our own ships.

Our veteran ball turret gunner so advised Eut over the intercom, then educated the rest of us. "You guys up top, don't worry about what's goin' on down here. Get your eyes on the sky above us and off to our left. There could be more coming in from the other way."

Good idea…I was glad we had an experienced man on board who wasn't too bashful to keep from speaking up. It was a lesson on which I drilled myself to not forget. Fighters to the right! You'd better glance over your left shoulder and keep your head on a swivel despite the obvious fatal attraction.

The rule was: if they are close enough for you to shoot at them, then you are close enough for them to shoot you. So the advantage went to the first one who saw the other.

The Messerschmitts went through us from head to tail six times before the flak near the target drove them away.

Getting into the flak actually made me feel pretty happy: "flak happy." Everything was relative; being shot at by impersonal flak from far below was better than being shot at by other pilots a few yards in front of you, like a shoot-out in a Western movie – face to face.

But what was the damage?

We lost three ships: thirty men, with no survivors reported. Pangle, Bailey, and…*Mullins*.

Mullins had been down in Coffin Corner again. I was thankful for having not flown with him just one more final time. I could see him in my mind, stoically riding it down. But already I was unable to recall his features, though I could never forget the figure of his unique flak helmet, goggles and oxygen mask that covered his face.

"God bless you Mullins."

"God bless us all."

Why hadn't I been assigned to fighters instead of bombers, like I'd requested? This was the *Shits*, sitting here with a wheel in your hand, instead of a stick with a trigger on it. It wasn't easy to just sit and watch fighters coming straight into you with pink flashes on their wings and in their noses, and the only thing between your chest and their guns was an instrument panel and a plexiglass nose…It really wasn't easy.

I noticed that it was around eleven-thirty right after we had dropped our bombs and were still in the flak, and I thought, Boy, this sure is a long day, because we're only about halfway through it and we've been going pretty strong for over nine hours since briefing…It sure was a long way back home. I couldn't help wondering what else was going to happen.

We were fortunate that the fighters were not waiting for us when we left the target. They were probably short of fuel, having stalked us for so long due to the weather.

But I wasn't complaining. I'd take the flak any day over the fighters, because of the human element. Flak seemed impersonal, while it was just plain scary to have a bunch of guys up there with you, coming at you with six machine guns and a 30mm cannon each. What I wouldn't give for a fighter plane. However, there weren't any. We didn't even have any escorts, because they didn't have the range to reach us.

The air battle and the target had been in the clear, despite their vague attempt to try and hide the target under a white smokescreen. Even so, we hit the target and after "BOMBS AWAY," we flew to the "R. P.," Rally Point.

Shortly afterwards we were back into the clouds and on our long way home, about 600 miles to the English coast. However, we would be passing within only 60 miles of the Swedish coast.

Now, there was a consideration.

Had we lost a couple of engines over the target – if the fighters hadn't gotten us – we could have cut the trip short, as well as all of our missions, by going to Sweden. After all, it was the thing to do, because Sweden and Switzerland were the only two neutral sanctuaries and a lot of crews had gone to both places where they would sit out the war. It sounded like going to heaven.

The older crews had told us about the attractions of such an option, but there was a made-up, unofficial requirement that you had to qualify among your peers by having completed at least twenty missions before you could take the coward's way out.

So despite all of the wishful thinking and joking about an easy way out of the war, it was generally considered better to be a dead hero than to bear the brand of COWARD the rest of your life.

Besides, nobody was shooting at us for the moment and the PRIDE OF THE YANKEES was performing nobly and the scenery was spectacular as we broke out of and through towering cloud formations. It was a piece of cake…food – which reminded me…

I crawled out of my seat and found my musette bag, which was a small knapsack usually issued to the copilots, that contained bailout packets and "K" rations, which I had distributed to the crew except for Moon's and my own.

The "K" rations came in a plain brown waxed box about the size of a Cracker Jack box. They were label "B" for Breakfast, "L" for Lunch and "D" for Dinner. Dinner was the favorite, because it had some meat packaged in a small can, like deviled-ham. Otherwise they were all about the same: three cigarettes; some chewing gum, what might pass for a couple of dog biscuits and a bar of dark bittersweet chocolate that was rock hard – not only at below zero temperatures, but even at ground zero on a warm day. Chewing it was not possible and it was difficult to melt by sucking on it.

I handed Moon a dinner box, put another in my seat for my return and signaled that I was going aft to take a pee in the bomb-bay. Moon called the ball turret gunner to advise him of my intentions so that the gunner would rotate his turret rearward. Otherwise, his single window would be iced up and he would be out of business.

Relief tubes were a devilish device that were best avoided, because they consisted of a small rubber funnel on the end of a tube that was plumbed to evacuate the waste to the exterior. With one end open into the slipstream, the other end acted as a vacuum hose. It was also at least as cold as the below zero temperature of the outside air, even without the wind chill factor, and its small opening guaranteed that it would make contact with your most private parts.

So, given a choice of disconnecting the wires and tubes for communications and oxygen, plugging into a walk-around bottle of oxygen, crawling out of your seat and fighting your way through the tight squeeze around the top turret to get back into the bomb-bay – or trying to use the relief tube after digging down through your flak suit, parachute harness, Mae West, flight suit, electric flying suit, long underwear and trying to find that little shriveled up blue thing – there was really no choice. The trip to the bomb-bay was better.

When I got back into my seat and took over the piloting chores, Moon took his turn to the bomb-bay. Afterward Ears took his turn, and stopped between us on his way back into the nose.

Even with the oxygen mask covering his face you could see the strain of a smile in his bloodshot eyes. It was obvious that he was not at all well and he was freezing because, having not brought his sheeplined gear and electric suit, he had only his light A-2 jacket.

I found an intercom extension for him to plug into and Moon asked him, "Cold?"

Ears just shook his head that he was cold. I felt sorry for him, but there was nothing anyone could do about his not having prepared himself for the flight. It was certain be would learn from this mistake.

"What about Eut?" Moon asked.

"I don't want to go back down there," Ears answered.

"What's wrong?"

"Eut's sick. I don't wanna go back down there"

"Why?" Moon asked.

Ears pointed forward, but we couldn't understand what he was trying to tell us. So Moon asked him to clarify.

"Astro-dome!"

We looked for the plexiglass astrodome located directly in front of us in the top of the nose compartment, but it was not in place. Strange we hadn't missed it, but then our focus had necessarily been on the ship whose wing we'd been flying on. So Moon asked what had happened to it.

"Eut's sick," Ears explained painfully. "He's got diarrhea. He took the astrodome out so he'd have something to shit into."

"Well," Moon asked, "Did he shit into it?"

"Yes and no."

"Yes and No?" Moon asked. "Either he shit into it or he didn't shit into it. What did he do?"

"Oh, Hell," Ears said, "He shit *in* to it – and then he shit out of it – and then shit all over everything down there…I really don't want to go back down there."

"Well you'd better get back down there," Moon said, "And you guys better get it cleaned up or that Crew Chief is going to kill us all for messing up his brand new airplane! He'll see to it that we get assigned some old patched up "F" model if we can't take care of this airplane."

Of course everyone on the intercom heard what had happened. Ears unplugged from the intercom and reluctantly went down and forward into the nose. I not only felt sorry for him, I pained for him. For as miserably sick and cold as he was, the nose compartment was the coldest place in the ship with a large hole that had been left in the ceiling where the astro-dome had been.

Eventually we saw the plexiglass dome replaced with its telling stain of brown. Hopefully the Crew Chief would have some forgiveness in his heart, having surely experienced even worse.

Flying on top of the overcast, five shells exploded above us and a bit off to the right.

I called Ears and asked, "Helgoland?"

"Helgoland," he confirmed.

I told him that I didn't want to add to his problems, but that I would appreciate his letting me know before we got into a flak area. I gave him a reading of fuel on board. And since we now knew where we were, asked him to calculate an ETA to England and to the base, because it looked to be a squeaker as far as our range was concerned. I also alerted Moon and he called for a reduction to seventeen-hundred RPM, and I gave him the lower revolutions on the engines.

Apparently, the reason the bursts of flak were above us was our having started a slow let-down and we were below their estimated altitude for us. It was also reassuring that the Lead Navigator knew our position in leaving the continent, which had allowed us to start our descent.

The Base Engineering Officer would not be pleased that we'd cut the RPM below eighteen-fifty, due to the strain on the engines, because the slower RPM meant the props were biting larger chunks of air. He'd shown an example of how such a strain had burnt holes through pistons.

Our justification was that it was better to blow some jugs than to lose the whole plane in the "drink" for having run out of fuel. Big bites of air gave better mileage. Besides, he didn't like us pissing in the bomb-bay either. So what was he going to do? Ground us? Not likely, because he might have to take up the slack and fly some combat missions for us.

Well, there it was. Great Ashfield! But there would be no celebrating until we got safely on the ground. And there they were. You could see the rest of the team waiting for us; everyone on the Base that could be there was there, as they always were; hundreds of them to welcome us back home and to count our losses.

We made the traditional pass over the field in formation. It came our turn and we peeled off, circled around and landed and not at all too soon. We had no more completed our landing role and turned to the right to get off the runway to make room for those anxiously coming in behind us, than the #1 engine quit from fuel starvation.

Burnell quickly transferred fuel to #1. We got it started and taxied out of the way and back to our hardstand. The Crew Chief was pleased to see his plane back and started immediately to inspect for damage.

He never did mention the mess left in the nose by Eut. However, he did tell us later that what little fuel remained in our tanks had all drained out on the tarmac from the flak holes.

I slept hard, but not for long, awakening while slapping and pulling at my face to get the spiders off. Thousands of little black spiders, even crawling up my nose.

The light made me squint, because it was still daylight and I was in the lousy billet. What was going on? I jerked a look at my hands to see if the spiders were also on them. As I sucked deeply for air it occurred to me that I had been dreaming.

God, I felt terrible. I was stiff all over and was partially paralyzed from the muscles that had also gone to sleep. I stretched my fingers then pulled at my face and massaged it in an effort to get back to living.

Sliding my feet off of the bunk to the floor, I put my elbows on my knees and my tired face into my hands. It was the fault of that damned *suck-sack*. I'd had the oxygen mask on for – how many hours was it? Seven or eight.

Jesus, what a nightmare – and it wasn't even nighttime. What time was it anyway? I looked at my watch and it wasn't yet seven o'clock. Where was everybody? I'd laid down on my bunk after eating and had dropped off – and was about to do it again when four new flying officers entered the billet as replacements: Second Lieutenant Turner as pilot with his copilot, navigator and bombardier. I did my best to make them feel welcome, because misery welcomes company.

Although cloud cover allowed you to play "hide and seek" with enemy fighters, it made it extremely difficult to hold formation. If you lost contact it was suicide to blindly try to rejoin the formation in the clouds.

THE WEATHER
CHAPTER 4

On the 1st of February 1943, President Franklin D. Roosevelt and Britain's Prime Minister Winston Churchill met for ten days at Casablanca in North Africa to reach "total agreement" on the conduct of the war. Only "unconditional surrender" of the Axis nations would be considered acceptable for the ending of the war.

As a result, the Combined Chiefs of Staff issued a directive code-named "Pointblank" whereby the U.S. Air Force would concentrate on destroying German fighter power, because there could be no victory until the Luftwaffe was no longer a threat.

Well, "Good Luck!" as they say, because these guys, unlike us inexperienced amateurs, were very experienced professionals who had captured and kept the airspace over all of continental Europe for Hitler's Third Reich, and we were supposed to go into the lion's den and defeat them in their own territory(?). We were supposed to out-bad the Bad Guys?

After all, we could hardly be the Good Guys if we took the war to their homeland by dropping bombs and blowing up the place. But then, Good Guys don't win wars, because WAR IS A BUSINESS OF BADNESS.

Be that as it may, I didn't hate anyone, not even my enemy. Sure, I hated going out to gamble my very life, but I sensed that my enemy felt the same way as I.

It was almost ironic, since my enemy over Germany was the Germans – as was I.

At least I was half-German, because my mother's parents were both from Germany. Only by a slight shift of Fate and I might have been in the Luftwaffe.

As aviators we had much in common and, without hate, we would fight each other in order to end the fighting. No hate, because hate is ultimately self defeating. I'd found that out early on as a boxer and from too many fist-fights.

Forget trying to find any logic in it. Just do your duty and sometime your future son might also sing the barracks ballad: "Flak suits, parachutes and wings of silver too. He'll bomb the target like his daddy used to do."

Well it was finally my turn. The Germans had bombed everyone in Europe until the Yanks showed up to poop the party by bombing Berlin in March 1944 and the Germans didn't like that at all.

So here it was the 18th of April and with the hornet's nest all stirred up, my chance had come to go to BIG "B."

MISSION #4
Berlin, Germany, 18 May 1944
Tuesday: 32 ships up, 2 down.
(9:15 Flying Time)

Moon and I, along with the Ears and Eut, were pleased to find we had been assigned the relatively new *"PRIDE OF THE YANKEES* B-17 "G," which meant we shouldn't have to worry too much about mechanical problems.

Ears had made sure to wear his sheeplined clothing, plus an electric flying suit underneath, and Eut was free of diarrhea, so the people-problems were probably under control. We were fortunate that the rest of the crew always did a good job of taking care of themselves. Maybe too good.

"You know," Moon said, as we waited for the briefing to begin, "We've gotta watch our gunners."

What did he mean? Our gunners had already been briefed and at 3 a.m. were now out at the ship in the dark under blackout restrictions loading their guns.

"B-R-R-R-R-R-R-R-R-R-R-R-R-R-R-R-R-R-R-R-R-T!!!!!!"

The sound of a 50 caliber machine gun struck silence over all of us in the briefing room and heads were ducked. Only pride kept everyone from diving to the floor. Some gunner had lost control of his weapon, which happened on occasions. Hopefully nobody got hit.

Moon looked at me and I stuck my thumb back over my shoulder as if to ask, "Is that what you're talking about?"

"No," he said. "Our guys take good care of us. But what worries me is, they don't want to get caught short and I noticed on the last mission that they stowed extra ammo on board. That damned stuff's heavy! There is a limit to what the plane can lift."

"HAT-TEN-SHUT!"

Everyone rose to attention. Colonel Vandevanter took the stage and was followed by his staff. Respectfully called "The Old Man," he had graduated from West Point, flown his first combat in the Philippines and was 26 years old. He seemed to suffer from a chronic throat irritation, because he could never get it cleared. Maybe it was nerves.

"At Ease…The target for today is…(ahem)."

"(Ahem)…The target for…(ahem)…(ahem)."

"The ahh (ahem)…The (ahem) for today is…"

Jesus Christ, let him say it. The suspense is brutal.

"The target for today is – BIG 'B'."

The drapery drew back from the operational map and the long red ribbon indicating the courseline, as usual, caused a reaction of moans to whistles and even a couple of cheers. Cheers? Who were they kidding?

The Intelligence Officer reported there were over 400 antiaircraft guns in the target area and I recalled a fact from high school history. Both the North and the South in the Civil War did not have more than 250 muzzle-loading cannon at Gettysburg…Berlin would be unloading at least 150 more automatic radar-directed, larger caliber guns at us than were fired at Gettysburg on both sides…Well, that should put it in perspective.

Then the Weather Officer gave us the bad news: "Weather-reconnaissance flights over the target report it socked in with clouds up to 20,000 feet. Although, it should clear by the time you get there. However, there will be a lot of weather along the way. But with the freezing level at 15,000 feet, you won't have icing above that."

Well, that was okay to not have ice building up on your wings, since everything at that level would already be frozen, but what guarantee was there we could get up to 15 Angels without getting a buildup of ice along the way? While we had alcohol anti-icing for the props, we didn't have de-icing boots on the leading edge of our wings

– probably removed to reduce drag. I guessed that somebody must know what they were doing to us.

Like Stettin, Poland, it looked to be a mixed bag, playing hide and seek among the clouds with the fighters. It was good we'd had a few days between missions for practice flights, but nothing could match the real thing.

Pilots were dismissed from briefing while navigators and bombardiers remained for details and to get their route-charts and flak maps with the updates on the flak areas. I picked up my ditty bag of K-rations and bailout packets when I left.

There was one packet for each crew member. Each packet, about $1^1/_2$ x 5 x 7 inches, contained colorful silk scarves (which were actually maps), benzedrine tablets for alertness, dextrose tablets for energy, a button that was really a compass when balanced on a sharp point, an empty water bottle and money. The packets were not to be used except for emergency and had to be turned in after the mission.

In addition to the bailout packets, we each carried our personal bailout pictures. These were pass photographs made on the Base that showed us in a civilian coat, shirt and tie. We carried them in case we were picked up by the Underground. The pictures could be given to the Underground who could use them to obtain forged passes. And by having the pictures with us it saved time and, more importantly, eliminated the chance of being picked up by the German authorities while trying to get our pictures made after we'd bailed out.

When not flying missions, practicing instruments in the Link flight simulator or flying practice formation, we attended briefings by the Engineering Officer or lectures on Escape and Evasion.

The in-person stories by those who had been successful in their escape and evasion, after having been shot down, were FASCINATING. After our last mission we'd listened to two different guys who'd made it.

One told how it was easy enough to escape a Prisoner Of War Camp, called a Stalag Luft (Stockade for airmen), but his warning was for us to make plans of evasion for after the escape.

A fellow POW of his was still in camp, even though he'd escaped seven times, because he had no plans to evade capture after his escape. The last time he'd gotten as far away as Munich, so close to Switzerland, when the girl who was hiding him caught him going through her purse and she called the authorities.

"Don't collect souvenirs," we were told at the second lecture. "If you're picked up by the Underground, these people who are gambling

"Moon" "Smitty"

Burnell Utrecht

• *Bailout Photos* •

their lives to get you out of the country will take no chances. They'll check you out while you're asleep. If your stupid enough to have somehow picked up a German Iron Cross as a souvenir and you've got it on you, you won't wake up. It's a very serious business."

He then went on to tell how he'd been rescued by the French Underground, the Maquis, in northern France and how they'd passed him all the way to southern France from one whore house to the next. He emphasized the importance of Top Secret to the subject, because his wife would kill him if she ever found out how he'd escaped the Nazis.

On the other hand, despite the seriousness and secrecy, he almost had a heart attack when the girl-of-the-moment, who had him in tow, took him to a surprise party to celebrate the "American Flier" in a village tavern in southern France.

"What a party!" he said. "The crazy goddamned French. I drank out of fear of being discovered by the Germans and – woke up in Spain."

The weather Officer was right about the clouds and wrong about them clearing by the time we got to the target. They only got worse along the way and we worked our asses off trying to hold in formation.

It wasn't just the simple task of flying instruments and boring holes through the clouds. We were 32 bombers trying to hold formation above and between the clouds where visual contact had to be maintained. For if you lost contact, it was suicide to blindly try to rejoin the formation in the clouds. Either you could see the ship you were flying on or rely on good luck, get the hell out of the way and pray you didn't run into someone else.

Of course, in the midst of 31 other aircraft, you were lucky if you could only see just the wingtip of the guy you were flying on, as all others around you were hidden by the clouds.

To keep your eyes glued to a wingtip – and straining to not collide with it – makes it impossible to also watch your instruments inside of the cockpit. This leads to spacial disorientation, or vertigo, and you can't tell rightside-up from upside-down.

Your only reference to the ship you're flying to the right of is his right wingtip. You jockey your controls to hold that position. The difficulty of maintaining the position suggests that he's changing flight attitude and, from what you're muscles tell you from experience, he is banking to the left. So be careful that you don't drop down on him, because in a left bank you have to stay above him.

While it seems to look correct, your sense of balance, which lies to you during vertigo, tells you that he has not come out of the bank, but that he has lost control and is rolling clear over to the left; that you are both inverted and about to fall into a spin.

Moon yelled to me, "YOU'VE GOT IT!" so he could look at the instruments for orientation.

I had it! But like the dog who catches the car he's been chasing, what do I do with it? I'd never flown a B-17 upside down in formation.

WHOOSH! We're in the clear and we're not upside down. We're flying straight and level. What a surprise!

Even in the clear it's not easy to fly cross-cockpit in formation, which is looking across the cockpit and through the opposite window about six feet away, to place your left wingtip, which is fifty-five feet away and out of sight, to less than fifty feet away from the right waist window of the ship on which you're flying – without colliding with its right wing – and…

WHOOSH! We're back into the "soup" and I yell for Moon to "*TAKE IT!*"

That's the way it went for over four hours!

Then flying momentarily in the clear at 27,000 feet, in a valley of clouds surrounding us, a P-38 fighter plane approached us from the east, passed high overhead and circled us three times.

He was a Target Ship, without armament and stripped down to outrun German fighters who might go after him. By radio he let our Group Leader "HOTSHOT YELLOW" know that Berlin was obscured by clouds and could not be bombed by visual reference.

Since we were not equipped with radar at the time, the alternate target at Barnewitz, Germany, was selected. Our course was changed and we went back into the clouds to head for Barnewitz. However, during the turn we lost visual contact with our Element Lead, on whom we flew.

Right smack-dab over the middle of Germany, we lost our whole bomb group!

And were we going to go looking for our Group somewhere in the middle of the clouds? It wasn't even a consideration.

Only our Lead and Deputy Lead had bombsights. Eut said he'd like to try to hit the target without a bombsight and Ears volunteered to try and find the target for us. The inmates wanted to run the asylum. However, a higher priority presented itself.

Since the main reason we'd lost the formation was that the supercharger on #3 engine malfunctioned and we didn't have enough power to hold formation. Therefore, it was idiotic to think we could help the war effort by jeopardizing any other planes in the clouds by pressing on blindly to the target. We had to get into the clear. Maybe then we could let Eut take a shot at something.

Surely Ears could find some sort of a military target and, hopefully, he would even be able to navigate us back to England.

We broke out into clear air and turned for home. Burnell called Rudolfsky in the radio room over the intercom from the top turret and instructed him on how to put a spare tube into the supercharger amplifier, which was located under the floor of the radio room in the camera bay.

Our later model airplane had a much better arrangement than the older hydraulic superchargers, even though it seemed to take Rudolfsky forever to get the job done. Part of his hangup was that he was also monitoring the Group over his liaison radio; and the Group was under fighter attack and had lost two planes. Counting us, they had lost three ships.

Despite the fact that Rudy frostbit his hands while fixing the supercharger, we were pleased to get power back on #3 engine and just in time. Ahead of us and slightly below was a B-24 bomb group headed back to England. Great! We would try and join them for protection.

No…It wasn't a good idea, because a dozen ME-109's had also spotted the group and steered in their direction for a head-on attack. What to do?

Hill called from the tail that another group of B-24's was behind us at six o'clock. Maybe we should turn back and try to join in with them for protection.

NO. The Bandits hit the group in front of us wounding six B-24's that started dropping out of their formation and the fighters kept coming – straight for US – and they would get to us before we could reach the the B-24 group behind us. So it was better to face them head-on than to catch it in the ass.

I hoped that Eut would get lucky with his twin fifties in the chin turret, as well as Corky in the ball turret, and I called Burnell to give him permission to fire forward from the top turret.

I felt this was necessary, because the first time he'd fired the twin fifties – whose muzzles were only a foot or so about Moon's and my head – was on a practice mission in Florida. It almost scared the life out of me and I'd told him I would "kill him" if he ever did that again.

However, today was different. It was again shaping up into the old fashioned Western main street face-to-face head-on shoot-out! Except, it wasn't a one-on-one.

They were favored by greater firepower: 48 machineguns, twelve 30mm, and twenty-four 20mm cannons against our six machine guns that could fire forward. The odds were ten to one in their favor.

Even so, we were not without advantage, because our guns were flexible, while theirs were fixed in their line of flight. This meant they had to be flying toward us to hit us. And since there was only one of us, they would have to take turns firing at us, because they couldn't all fly into us at once. Also they knew, as did we, that the B-17 could withstand a lot of battle damage. That's why the Luftwaffe strategy had evolved into head-on attacks to KILL THE PILOTS!

I bumped Moon's arm and pointed to our autopilot, which we always kept on, but not engaged. He nodded, I fine-tuned it and he engaged it. PRIDE OF THE YANKEES flew by herself as stable as

Gibraltar and would continue to do so without pilots or flight controls or control cables should he and I both get killed.

That's why we always kept the autopilot on standby. It was worthless in flying formation, but it was worth more if the flying cables got shot out or anything happened to us. This was because each control surface was controlled seperately by individual servo motors guided electrically by the autopilot.

With the rate of closure at almost 600 miles per hour, the Bandits got to us in seconds! And to our surprise, they passed us by, keeping out of range of our guns, as they continued on back to the B-24 group behind us.

Hill reported them hitting the B-24's, knocking two out of formation and continuing on eastward out of sight.

We felt vulnerable at that altitude because that's where the Bandits were, but that's also where the flak was.

Ears called and said we were headed for a flak area...which suggested a change in course...which he had already figured out...

By golly, Ears was actually awake and ahead of us. Bless his heart.

So changing course we also started a descent, which increased our speed. All we needed was MY FRAN, the American P-47 escort, to show up – but he didn't. Where were those fighter escorts to protect the bombers that we kept hearing about, anyway?

For the Great "Experiment" of Strategic Bombing to work, the Master Plan had been modified to include fighter escorts. But where were they?

The P-47 was a great fighter, but it didn't have the required range. The twin engine P-38 had the range, but there weren't enough of them. There were plenty of P-51's set up for production, but they didn't have the necessary power – until it was discovered that the British Merlin engine could provide enough power. So the *word* was that the P-51 Mustangs were on the way, but not today.

Ears picked a target for Eut and we dumped our bombload at a minor railroad marshaling yard that didn't throw up very much flak.

At least Ears *claimed* the target was of military importance. We could not tell from the cockpit, as we could not see below us, and normally at altitude it was difficult to discern anything on the ground in detail.

Lacking a bombsight, Eut claimed he'd taken his shoe off and aimed between his toes, but we knew that to be fiction.

C aptain Cerrone, our Squadron Operations Officer, drove up in his jeep when we parked on the hardstand and he waited for us to walk over to him, which we did.

"We got a call from the middle of Germany that you were *missing*."

I was a bit disappointed that he wasn't happy just to see us, because I was certainly happy that we'd made it back.

"So who's the first ship back?" he asked. "You are!"

Was that some sort of a reprimand? What had we done that was so wrong?

"I was prepared to wait for you all night, but you're the first ones back."

Well, he did care that we'd gotten back. So what appeared as controlled anger was his adjusting to the good news. However, he still couldn't let down, because all of his chickens had not yet come home to roost.

"By the way," he said, as he reached into his jeep for a coiled up trailing antennae with its customary egg-shaped lead weight on the end of it, which allowed it to stretch itself out and below the plane for better radio reception, "Here's your *Bull's Nut*."

He handed it to Moon, then got into his jeep and drove away.

I knew that Moon had the urge to wrap the antennae wire around Rudy's neck for humiliating the entire crew by having forgotten to reel in the lead-weighted aerial before landing. It had been the third time for Rudy to have made such a stupid mistake.

So in disgust Moon shoved the coiled wire toward Rudy and said, "Here! I think this is yours."

Automatically Rudy reached out to take it, but he couldn't, because he'd tried to bandage his frostbitten hands with compresses by himself and hadn't done a very good job of that either.

Hill reached in and took the antennae for Rudy.

It was obvious that Moon was both angry and sympathetic. He tried to make the best of it by saying, "Somebody take care of Rudy's gun an' stuff. We'll get him to the Infirmary."

I felt a twinge of emotion, because little Rudy was more than tired, disappointed in his lack of performance, and suffering from the pain of his frostbitten hands that should have been cared for hours before. He was simply used up and old.

I was certain that Rudy had lied about his age and that he didn't seem to fit the role into which he'd been cast. He probably even had a son in service someplace and was trying also to do his bit. It wasn't uncommon for men who had missed the action in World War One to try and make up for it in Doubleya-Doubleya Aye-Aye.

I knew this, because my dad, a Private in War One, had volunteered before I had when War Two came and he was serving as a Captain, Post Exchange Officer, at a Troop Carrier Air Base in Sedalia, Missouri – within only thirty miles of where he'd been born.

MISSION #5
Le Grosseiller, France, 20 April 1944
Thursday: 36 ships up   (5:15 Flying Time)

One day off – not even a practice flight, Link or lectures, and for some reason we were assigned an older "F" Model to make a shorter mission, called a "Milk Run," to France. It was referred to as a "No Ball" mission, which had something to do with what was rumored to be a launching site for Hitler's new "Secret Weapon."

Well, classified information was on a need-to-know basis and I guess they figured that we didn't *need* to know what it was, so they didn't tell us. Just go bomb the goddamned thing. And we did.

It was a short trip with light inaccurate flak and no fighters. I decided that I preferred flying Milk Runs. However it proved to be a rarity.

The Milk Run was gratefully accepted, along with an Air Medal for having completed five missions. Only twenty more left to fly. I thought, at the rate I was going it would all be over before very long and I would be awarded the Distinguished Flying Cross for "Heroism and/or Extraordinary Achievement while participating in aerial flight," and I would be on my way back home soon.

Well, that's what I thought at the time.

I also appreciated not being scheduled for combat for the next eight days. Three of those days didn't even involve flying practice missions or Link Trainer. I actually got Saturday off and jumped onto a truck with a lot of troops my age to go to an afternoon community dance in the village of Stowmarket.

Well chaperoned, it was an enjoyable affair and a young lady invited me to her home for tea. Her parents were gone and we had the house to ourselves, so I looked forward to possibly adding some much needed tenderness to my life.

She excused herself to go make the tea and I settled onto a comfortable sofa that had ample room for two. It was covered with a colorful afghan, which I found interesting. The geometric designs were intricate. So to pass the time I traced them with my finger until I reached the fringe at the edge of the piece that happened to be on the floor. It was too nice to be on the floor, so I lifted it up – and found a pair of black shoes.

Now, I wasn't necessarily surprised that they were men's shoes, which could belong to her father, but those were the BIGGEST goddamned pair of men's shoes that I had ever seen in my life! I guessed that they were no smaller than a size fifteen. I couldn't even imagine the giant size of the man who wore them, nor was I the least interested in finding out.

Good manners be damned. I left without a "Thank you" or a "Goodbye." My life was already too uncertain and too insecure. I would save my bravery for the war.

I t was nice to get back home in the billet. Captain Stern, our Executive Officer had acquired us a replacement stove and also some coke for fuel. Someone on Turner's crew even knew how to make it burn and it was rather cozy with hot chocolate, some grilled cheese sandwiches and good companionship, because another replacement crew had arrived and the place was less like a mortuary.

The new crew was McDonald, his copilot Ryan, his navigator and bombardier. Ryan even had a radio on which we discovered Lord Haw Haw, a very erudite announcer from Germany with a distinctive British accent.

While I'd never actually heard Lord Haw Haw until we had Ryan's radio, I had heard a lot about him and his broadcasts. Lord Haw Haw's favorite subject was the Eighth Air Force. His audience, therefore, was mainly the members of the Eighth Air Force to whom he spoke directly.

So with the benefit of Ryan's radio we listened to Lord Haw Haw tell us the futility of our efforts in attempting to destroy the Third Reich and lecturing on the immorality of our bombing children's hospitals and nursing homes, which he identified.

"Lord Haw Haw," as he referred to himself, was the male counterpart to Axis Sally who was also in the business of broadcasting propaganda.

To assume that propaganda meant the same as telling lies would be a mistake, because it is more believable and effective when truth is used to persuade others to change their beliefs.

It was true that Lord Haw Haw would broadcast the names of the targets struck by the Eighth Air Force – and what bomb groups flew to which targets, because he somehow had access to inside information. Sometimes he would welcome replacement crews by their names. He once told a specific bomb group to check the clock in their Intelligence Section, telling them it was fourteen seconds slow – which it was!

McDonald's and Turner's crews were not offended that Lord Haw Haw had not mentioned their arrival; at least while we listened to the broadcast.

I also got two more days off during the last full week of April. And while there were practice flights and Link, there was no combat until Saturday the 29th. This finally gave me a chance to settle down a bit, have my laundry taken care of, and pick up some candy bars and rationed cigarettes at the Post Exchange for a dollar a carton.

I couldn't get too much because payday wasn't until the first of May. I looked forward to the addition of Combat Pay onto my Flight Pay, which amounted to about $240.00 before taxes.

Well, not exactly. There were deductions for meals, Officers Club dues and miscellaneous. There was also a rumor about some sort of a withholding tax that was to be enacted into law.

But what the heck, I'd gone into the service at $21.00 a month and in only 20 months I would be earning twice that amount a week to spend any way I liked.

Since I didn't have any deductions for dependents, I did make some effort to save a bit and had also agreed to a deduction for War Bonds. However, there wasn't much planning for the future, because the odds almost guaranteed that there was to be no future.

How lucky could I get? Just two years before, I had saved my lunch money by getting free meals for working in the high school cafeteria so I could pay for flying lessons.

But in the meantime, the Air Force had taught me to fly and provided a four engine bomber to practice with. Using 200 gallons of fuel an hour, at thirty-five cents a gallon – WOW! That was more than I made in a week as a Second Lieutenant. It was great. I could have never afforded to buy such training. Of course, there was that one problem of the Luftwaffe trying to interrupt my career.

The Noise Maker. *With two 50 calibre machine guns, the top turret fired only inches above the heads of the pilots.*

THE WORST
CHAPTER 5

MISSION #6
(Berlin) Magdeburg, Germany, 29 April 1944
Saturday: 28 ships up, 7 down
(8:20 Flying time)

It was a navigational error. Ears could not be blamed, because he was not on the mission. None of our crew went on this mission except me. For some reason I had been selected to fly copilot with Captain Vance and what started out to be routine turned out to be THE *WORST DAY OF MY LIFE!*

When possible, a "Spare" ship or two were assigned to form up with our Group in case someone had to abort before departing England. And sure enough, after 30 ships took off, two aborted just as we headed for Germany, and we filled into the tail end of the High Squadron as a "Spare."

Three Squadrons made a Group; Four Groups made a Wing; Four Wings made a Division; and Three Divisions made the Eighth Bomber Command, at the time. Numbers varied, but an all-out effort could amount to a Force of a thousand bombers or more, depending on losses and replacements. Therefore, organization and scheduling were important to overcome the natural chaos of getting that much traffic, hopefully, to the target and back.

Thus highways, called "Bomber Streams," were set up in the sky. Due to the difference in airspeed, the Second Bomb division, consisting of B-24's, had their Stream. The First and Third Divisions of B-17's had their Stream. We of the 385th Bomb Group were in the 93rd Combat Wing of the Third Division.

Each Bomb Group had a precise time and altitude from which to drop bombs from above the target, otherwise there would be collisions and dropping onto each other. Even so, there was no absolute guarantee that accidents would not happen; because they did.

With the development of more high-altitude flying a new phenomenon was discovered. For lack of a technical name it was just called a "Helluva Wind." It was unpredictable, over a hundred miles and hour and it could be a real threat.

Springtime weather was a bitch! It was everchanging and handicapped visual reference to checkpoints on the ground. However, some aircraft were equipped with a primitive radar called "PFF" or "MICKEY," which allowed navigating and bombing through the clouds.

Our Group did not have such a highly specialized ship or crew, but one of them was assigned to us for this Berlin mission.

From inexperience, or whatever reason, the Mickey operator led us about forty miles out of the Bomber Stream and we had to pay the price.

As copilot, riding in the right cockpit, in the last and highest ship on the right side of our Group in the High Squadron, my view to the right was unobstructed, except for the tops of the clouds that seemed to drift slowly by.

I did not know any more than anyone else at the time that we were actually outside of our Bomber Stream.

JESUS – CHRIST!

Unannounced, I was the first to see, off to the right at a great distance, what appeared to be a swarm of hornets beyond the tops of the clouds. They were insect-small, not because they were insects, but because they were so far away – too far to count or to determine if they were even aircraft.

Yet, they had to be airplanes, because insects, nor anything else, could live at that altitude. And if aircraft, they had to be fighters, because they were not flying bomber formation.

"BOGIES – THREE O'CLOCK HIGH!"

Our Group Lead spotted them and gave the alert. As "Bogies" they were yet unknown and unidentified. This meant to me that they were assumed *enemy* aircraft, because our Group Leader would have known if they were "Friendly" and not have called them unidentified "Bogies."

Besides, there had been no mention of friendly fighters at the briefing, since our planned-for fighter escorts were still presumed to be somewhere in the "pipeline."

I couldn't see any other bombers in front or to the side of our Group. I checked with the tail gunner and there were none behind us. We were alone. Twenty-eight of us and – how many of them?

There were over a hundred of them!

As I studied them and they slowly moved closer, being joined by more of their own, I could identify them and I revised my best-guess-count to at least *TWO-HUNDRED* Focke Wulf 190s and Messerschmitt 109s! It looked as if they had combined the entire Luftwaffe.

I had trouble figuring math in my head under the circumstances, but we seemed to be outnumbered by seven to one and that came to me as the odds that Custer faced at Little Big Horn.

SHIT!

DANGER! Fight or Flee was the natural response. Yet, we couldn't flee and if we fought we couldn't win. It was PANIC TIME!

I had a Panic Attack. I couldn't think. A jolt of adrenaline hit me and I shook all over. I felt the hair that I didn't have try to stand up along my spine, not unlike a threatened dog or wolf reacting with basic instincts.

Fight? I couldn't fight. If I wasn't sitting down, the fear of what was about to happen would have knocked me down. I didn't seem to have a muscle in my body and my brains had turned to mud.

I'm going to die! I'm going to die from fright alone.

"You sure as hell are if you don't get with the program."

I don't know where that message came from, even though it was in my own head, because I was incapable of thinking. It might have come from somewhere in the past, like Coach Sullins in one of those losing football games back in high school, or Coach Claudfelter during a wrestling match when I wanted to quit.

But this "game," the one that was about to begin, was the most important one in my life, because my LIFE was at stake. It was the ultimate test. A lot of people were going to die right here in the sky above Germany. Within moments I would experience *DEATH* – and I really wasn't ready for that.

No matter. It was coming. There was no place to hide nor any way to avoid it.

Feeling helpless and scared, I wanted to cry.

I was a child about to recieve a deserved and painful switching from my father. My father had whipped me only twice and it had never been administered out of rage. It was the damned logic of it that I had difficulty understanding.

"You must assume your responsibilities," he had said. "Grow up and take your punishment like a man."

He was right of course, which had been reinforced in sports. No Pain, No Gain. Play through the pain. Regain self control and never – never – NEVER – quit!

But against more than *TWO HUNDRED ENEMY FIGHTERS?*

There was one hell of a collision about to happen. Twenty-eight American bombers were in a box formation that was the size of three city-blocks high, three city-blocks long and seven city-blocks wide.

Two-hundred German fighters were going to attempt to penetrate the congested 63 cubic city-blocks of American bombers at near the speed of sound – in a head-on attack!

Since fighters also need their space, it would be much like trying to pass one solid mass through another solid mass even though there was supposed to be fifty-feet between each bomber.

But because the bombers would be using the space between them to maneuver with evasive action, what might be an empty space for one brief moment, would be filled by some bomber within seconds with 63,000 pounds of bombs, gasoline, metal and men that could not be avoided by any one of 200 fighters.

Well 200 will not go into 28; at least not safely. All of which meant, a lot of men were going to die within a short period of time.

That's the way it was going to be without a shot being fired. But add to the imminent disaster the fact that the fighters would be trying to cut holes through the bomb group with their 800 machineguns and 200 twenty-millimeter cannons. We would be firing back at them with our combined 168 forward-firing machine guns. It was going to be one hell of a battle and the suspense was almost paralyzing.

Flying parallel to us off to the right they moved closer as if in slow motion; as if there was all the time in the world before this terrible thing was going to happen. And the closer they got, the more real it became.

I couldn't help but think about tornadoes back in Oklahoma that made people run to hide in a "Fraidy-hole." Except, there was no place to run to and no place to hide up here in the sky.

The bastards. They were showing off, weaving back and forth, bouncing up and down, some of them rolling as if to demonstrate a victory roll – before the fact. The impression they gave was that they were fearless and could not wait for the slaughter to begin.

Then it occurred to me that they were psyching themselves up and trying to psych us down in the performance of their "war dance." That's what it was, a primitive "war dance" just before the battle.

Captain Vance pushed forward, dropped our nose and slid under and to the left of the last ship in the top Flight. I could see our Group in front and below us as we relocated and we too were limbering up, bombers oscillating up and down like a giant school of porpoise, large as whales. Such was our "war dance."

Vance switched to intercom and said, "When we get into this, be sure to use plenty of evasive action."

I shook my head as if I understood, but I didn't. We hadn't done what he must be talking about when we got hit by fighters at Stettin. It must be something new, because I hadn't been checked out on it. But, I was ready to learn.

We were at the tail end of what was turning into "crack-the-whip"; trying to fly formation on a ship that was undulating up and down, trying to fly in formation with another ship that was dancing down and up. As a result we almost collided with the ship on which we were flying. So I grabbed the controls and avoided the crash.

"I can't see from over here!" Vance said, "You've got it!"

Well, SHIT, I thought. Of course he can't see, because he's flying cross-cockpit and has to look through my window. Even with the clear view I had, I had trouble flying on my fluctuating guide. The command performance was about to begin and I could not have felt more incompetent than if I'd been handed a violin for the first time at a great concert and told to "*PLAY!*"

Well, by God, sour notes or not, I was going to PLAY!

Beyond my guide I caught glimpses of the Bandits high off to our right at 3 o'clock High pulling slowly forward to 1 o'clock High in front of us. Slowly they turned to their left toward 12 o'clock High, from where they would begin their head-on attack.

As busy as I was with left hand on four throttles and right hand on the wheel, I quickly switched to Channel "A" on the radio and heard our Lead, 'Hotshot Yellow' say, "Okay boys. On your toes! THIS IS IT!!!"

"God, if you're there, I'm sure you're getting a lot of requests just about now from both sides, but I do want to remind you of our deal: I'm going to do the very best I know how and the rest of it I'm leaving up to You, because it looks like I'm going to be too busy to be worrying about what I have no control over anyway. So please clear my mind so we can get this over with successfully; whatever that means."

It was dramatic!

If the encounter had not been so deadly and terrifying, it would have been beautiful. It was even more than a combination of ballet, football, airshow, hockey or championship boxing, because the final score would be measured by life or death!

Even so, devoid of morality or intelligence, it was sensual. It exceeded all limits of emotional feelings. Physically my muscles trembled. There was an urge to let go of everything; bladder, bowels, my grip on the flying controls and to let my eyelids close – and what? Miss the greatest show of my life on my way out of it?

"COME ON GOD! Don't let me lose control now! It's just beginning!"

Two hundred of those sonsabitches curved downward and into us. Some had their prop-spinners painted yellow, as members of Goering's elite. The leader was in an FW-190. And as the first, he was one gutsy bastard...Or was he?

Fascinated, as well as not wanting to collide with the bouncing Seventeen on my right, I banked to the left in a shallow dive to watch the leader, firing into our Lead, rolling upside down to protect himself with his armor-plated belly and electing to drop below our Group instead of trying to penetrate.

No wonder he was the leader. . . He knew how to survive.

Even with their advantage, outgunning us seven to one, they had to know we were no pushover, because Colonel Vandevanter was correct in having drilled us in flying a tight and solid formation. We were more invincible as a stone than a sponge.

While the leading "Bandit" might have had the option to avoid us by flying under our Group and picking up his "gaggle" of birds behind us, his followers were as unfortunate as were we.

BOOOM!!! Bandits and bombers collided!!

When two aircraft met they exploded instantly into a giant flaming red fireball! Such dazzling crimson against the white clouds in the background, at the same time imploding back into the black hole in the center of itself. Sucking back into the vacuum of the explosion, it was both there at the same time it was gone, yet flinging debris in all directions: engines, metal, bodies, props, undefinable pieces, pieces, pieces. It was MAGNIFICENT.

Vance hit my left arm and ordered me to "Get back into formation! EVASIVE ACTION!!" he yelled.

What I saw had hypnotized me and I could hardly pull my attention away from the shooting and the total and partial collisions. So much was happening at the same time that I couldn't get it all into my head. However, I did realize that the distractions had caused me to drift out of formation and away from my duties.

"God, DAMN IT, let me focus on my job!"

Vance got on the controls and drove us toward the ship we were supposed to be flying on. Unable to see clearly, he nearly rammed us into our guide and it took all of my strength to prevent a collision.

Captain Vance was not a big man. The B-17 did not have power-assist or power-boost on the controls. With stable characteristics, it took a lot of muscle to change its mind. It could be thought of as having obstinate "mulepower" instead of horsepower. Yet, the little Captain kicked her in the ass. And as heavy as she was on the controls, he made her jump to his will.

It was my will that we should not slam into anyone else and to avoid getting behind another Seventeen, because the propwash behind another bomber with four fans driven by 6,000 horsepower created a tornado effect that could flip a 60,000 pound bomber onto its back and send it earthward in a spin. I knew that, since it was happening to others in the formation. Some were able to recover; some were not.

The tail gunner called, "It looks like a Christmas tree back here with all those cannon shells exploding!"

The Bandits had hurt us badly on their first pass through us. Actual damage was hard to assess. We were obviously not the same, since those of us left in the formation were strung out.

Maneuvering in evasive action had reduced our forward speed and those of us at the rear had dropped farther behind while our leader, Lt. Colonel McDonald, pulled farther ahead, as if he was in some kind of a goddamned race. To where? There was no place to race to.

I switched from intercom to Command Channel to request our Lead to slow down so we could catch up. As a Second Lt. at the tail end of the pack, I had no authorization for any such communication, but it was critical for our Group to maintain its unity. However, someone else beat my transmission:

"HOTSHOT YELLOW – GOD DAMMIT!!! *SLOOOW DOWNNN!*

The fighters, too, had gotten themselves strung out and were regrouping back up on their "perch" at 3 o'clock high for another attack, but it looked like they were having the same problem as we had.

Their leader, the sonovabitch who had avoided the attack so he could keep on leading, was pulling ahead of them in a "race" to lead them into another assault.

I allowed myself the luxury of a moment's mental jump into the Luftwaffe, as if I were in their place: Go ahead you sonnovabitch. If you want to be a goddamned hero, you just run the ball over the goal line for a touchdown by yourself.

What the hell difference did it make anyway if we collided at 500 miles per hour or at 600 mph? The ideal strategy in any conflict is to do the opposite of what your opponent expects you will do – if you can. I'd learned that in wrestling – and football.

Of course we couldn't have done it, but wouldn't it be a surprise if we could just slam on the brakes and stand still just when they were ready to penetrate.

Well it had served me well when I had to run the "belt-line" in basic training, because it threw off the rhythm of those swinging at me with their belts...

Where was my mind going, anyway? I had to get it back into the game. I had to get REAL – as long as reality might last.

Vance took the controls away from me, banked left and dove for our Low Squadron. That is, what was left of it. For as usual, it seemed to have been hit the hardest.

Some ships not immediately destroyed were nevertheless wounded and were falling back and downward. Our dive added to our speed and we were able to catch up and we slid into the Low Squadron in time for the next assault. This time Vance was on the driver's side and I was the spectator.

Instead of being Tail-end Charlie in the High, we had dropped down into the Low Squadron and were Tail-end Charlie in *Coffin Corner*.

I took the opportunity for a "Crew Check" and each station from tail to nose acknowledged. We were all in good shape – so far.

HOLY SHIT!!! The goddamned twin fifties in our top turret, their muzzles just inches above my head, cut loose!

B-R-R-R-R-R-R-R-R-R-R-R-O-O-O-O-O-O-O-O-O-M!

I almost jumped out of my skin and my heart seemed to knot and stop.

I was staring straight forward at the leader of the Bandits in his fucking FW-190! Pink flashes on his wings meant he was shooting at me!

ME!!! He wasn't firing at our Group, Squadron or our ship. The sonnovabitch was trying to kill *me* personally! I naturally wanted to shoot back, but all I had was a damned steering wheel.

B-R-R-R-R-R-R-R-R-R-R-R-R-R-O-O-O-O-O-M!

B-R-R-R-R-R-R-R-R-R-R-R-R-O-O-O-O-O-M!

I grabbed my chest, because I heard what seemed to be glass tinkling in the pauses between the bursts of the twin fifties.

PUNK…BANG…TWANG…THUMP!!!

We were in a hail of fifty-caliber spent shell casings spewing out of the ship above us. Only four inches long, the hundreds of falling brass casings from one of our own ships punched holes into the leading edge of our wing, engine cowlings and shattered our plexiglass nose. What I thought was breaking glass was brass casings from our own top turret spilling into the canvas bags attached below each gun to catch them.

The attacking Focke Wulf was long gone before I checked to see if my hand-to-chest had collected any blood.

It had not.

Maybe?

I checked on my feet and the rest of me. I seemed to be okay.

Although millions of times larger than the exploding twin fifties, the distance and thin air muffled the sound of the exploding B-17 just ahead of us.

FIREBALL RED against the white clouds! *BLACK* oily smoke! A PROPELLER by itself spun and slashed toward us like a giant whirl-a-gig, which fortunately missed our wing.

A DOOR! I ducked.

A BODY tumbled toward me and barreled past me!

PIECES!

PIECES! PIECES!

AWESOME…!

It happened so fast that we flew right into the middle of the explosion and out the other side within fractions of a second!

Only by trying to replay it in my head in slow motion could I begin to understand its impact. But there was no time to dwell on it, because the Bandits were pouring in on us; guns blazing and us shooting back. It was truly a *goddamned WAR!*

Vance somehow "wished" us forward to replace the missing bomber. But even with throttles wide open, it was a struggle. He tagged onto another ship, but it failed and dropped back. He then joined us onto the left wing of another Fortress and hit my arm for me to take over as it was on my side.

I preferred the role of spectator, but I was forced to focus on the guide-ship to hold formation. This spared me seeing the Bandits coming straight at us, but the *sound* of the twin fifties above my head confirmed their presence, as did the blur of them sliding past us and the shooting back from the ship on which I was flying.

The ball turret on the bottom of the ship on which I was focused took a hit and was disabled!

What followed was a heroic act that was lost in the business of the day, but it was impressive.

Having personally flown and fired from every gun position in a Seventeen on practice missions, I considered the ball turret the worst. It was even more isolated than the tail gun and definitely more uncomfortable, because you sat on the small of your back with legs flexed and your knees almost in your ears.

There was no way to stretch or to relax. It triggered both claustrophobia and acrophobia, since you were hanging outside, alone, on the bottom of the ship at the mercy of a single "Jesus Nut." If that nut or bolt came undone? "Jesus," what a fall!

There was no room in the ball for a parachute. So if anything went wrong, it was hoped that one of the waist gunners would be there to help you get out of the ball in a hurry and get your chute on before bailing out.

There was also no heat. So cold and cramped muscles inside of a burdensome sheeplined flying suit guaranteed slow and restricted movement.

I watched the forward pointing and silent barrels of the ball's twin fifties starting to move slowly after the hit. Ever so slowly they move downward.

So despite the direct hit, the gunner was evidently still alive. And without electrical power, he was cranking the turret by the hand cranks between his feet in order to get his guns pointing straight downward. For with his guns pointed downward, it would allow him to escape into the waist of the ship from the door in the back of the turret.

Good. I could see that he apparently was able to extricate himself from the ball. But there was even more to it!

The ball gunner is held in his position with a safety belt that is snapped across his back. To snap it on or off usually requires assistance from a waist gunner. There are also two latches on the door at the back of the ball that are difficult to manage alone.

So with everyone else on their guns, the ball gunner was on his own.

Having gotten himself out of the ball, it must have dawned on him that the only guns for him to fire were still in his ball turret and the Group needed all the firepower it could get...At least this was what I imagined was happening. What followed confirmed my thinking.

Slowly the guns that were pointing downward from the ball turret started to move upward and pointed forward to aim at the incoming fighters. Then the twin fifties in the ball turret started firing!

My God! It was really unbelievable. The gunner had gotten himself back into the ball and had gone back to work aiming his guns manually by the hand cranks. He'd had no assistance, because he'd not been able to secure the safety belt across his back, nor had he been able to snap the latches closed on the door, because the door was open and waving in the slipstream, as was his safety belt!

To duplicate his position would be to sit backward on a dining room chair with your knees over the back and keeping yourself from falling off by holding onto the back of the chair while being pulled through the air at 150 mph at fifty-degrees below freezing – five miles above the earth!!!

I could only support him with prayers for strength and enough oxygen. There was nothing else I could do. I dreaded the fact that he could lose his grip and fall backward out of the door without his parachute. How long could he keep it up? How long could any of us expect to survive?

What had begun with two waves of attacks was changing into a non-interrupted assault, because the Bandits were no longer pausing on their "perch." Instead, they had formed a circle and were flying "circuits and bumps." It was as if the merry-go-round was running into the roller-coaster – with everyone shooting!

While we had started as a Spare as the last ship in the High Squadron and moved to the last position in the Low Squadron, we were working our way forward through the Low whenever someone in front of us blew up, was shot down, or dropped backwards.

Unable to see to the rear it was only a guess as to what our Group looked like. However, it was definitely being altered. There was no reason to believe otherwise than that the battle would not end until we had all been destroyed.

I had a fleeting thought of Ears and wished he had come along, because he could have found us a flak area. I wished for flak, because the fighters would not follow us into it.

Then my wish came true.

Hotshot Yellow had elected to drop our bombs on the alternate target of Magdeburg.

The flak started coming up, light at first to warn away our attackers, then more concentrated as the fighters left us alone and we neared the target. Even so, it was relatively more comfortable and gave us respite from the fighters – for awhile.

Getting rid of our bombs also eased the stress. But with "Bombs Away," leaving the target and diminishing flak, the fighters were waiting for us.

Having done our job in delivering the bombs we were headed back home. Even so, the Bandits continued to hammer on us, although not as ferociously as in the beginning.

Having dropped our bombs, we were not the threat we had been and our value was reduced. The length of battle had also used up the small fuel load of the Bandits, as well as about fifty of their number, and they eventually left us alone to struggle with our everpresent battle of simply staying in the air long enough to get back home.

So in our exodus, without fighters or flak shooting at us, the battle damage still caught up and took ships out of our formation along the way.

Out of the thirty ships that had started out early in the morning, only six of us were still in formation eight hours later as we approached and contacted our "HARDLIFE" control tower.

It felt good to get back. It should have felt GREAT, but our losses and just plain fatigue downgraded any exuberance and took any glory out of it.

It would be several hours before it was determined that we had actually lost only ten ships and seventy men, because the others who had dropped out of formation would straggle in later or put down on other airfields. Even so, there were also casualties among those who had managed to get back to the base.

The debriefing was not as crowded as usual. I got my standard large cup of coffee and peanut butter and jelly sandwich from the voluntary Red Cross ladies.

At mid afternoon it was the first food or drink I'd had for twenty hours. We had simply been too occupied to snack on "K" rations while on the mission. So the aroma and taste of the coffee and the flavor and texture of the sandwich was wonderful.

Waiting my turn for debriefing, while enjoying my refreshments, I strolled over to the Formation Boards along the wall where crews, ships and their locations in the formation were posted.

I noticed that Colonel Vandevanter was staring at the Formation Boards. It looked pretty grim at the time, since the final count was not in and all crews had been "X"ed over, except the first six of us that had returned together. So it appeared that our casualties were 80% at first-count.

Colonel "Van" had been staring at the Boards before I got there and he remained motionless even as I drew near. He had not moved and was not going to move. He was locked in place.

He had a reputation of leading the tough missions himself. We respected him greatly for that. I guessed that he might even be blaming himself for us getting busted up so badly, feeling that if he'd been our leader we wouldn't have strayed out of the Bomber Stream.

I wanted to speak to him, but what could I say?

While he was physically there I was sure that he was mentally back over Germany, somehow sharing our experiences of the day through his own adventures. So as he stared at our losses displayed on the Formation Boards, I stared at him. There we stood, Colonel Van staring at the losses and me staring at him.

It was a moment of reverence. In time I saw the tears come to his eyes.

There was to have been a large party in the Number One hangar that night to celebrate the Group's 100th mission, but the worst disaster the Group had ever encountered in combat dampened the spirits of everyone on the base.

I didn't go to the party.

E veryone "crawled back onto the horse" the next day, which was Sunday. Twenty-four crews in the Group went to France for a shorter mission and the rest of us flew a three-and-half-hour practice mission over England to improve our skills and to get ready for Monday's mission; a "Milk Run" to Le Grosseiller, France – where we lost only one crew:

MISSION #7
Le Grosseillier, France, 1 May 1944
Monday: 22 ships up   (6:30 Flying Time)

A day or two off would be appreciated, because I was fatigued. But even when we didn't fly combat missions, there were practice missions and drilling on instrument flying in the Link trainer, since we needed all the practice we could get. I wasn't complaining; just bushed, because

I couldn't relax. Sure, we had beds, but that was no guarantee of a good night's sleep.

Actually I felt very lucky, because my only physical wound was the damage I'd done to my hand on the manual fuel primer. Each of the four engines had to be primed individually in starting them up and there had been a lot of that lately.

It was no wonder that I had blisters on my right hand. Even my blisters had blisters from being ripped open before they could heal. However, the blisters were beginning to turn to tough callouses...If only my mind could do the same.

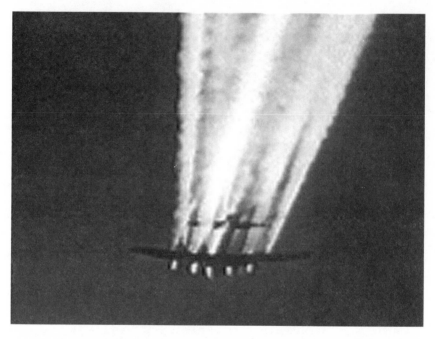

Contrails were beautiful to see but made the bombers easy targets for both enemy fighters and flak crews.

A BUSY WEEK
CHAPTER 6

Two ambulances were coming my way. I stuck my thumb in the air and signaled to hitch a ride and they both coasted toward a stop.

I didn't have a three-day pass, but it was Thursday and I wasn't scheduled for anything until Link Trainer on Saturday. So I decided to catch a ride to visit Corporal Walter "Bud" Bishop from my hometown who was stationed just east of Cambridge at the 361st Fighter Group, 376th Fighter Squadron at Bottisham.

The ambulances stopped long, so I ran toward the rear one and unfastened the latch on its back door.

"NO, Lieutenant!" I heard someone call to me. "Up front!"

Too late. I'd opened the door and was shocked to see what had to be nine cadavers in white sheeting on stretchers. A PFC closed the door and escorted me to the cab up front, because what I had unexpectedly encountered had immobilized me. This was what was going on behind the scenes and was best kept hidden from those of us who faced such fate.

The PFC and the Sergeant at the steering wheel must have had some idea of what was on my mind and they tried to cheer me up as we drove toward Cambridge where the bodies would be interred in the Eighth Air Force Cemetery. Then just before Cambridge, they let me out at Bottisham; a fighter base with P-51 Mustangs.

Seeing Bud lifted my spirits, because he was a small, hyper and witty individual, undaunted by military protocol.

"What took you so long to report in to me, Junior?"

I was not a "Junior" and he knew better than anyone, but he was making a show for his five buddies that he, a Corporal, working as a radio technician, was not intimidated by some shavetail Second Lieutenant.

They were returning to quarters from their duties. Bud introduced me to his happy "fan club" and I was invited to chow with them; "Unless you want to take us all to the Officers Mess" he bantered.

At Bud's prompting they scrounged up a mess kit, canteen cup and some "tools" for me and said they'd have a place for me to stay overnight in their billet.

We had been fortunate that Bud had come to work for our family's boys and mens store in Ponca City in 1942 when my dad got a direct appointment as a First Lieutenant into the Air Force. While Bud was not a surrogate father for my younger brother John and myself, he sort of played the role of an older brother and was still at it.

"Mom says you should write home more often." and, "What are these medals you're wearing? You're not supposed to be a bloody hero, so don't do anything daring. . . Now, listen to me, because I promised Mom I was going to take care of you and I don't want you taking any chances."

And so it went until I departed the next morning after Bud told me, "You know, I pray for you every night. . . In fact I pray for all of my friends every night. I don't just say, "God bless 'em all," but I pray for each and every one of them. . ." He stopped in thought, then added, "No wonder I'm not getting enough sleep any more. Everyone I know is somewhere in the military."

MISSION #8
Berlin, Germany, 8 May 1944
Monday: 31 ships put up, one lost
(9:00 Flying Time)

With more American fighters becoming operational; so they said – although I had yet to see any of them flying support for us – the strategy of our mission to destroy the Luftwaffe was changed: The bombers would be used as "bait" to draw the Luftwaffe into the sky, then our fighters were to shoot them down, in the supposition (I supposed) that the Germans would run out of fighters before we ran out of bombers. For me, however, fighter support was a fairy tale.

For example, on the mission to Berlin we headed toward Osnabruck and German fighters were dispatched to save Osnabruck. Our fighters were to shoot them down. Then we headed toward Hamburg and German fighters were sent up to protect Hamburg. Our fighters were to shoot them down.

And so it went across Germany; the bombers attracting the Bandits for our Friendlies to shoot down. But wouldn't you know, before we got to Berlin, picking up Bandits along the way like a magnet, there weren't enough Friendlies to protect us, even before we got to the target.

Since our fighters didn't have the range we had, they were designated to Sectors through which we flew. I was assigned to guard the Fighter Channel: "C" for Charley. The code name for our Group was "Vinegrove One" and their's was "Balance One."

When we entered the "F" Sector about thirty Bandits started queuing up to attack us. So I called, "Balance One, Balance One, this is Vinegrove One in Sector "F" with thirty Bandits."

"Roger, Vinegrove One; Balance One. We can't help you right now. We're in Sector "G" and we've got our hands full."

Well, thanks a bunch to whoever dreamed up this scheme. We drew the Bandits alright, but we had to fight them ourselves. And our Group wasn't the only one.

"BALANCE ONE! BALANCE ONE! VINEGROVE TWO IN SECTOR "E"! THEY'RE SHOOTIN' THE SHIT OUT OF US!! HELP!! HELP!! OHHH MY GOD!!! The panicky voice faded into sobs, totally out of control. The sound of it was chilling.

The Luftwaffe was out in full force: Behind us in Sector "E"; ahead of us in Sector "G" and definitely with us in Sector "F."

It was a real shoot-out and I was fighting the tendency to slip into the panic mode, knowing I couldn't allow myself such luxury; when I was jerked from the horror of the situation into the weird reality of what was actually happening.

We weren't fighting some faceless monster or the Master Race, but the fight was with humans like ourselves. It dawned on me when I saw for a fraction of a second a German pilot, only 10 yards away, *thumbing his nose at me* as he zipped by.

I threw a finger back at him, but it was too late for him to see. He was gone. REALLY GONE!

Burnell had fired over my head and called, "I GOT HIM! I GOT HIM! SOMEBODY CONFIRM IT! HE'S SMOKIN' DOWN!

Hill confirmed the hit from the tail.

I was ready for the next one and presented myself to him with a one-finger-salute. He damn near collided with me, but shot straight-past over the top of us. I hoped he got my message.

Now, Rudy should have been grounded with his frost-bitten hands, but he'd convinced the Flight Surgeon he was not handicapped; could do his job and wanted to fly every mission with our crew so he would finish his tour of combat with the rest of us.

When the latest ME-109 shot by overhead, Rudy called from the radio room for a confirmation, but nobody would verify that he'd shot the fighter down, because there was no way he could have shot anyone coming at us head-on when his single gun was restricted to fire only upward. In fact, he lost his credibility with the crew for even claiming such an inconceivable shot. However, Rudy had invented how to make the incredible shot work.

All Rudy could see of the fighting was through the top window of his radio compartment where his single .50 Caliber machine gun was mounted – pointed *upward*. He couldn't see the fighters coming in on us head-on. However, he noticed that the tracers from the guns of a Bandit were – followed by the Bandit himself – as he passed right above the muzzle of his gun.

So Rudy figured, if he started firing between the lines of the tracers, it wouldn't be long before the ship would follow. Therefore, he aimed his .50 straight up and waited for the tracers. When they appeared, he held down on the trigger, firing between the lines of tracers.

The excitement of battle had raised his pain threshold. But even so, the jerking .50 Caliber machine gun delivered pain to the raw nerves of his hands. But as he'd planned, it didn't take long for the Messerschmitt to follow the tracers and Rudy's .50 Caliber ripped its belly open from nose to tail as it passed overhead. Unfortunately, nobody could testify to Rudy's kill.

Enemy gunfire shattered the plexiglass in our nose, but somehow neither Eut nor Ears were hit directly. However, shards of glass struck Eut in his face and eyes knocking him off of his bombardier's perch. Ears tended to him and toggled out our bombs when we got to the target.

The Bandits did not follow us into the flak over the target, of course, and there was time to try and sort things out, which was greatly needed.

What a mass of confusion. The fighter attacks had damaged all of the bomb groups and screwed up the scheduled times over the target. Nobody seemed to be at the correct altitude or position. High groups were dropping bombs through the lower groups. Individual damaged and malfunctioning bombers were trying to form up with anyone they could keep up with.

After the drop I watched a smoking Seventeen off to the right of us with bomb-bay doors still open. The first guy to jump or fall through the doors must have accidentally opened his chute too soon, because the canopy caught up inside of the bomb-bay and it didn't tear loose when his body jerked at the limits of the shroud lines. He was *stuck*, tethered to the bottom of his ship by his parachute and swinging in the slipstream.

Since the airpressure pushed him back toward the rear of his ship, those jumping after his exit were evidently unaware of his crisis and failed to cut him loose. For even a free chute with a hole in the canopy would have been better than what he suffered.

The poor guy tried climbing up the shroud lines against the 150 mph wind and minus 40 degrees temperature to try and get back up and into the ship.

About half way up, when he reached the silk, he lost his grip, fell, and bounced at the length of his tether. More members of his crew fell from the bomb-bay past him.

Again he tried climbing up the lines of his chute, but the subfreezing temperature, lack of oxygen and slipstream defeated his efforts and he dropped back again to the limitation of his restraint and dangled there like a puppet on strings in a hurricane wind.

It was a morbid performance witnessed by so many who were powerless to help.

Thank God for the effects of anoxia, because his departure from life was eased by a state of euphoria.

MISSION #9
Leon Couvran, France, 9 May 1944
27 ships put up   (5:25 Flying Time)
Target: "No Ball" Buzz Bomb Site
Next day: "Practice (?) mission," 10 May 1944

Eutrecht called us from the main hospital where he'd been taken. He had not lost his sight and would be okay. A P-47 had flown low over the hospital yesterday to "buzz" everybody. It had created a lot of excitement, but he wanted us to come over and lay on a *real* "buzz job."

It was the first best-day of the year with sunshine and warmth. Perhaps a hundred ambulatory patients in maroon colored robes lined an embankment next to the hospital to enjoy the out of doors. It would take only one of them to get our aircraft number and turn us in. But we gambled that none would object to a closeup view of a B-17.

We were out of sight until we popped up and could see them. Their first view of us was four Wright Cyclone engines held in a tight formation by a single wing spar that measured one-third of a city block. We were coming at them at eye level. As they lay down on the green embankment it looked like a maroon wave.

Together, Moon and I pulled back on the controls to jump up over them on their rampart -- and then pulled back even harder to *just miss a barn behind them*, which was a surprise to us. Burnell fired a yellow/ yellow flare as a greeting.

One pass was enough to impress us on board and to satisfy Eut's request for a "buzz-job," without us getting caught.

Eut, on his return from hospital, reported the success of the short performance, adding that it was unfortunate that we were so low that the flares had not burned out before falling onto the thatched roof of the barn next door and had set it afire.

Why did things have to go so wrong like that?

MISSION #10
Brussels, Belgium, 11 May 1944
Thursday: 33 ships put up. (6:00 Flying Time)
Target: Railway Yards.

Minus our bombardier, Carmen, our Armorer, was moved from his right waist gun position to the nose as Toggelier. All he had to do was man the nose guns, open the bomb doors and push the toggle switch to release the bombs on cue from our Lead.

Carmen's cue was a verbal radio command, "BOMBS AWAY!" and the sight of flares fired from the Lead and bombs falling out of the Lead ship that were marked with smoke. Well, as simple as it appeared, it didn't happen as it should have, because something went wrong.

For some mistaken reason we were assigned to fly in the Deputy Lead position, which takes over in case something happens to the Lead. Because of this the Deputy Lead has a bombardier and a bombsight. However, we didn't have either one. What we had was Technical Sergeant "Yeh-Yeh" Carmen.

We approached the target on the Bomb Run and a couple of miles before "BOMBS AWAY!," our bombs were *away!!!*

We did the customary jump-up from the loss of our three-ton load and Carmen started yelling on the intercom, "YEH-YEH! It's my fault!," and tried to explain what he'd done.

He'd had trouble with the lever that opens the bomb doors. And when he finally forced it to move, it went all the way to the manual Salvo position and our bombs left. And – we were the Deputy Leader, right(?). So what happened?

Ironically, the Lead Bombardier had mis-calculated and decided *not to drop*. But the Group was already dropping on our cue, as Deputy Lead, and ninety-nine tons of bombs plowed up an unknown amount of Brussel sprouts along the Bomb Run to the target in the city of Brussels.

Since the flak was lighter than usual, I couldn't help imagining antiaircraft gun crews looking up, discovering the bombs falling everywhere except the target, running for cover and swearing at us for not playing by the rules.

Every ship in the Group had unloaded their bombs, *except our Leader*.

"Hotshot Yellow! WHERE IN THE HELL ARE YOU GOING?"

Somebody was pissed off badly enough to break radio silence and to question our Leader. It was a no-no, but not the only one.

"Goddammit Hotshot! Get us outa here!"!

"What's your problem, Hotshot?"!

"GIT OFF THE AIR! MAINTAIN SILENCE! This is Hotshot Yellow. We didn't drop and we're making a three-sixty to go in again."

"FUCK YOU, HOTSHOT!"

"Everybody's dropped but YOU, Hotshot!"

"Get us the Hell outa here!"

Time over the target is Lethal-Time. Having let the flak guns rehearse their calculations on the first pass over the target is bad enough, but to give them a second chance is suicidal.

Fortunately our Leader was made to see the logic of it, even though he was the only one to bring his bombs all the way back to Base and had to land with them.

That night all radios were "safetied" and anyone breaking a safety wire to transmit would have some explaining to do.

As this was my tenth mission, I was awarded an Oak Leaf Cluster to my Air Medal.

MISSION #11
Zwickau, Germany, 12 May 1944
Friday: 28 ships up, one down   (9:15 Flying Time)
A long-day at the end of what was a long-week.

Moon and I had worked out a routine to get a little much needed
rest. With emotions up after a mission and emotions up before a mission,
the only time for rest was in forming up into flying group-formation
after finding out what the target of the day was. The strain effected the
whole crew, but they, unlike the pilots, could sleep after takeoff during
assembly.

Flying in circles around the radio Buncher-beacon was an invitation
to sleep. So Moon would fly for fifteen minutes, then I would fly fifteen
– and so on and on. We were so good at it and desperate for sleep that
on the quarter hour – counting down the seconds – one of us awakened
and the other was immediately asleep, sitting upright. A bump on the
arm and the sleeper was awake and the *awaker* was asleep.

Except, there was one morning when it didn't work out right.

I agonized in trying to stay awake as I counted the seconds: Three.
Two. One. There! Moon's turn. I hit his arm to awaken him, my eyelids
seemed to "clank" shut, my head dropped to my chest and my hands
on the wheel awaited the cue that Moon had taken control, but it
didn't happen.

I heard Moon yell, "I can't take it!"

"WHAT?" I was awake. I looked at Moon and he was still asleep.

"You've gotta take it, Moon! I can't fly anymore! I'm falling asleep!"

MOON!! I hit him on the arm and he opened his eyes in my
direction, but he wasn't even seeing me.

"I'll tell you what," he said, closing his eyes," You take it, just fifteen
minutes more – an' I'll take it for – thirty minutes."

I had no choice. I couldn't wake him up. It sounded like a good
deal, because I could sure use a thirty minute nap. Okay. We were
orbiting at 10,000 feet and not yet on oxygen, so I lit up a cigarette.

Moon had taught me to smoke when I'd first joined the crew and
his smoking made me airsick – just like my dad's cigars used to make
me carsick. He'd offered me a cigarette, I tried it, got unsick and became
addicted.

Well, the cigarette alerted me a little, but not for long. I thought
about my great responsibility, because I was the only one of the crew

awake and I had to be cautious of thirty other aircraft, whose crews were probably also asleep.

No wonder planes collided during assembly. And to think, last night when I could have, and I should have, I could not go to sleep for the life of me and now I could not stay awake.

I couldn't help thinking about the rest of the crew, all asleep, especially Ears and Eut up in the nose, probably already on oxygen to help them sober up.

Things were certainly mixed up to be sobered up on oxygen when you were being shot at and to numb your brain with alcohol when you were not being shot at.

"Man," I shook my head and talked to myself, because it sure as hell wouldn't bother anybody. I sang allowed, "I walk alone. For to tell you the truth I be lonely…" What were the words anyway? "A children's carousel, a chestnut tree, a wishing well." Well, it wasn't keeping me awake.

I got a great idea. The bailout packets had benzedrine, in case you had to stay awake, and "Boy Howdy," did I ever need to stay awake.

In an emergency I might even try some of the morphine in the First Aid packets on board. However, I'd heard that the morphine was usually missing; taken by some addict.

No, it would be better to take one of the white benzedrine pills from my bailout packet.

But, wait a minute. What if we got a Recall and the Group returned to Base? If I took the "benny" I wouldn't be able to sleep when I got back – unless I took some of those red sleeping pills – and then they'd wake me up for a mission and I'd have to take some more bennies and – all of that could make me crazy…

I awoke to see the big tail of a B-17 right in front of me and tugged at the controls to miss it!

Somehow we missed and I spoke to myself aloud, "DAMN, I've GOT to stay awake!"

Having dropped off into sleep, I'd almost killed twenty people!

It occurred to me that one of the problems was the steady drone of the engines. Steady engines were as comforting as a mother's lullaby. Let an engine stutter and that was a wake-up call for sure.

I wasn't about to shut an engine down just to stay awake, but I could alter the drone-sound by unsynchronizing the props.

While it took some talent to get the engines to run in sync, it was quite simple to move an RPM control lever to throw the rhythm out of balance. This way, with the sounds of the engines fluctuating, flashing yellow lights in my head should keep me awake…

I heard Moon say, "I've got it" and felt his tug on the controls.

My God, I'd been flying while I was asleep. I wondered if I'd been asleep with my eyes open and for how long.

Zwickau, Germany is located equidistant between Berlin and Munich, almost on Germany's eastern border with Czechoslovakia.

The mission to Zwickau on the 12th of May, 1944 is considered the most outstanding sortie of the 385th Bomb Group in the unit's history. It was led by Colonel Vandevanter and the 385th received the Presidential Unit Citation.

EXCERPTS OF THE CITATION FROM
THE HISTORY OF THE 385TH:

"The assigned high priority on this date was the aircraft repair factory of G. Basser, K.G.. On this highly successful operation, the 385th Bombardment Group (H) (for Heavies) led the Division forces and the 4th Combat Bombardment Wing. The flight was a distance of 1,270 miles. Four hours and forty minutes, over a distance of 965 miles, were over strongly defended enemy territory. Of the 95,000 pounds of bombs dropped on this visual operation, 97% struck within 2,000 feet of the preassigned aiming point, 51% within 1,000 feet and 18% within 500 feet.

"Between 100 to 150 hostile fighters began to attack the force just south of the Koblenz area. So determined were their head-on attacks, in waves of 20 to 30, that friendly fighters were unable to break up their formations…

"While skillfully and courageously maintaining close defensive formation in the face of this fierce enemy opposition, the 385th purposely slowed down the entire division formation until groups of the straggling wing formation, trailing the 4th Combat Bombardment Wing, could reform.

"As a result of these attacks and antiaircraft fire from enemy ground positions, 18 of the 28 airplanes belonging to the 385th Bombardment Group sustained battle damage. All participating aircraft of the 385th Group bombed the target.

"On the return journey, two B-17's were lost as a result of enemy action. Thirteen officers and men are missing in action. The 385th

Bombardment Group is officially credited with destroying 15 enemy aircraft, probably destroying three and damaging two more.

"Undeterred by the vicious enemy fighter attacks and antiaircraft fire, the officers and enlisted men of the 385th Bombardment Group (H) displayed extraordinary heroism in fighting their way to the target. The determination, devotion to duty and total disregard for personal safety above and beyond that of all other units participating in the mission are in keeping with and add notably to the highest and most cherished traditions of the Armed Forces of the United States."

T he official citation did not cover such details as when I came back from pissing in the bombbay, sat down and forgot to fasten my seat belt, because Burnell interrupted me.

"Bogies eleven o'clock high! I think they're Bandits!! They're crossing over us and – THEY'RE DROPPING BOMBS ON US!"

That's when I forgot to fasten my seat belt, because I'd never heard of Bandits dropping bombs on anyone – rockets and ramming, but never any bombs. I scooted forward, without my seat belt on, to look up through the windshield to try and see this phenomenon.

"They're not bombs," I reported to everyone on the intercom. "They're dropping their auxiliary fuel tanks before they attack."

Those cunning Krauts. They had been waiting for us up there and they weren't about to waste anything. So they would drop the tanks on the Yanks and maybe get lucky.

The damned tanks caromed and banged off of the ships in our Group, but apparently did no great physical damage. Although, it is mentally disturbing to be as high as 27,000 feet and have *anything* dropped onto you from above, even if they're only partially empty tanks of metal.

There were about 60 of the Bandits – obviously not Friendlies – and they queued up above our right flank. It was certainly not a pleasant prospect, but thankfully not as bad as the Magdeburg encounter. And since Moon had missed that one, I told him, "When they come in on us in a little bit, we're going to shake the SHIT out of this bucket of bolts."

After the Magdeberg slaughter I'd given some thought to evasive action from the attacker's point of view:

(1) You could only fire straight ahead in line-of-flight

(2) Your time to focus on the target is only seconds

(3) If your target moves, focus on the next target

From the target's point of view:

(1) MOVE out of the line of fire! It forces the attacker to refocus on the next available target.

(2) Do not fly back into the line of fire!

(3) Fly erratically. If you don't know where you're going, then the attacker cannot know and anticipate your move.

The strategy I developed was a contradiction, because it required going crazy to deceive the attacker, while sanely focusing precisely on the one-at-a-time attacker.

This required ignoring the natural curiosity of observing the overall pandemonium. It demanded total concentration and looking your enemy in the eye.

The Bandits turned in on us at 12 o'clock High, selecting their targets, like shooting whales trapped in a bay. But I was determined that we were one whale who wouldn't sit still for it.

Of all the fighters, one selected us and bore in, but Moon and I hauled back on the controls and jumped up about thirty feet above his tracers.

So as not to fly back into his line of fire we jumped up again, instead of porpoising along a straight line. He shot beneath us and we shoved forward to pitch back down and get away from another fighter who thought he had us, but we went under him.

However, without my seatbelt fastened, I flew to the ceiling!

We were going down at an extreme angle. Moon hauled back on the controls to pull us out of the dive. It eliminated the negative G-force that had trapped me in the top of the cockpit and my butt slammed down into my seat. At the same time I also pulled back on the controls with Moon and together our big bird lurched up like a breaching whale: "KABOOM!" Something big broke loose!

Rudy called from the radio room, "BOMBS AWAY!"

"What?" I asked, while working with Moon to avoid our next attacker.

"Bombs Away!" It was Rudy's job to check the bomb-bay.

"Where in hell did they go?"

"Right through the bomb doors!"

"But the doors weren't even opened."

"They are now!"

Ohhh Shit! I'm glad we didn't have a loose fuse.

Eventually, the flak started and the fighters withdrew to wait for us to exit the target area. And there they were, as we came off of the target and out of the flak.

I switched to the Fighter Channel to hear if anyone had called Balance for support. What I heard chilled the pee in my bladder, because I had never heard such terror in a voice. It sounded more like a woman screaming for her life. Not a yell. Screaming!

"BALANCE-ONE, this is VINEGROVE ONE! OH, MY GOD! HELP US! BANDITS! COME HELP US!! THEY'RE SHOOTING THE SHIT OUT OF US!! BALANCE – VINEGROVE, OHHH MY GOD!!!"

The voice faded into sobs and was unintelligible. It hit me in a strange way as embarrassing to hear the pleading and uncontrolled hysteria of a man. Maybe it triggered my own feeling of shame at having almost lost control on my sixth mission when we had gotten out of the Bomber Stream and they did shoot the shit out of us.

But, this battle didn't even compare. There were only about 60 Bandits. Not over 200.

True, they had knocked down one of us so far, but our Group was holding good formation and not all strung out like before. And as far as I could tell, we were making them pay for it.

Until I heard the guy with the girl's voice screaming, my thought was that we were scaring the Hell out of the Bandits and we would end up with smaller losses than they. At least I was happier where I was (a relative term) than if I had been flying with the Bandits. In truth, 'It weren't no picnic for nobody' because it was a goddamned WAR!

But there was this *sissy* screaming for help that was most demoralizing. He had to be inexperienced to even expect we would get any help from our scheduled escort, BALANCE-ONE.

"VINEGROVE-ONE, this is BALANCE-ONE."

No shit! There really was a Balance-One out there someplace. He actually answered the call for help. I couldn't believe it, because nobody had ever come to our rescue before, except that one time MY FRAN checked on us.

"BALANCE-ONE, this is VINEGROVE-ONE," came the reply from our Fighter Channel Guard, "We're south of the target. Where are you?"

"Well, we're just a little busy right now Vinegrove-One."

I couldn't believe the calmness in Balance's voice. If they were "busy," there was a slaughter going on in the busy-ness of killing and being killed. Yet, his voice was unruffled, as if he were a salesperson willing to wait on you as soon as he was free.

It might have been assumed that, going deep into Germany from England, we would have approached the target from the west; and having dropped on it, we would make a 180 degree turn and head back west to England. Not so.

Strategic bombing was more like American football tactics. What might appear as a direct drive to one target could turn into an end-around to a different target.

So, headed east to the border of Czechoslovakia, we cut north to Zwickau, dropped, and made a 180 degree turn back south, instead of east for England. It was designed to keep them guessing and ending with us flying over more territory as fighter and flak "magnets."

God, how I wished again that I'd gotten assigned to fighters instead of bombers: Shorter hours, faster planes, smaller targets, more independence...Hell, they could even be back partying in London Town before we got back to the Channel – if we were lucky.

Well, that's the way it was. We still didn't have fighter protection. Somebody must have, but we didn't have it. So here we were, coming off of the target; the Bandits were queued up to have at us again and we would be fighting our own battle.

There was no doubt that the strategy of using us as "Bait" was premature. But what the hell, it was all one grand "experiment," because it was a new type of warfare and we had to do THE WRONG STUFF in order to find out how to do it the right way.

This time the Bandits queued up on our left flank at 9 o'clock high and their number seemed to have diminished to about fifty, still outnumbering us two-to-one, ship for ship.

Out of the habit I had formed, I looked over my shoulder in the opposite direction of the obvious threat, so as to avoid any surprises – and was I SURPRISED!

There were two little "dots," way up at 3 o'clock high and they were coming in our direction in a hurry. They were aircraft. I could even make out, as they neared, that they had twin engines and twin-boom tails. That could mean only one thing. They were American P-38 Lightnings – BALANCE ONE!

Before my goose-flesh got too happy, I thought, BALANCE? That was no balance. Two Friendly fighter escorts and FIFTY BANDITS?

Make that FIFTY BANDITS and only *one* Friendly, because one of the two Friendlies started flying zig-zag over the top of us, like a mother hen protecting her chicks, and the other Friendly kept going until he was above the group of FIFTY BANDITS.

Boy, this was going to be some kind of a performance. One P-38 was going to protect the bomb group by himself and the other P-38 – by himself – was going to take on FIFTY BANDITS(?).

Now I had seen all kinds of competition, but this was like a single matador jumping into the arena with 50 killer bulls. Somebody was going to get killed for sure. But if victory was going to go to the guy with the biggest "balls," then BALANCE-ONE was, unbelievably, the 50 to 1 favorite.

My God! Balance One flew out over the top of the Bandits, rolled upside down into a "split-S" and dove straight down for the FIFTY BANDITS!. He must've eaten nails for breakfast.

Goddamned American fighter pilots: vain, insolent, conceited, arrogant, cocky and impertinent Fighter Jocks! God bless 'em all. My skin crawled and my eyes got moist – "Greater love hath no man than to lay down his life for another."

There was no doubt, it was a "gutsy" move and I was impressed. Such bravery also impressed the fifty Bandits, because – as if one plane – they all pitched forward into a vertical dive to get away from my hero, the "Forked Tailed Devil," as the Luftwaffe had dubbed the P-38. This was the cool voice on the radio who had been "Just a little busy right now."

Swinging back and forth behind the Bandits, he blew up two ME-109's before they all dove into the cloud deck below us – with Balance One still tailing them.

WOW! What a show! It was well worth the high price of admission. Only the inside of my oxygen mask could have heard my "Thank you Mr. Balance," and – "Where in hell are *you* going?" as I addressed our Top Cover who also took off for the wild blue yonder at the conclusion of their performance.

I t was time for a break and I wanted a cigarette, but my lighter wouldn't burn for lack of oxygen. I hadn't thought of it before, but we had oxygen.

So while Moon was flying, I flipped my oxygen control from Demand to Full and inhaled, while digging out my cigarettes and lighter.

Okay, I was ready. Put the control back on Demand, hold the pure oxygen in my lungs – mask off, cigarette to lips – blow through the cigarette and strike the lighter.

Whoosh! Fire shot from the end of the cigarette like a blow torch. Inhale quickly to pull the fire back to ignite the tobacco and I was smoking. It didn't even occur to me at the time that I could have been burning. In fact, I could have blown up the whole goddamned airplane.

In the rarefied atmosphere at altitude that cigarette lasted me almost an hour.

But then, the trip home still took many hours more. The point of it being that combat-flying was either endless hours of boredom, or it could be shattered by moments of total terror. So what was required was a sense of balance, in coasting when you could to save yourself for the high points.

However, one thing out of balance was the schedule. We hadn't had a day off for a week and a mission was scheduled for tomorrow. There was no Interlude.

Piccadilly Circus

LONDON TOWN
CHAPTER 7

I was bushed, finally in bed, but I was wide awake. In too short a time I'd probably be back in the cockpit, sleepy as hell, and wishing I was back in bed. But since I wasn't about to get drunk or ask for medication (to screw me up), I would just have to think myself to sleep...So what I thought to do was to hypnotize myself.

I'd gotten into hypnotism back in junior high school by answering an advertisement in a magazine.

Sometimes I could make it work on others, but not on myself, which was the real point of it in hopes of improving my school grades. You know; hypnotize myself, do the required lesson and "Shazam," I would have the answers through auto-hypnosis at test time.

Except, I couldn't auto-hypnotize, nor could I be hypnotized by anyone else, because I couldn't follow the first instruction,"Clear your mind."

That was the problem I was having. There was some pretty heavy stuff to clear out of my mind and I couldn't even evacuate the easy stuff, because it was impossible for me to clear my mind, to think of nothing. I'd push out one thing and something else rushed in to replace it. So, how do you remove a thought?

Since it's difficult to outsmart yourself, I conceded that I could not remove any thoughts. However, if I invited a new thought my mind would accept it and, by this trickery, would be forced to give up the old thought.

Now this focus on mental gymnastics might seem inappropriate to aerial combat, and there had been no military training in the area of mind control – most probably because no psychiatrists were actually being shot at – but you had to have some control over your mind, since your mind is what controlled everything else. Otherwise, I suspected that my mind might shut down on me in a critical situation.

So it was, that lying awake for many nights I developed a much needed technique to go to sleep. While it took longer and some training, I thought it was much better than sitting down with the Flight Surgeon and him handing me a bottle of booze to dim my wits, which was the only remedy at the time.

I felt I had discovered the key to the whole concept of clearing the mind, so I tested it and it worked. The trick was not only overloading the system with thoughts that the mind accepted and then discarded at the next thought, but in not allowing the mind to trick me with the pleasure or fascination of dwelling on a thought. That was it. That was the secret – DON'T DWELL ON ANY SINGLE THOUGHT!

For instance, an airplane blows up. Avoid recalling the details. Replace it with something more important. What could be more important than an airplane blowing up? Sex, of course. Now that's a fun thing to think about, but no, DON'T DWELL ON ANY SINGLE THOUGHT. Keep moving. Don't worry about finding a thought, it'll be there.

But focusing on the trick of not-focusing on anything gets to be a job. It's tiring. Forget tiring. Get abstract. Cloud formations are abstract. There…I can coast now without working to change my mind, because the clouds are changing…Boring? Well, add color. What color? Pick one, but DON'T DWELL ON IT! Pick another, and another, and another…

Sergeant Gatt stuck a wake-up cigarette between my lips.

I awoke to a lot of commotion in the billet and what appeared to be everyone preparing to go on a mission.

MISSION #12
Osnabruck, Germany, 13 May 1944
Saturday: 21 ships up.   (6:35 Flying Time)
The fifth mission of the week…Give me a break.

Osnabruck was in the middle of "Flak Alley" in the mining and industrial Ruhrland of Germany. And while I liked to think I had a scheme to increase my odds against fighters, flak was a different threat, because it was so impersonal. It was just there and there was no way to avoid it, except good luck. However, the odds favored the flak winning before completing a tour of 25 missions.

Yet in spite of this, a mystery presented itself on the Osnabruck raid.

I was watching Turner's ship as we started picking up flak on the way into the target. Rather, the flak started picking us up.

The German antiaircraft guns were controlled by their infared radar and fired in bursts of three to four-at-a-time in fusillades of three that exploded along our flight path: Bloom-Bloom-Bloom/ Bloom-Bloom-Bloom/ Bloom-Bloom-Bloom!

Without any apparent reason, Turner banked to the right, then back on course. Had he not made the deviation he would have been destroyed by direct hits from three volleys of four bursts-at-once.

What it looked like was a guy driving down the highway and changing lanes to pass a truck, which just happened to explode.

I couldn't believe it. It was as if Turner knew he had to alter course to keep from being blown up, but that wasn't possible. However, it was so unusual that it was all I could think about for the rest of the mission.

To leave the formation and go off on your own was just not done. Yet, that's what Turner had done. He had abruptly banked to the right, avoiding the volley, and circled around it and back into formation. It was incredible. How did he know when to do that.

It wasn't until we were standing in the chow-line after the mission that I saw Turner and asked him if he recalled pulling out of the formation.

Yes, he remembered.

Did he realize that they would have been blown up if he hadn't pulled away?

Yes.

"What I want to know, " I asked him, "Is HOW did you know to pull out of formation when you did?"

He had a look of bewilderment. His eyes wandered and then he looked straight at me and confessed. "I have no idea, Smitty…It was just an impulse…It just came to me."

"Man, that's strange."

"Yeah," he said, "I wish I understood it."

"Me too…That's one special talent."

Moon, Ears, and I boarded the milk-run train at Elmswell, the closest railway station to the base, and endured its slow progress to Ipswich, where we planned to transfer to the London Express.

Since we had a three-day pass, with plenty of time between bottle and throttle, Moon and Ears placated themselves with the contents of a bottle of Vat 69 whiskey . We seemed to crawl along in the typical and quaint little British commuter train through what seemed to me was a miniature English countryside.

Unlike American trains, it was smaller and its whistle sounded like a woman's scream instead of tooting. But the main difference was the absence of a passageway down the center of the cars.

Each car was made up of compartments and there was no access between the cars, nor even between compartments. It was Third Class. You got into a compartment at the station and there you remained until stopping at the next station. All of which led to a problem, since we were actually impounded.

"I've gotta take a piss," Ears said.

The remark was not offensive since we were the only ones in the compartment. Moon stood up and was forced to pace around to hold his balance against the jostling of the train and commented, "I've gotta go too, but I don't see any relief tube in here. What in hell do these people do anyway? Loan me your cap, Smitty."

"Use your own," I said, "or hang it out the window."

Looking like Buster Keaton, Moon struggled to get to one of the windows located in each of the two doors at the ends of the compartment. Once – twice – three times he tried. There, he grabbed the leather strap that controlled the window, pulled it and dropped the window open. He then attempted to present himself to the window as if it were a urinal. But it was not such an easy task.

For one thing, we bounced around a curve and Moon, his equipment in hand, waltzed backwards – and I moved away from the targeted window. Ears, bottle in hand, remained seated next to the window, curious about procedure, since he was up next.

Moon was able to reclaim his place at the open window, but discovered that he was either not tall enough nor long enough to manage the job, so he stood up on the opposite seats and spread-eagled himself up against the window tightly and released.

"Ohhh, yesss! Ohhh, boy! What a relief."

There is no warning when trains pass each other going in opposite directions and the sound of it is startling in proportion to the nearness to the window.

"ZOOMITY-X-ZOOMITY-X-ZOOMITY-X-ZOOMITY-X-ZOOMITY!!!!!!"

Moon thought he'd lost it and jumped back from the window before he could stop the flow, that was sprayed downwind from the force of imploding airpressure which was not in Ears' favor.

Ears in his characteristic, unrattled, slow motion way, reacted by drawling out, "Welll, I'll beee godd-damned."

I had a great urge to say, "That's one way to get pissed off," but kept painfully quiet because the situation was funny only to me.

With a slight slur in his speech. Ears said, "I ought to do that to you, but I'm more con…con…You know what I mean."

Still in need to relieve himself, Ears had a better idea. He searched his pockets and produced a condom.

"Now I know why they make us carry these G. I. rubbers. It's in case you're riding one of these godd-damned trains without a toilet."

So to avoid the problems that Moon had encountered in trying to use the window, Ears proceeded to relieve himself into his rubber reservoir. I thought it was rather ingenious and even considered doing the same, until he tried to throw it out of the window into the slipstream. "SWOOOSH!!!"

The experiment failed at the expense of Moon, who got his payback when the pee-filled balloon exploded.

So considering the unfortunate beginning of our time off, I felt my luck would improve if we parted company; they to a pub in Ipswitch and me to catch the Express Train to London Town.

The Express, while extremely crowded, was a bit larger, faster, had a passageway, not down the center like American trains, but along one side throughout and from car to car, and a lavatory at the end of each car, even though they were perpetually occupied from the overcrowding.

One thing about the war was that it seemed that everyone was involved with something that was somewhere else, because public transportation was overburdened with everyone trying to get from where they were to some other place. But then, everything was in short supply. Even the traditional British reserve.

In search of a bit more personal space I pushed slowly through the tightly crowded corridor, struggling to make my way to someplace that was not so claustrophobic when I was physically trapped in a scene of khaki. I was attacked.

Yes, I was actually hooked by a firm grip onto my left buttock. It was a commanding grasp of a heavyset middle-aged woman in uniform who wore Sergeant stripes and the emblem on her cap had the letters ATS, which stood for Auxiliary Territorial Service, the British equivalent of the American WACs, or Women Army Corps.

I was shocked by this new experience of being put upon by the aggression of a female. It was scandalous. No…I was actually more frightened than shocked, since fear is based on the unknown and I certainly didn't know what was going on. I was more familiar with aerial combat, but being groped on the butt by a hefty female British Sergeant who had more hair on her upper lip than I; well, it scared me. I was frightened because I was not in control of the situation.

Was I going to be raped?

Was that even possible?

Should I call out for help?

No. She was not alone. She had a dozen other uniformed women under her command, all giggling, shouting – gone crazy like the bobbysoxers at a Frank Sinatra concert that I'd heard about.

The situation was not only scary, but humiliating, a commissioned officer of the United States Army Air Force being attacked by loopy and turned-on females in khaki who had captured themselves a naive twenty year old American Lieutenant, spit-n-polished in his Class "A" dress uniform with silver "leg-spreader" wings.

"Roll me over Yankee soldier," the Sergeant sang and was joined by the others, "Roll me over, lay me down and do it again."

I was bagged!

It was a primitive frenzy of bawdy behavior. I was completely surrounded by a superior number of flighty females, singing their loudest and noticeably enjoying my discomfort.

There was no choice but to abide their merriment and to sweat out the lengthy lyrics from,"This in Number One, the party's just begun…" through, "This is Number Two,Shoe…" to "Three, his hand is on my knee…" then "Five, the bee is in the hive…" – until the whole bloody thing should have ended with, "Ten…" But it rhymed with "again" and the entire thing was repeated with the chorus, "Roll me over Yankee soldier. Roll me over, lay me down and do it again!"

I was happy to see, therefore, another "Yank" enter the melee from the opposite end of the corridor.

Dressed the same as I, his over-six-feet-tall stature and toothy grin made him more attractive than I and he welcomed the attention turned his way. He grabbed almost six women into his arms in a giant bear hug and joined in the chorus of "Roll me over Yankee soldier. Roll me over, lay me down and do it again."

His name was Tom Schneider and he invited everyone to call him T.S.. He too was a copilot, assigned to a different bomb group. Hidden behind him was his pilot, Stephen Stein, much smaller and more introverted than T.S., which seemed to make for a good combination in sort of a flip-flop fashion, since Stein was the senior pilot and, by rank, the leader. But it was T.S. who was obviously the social animal and, like the Pied Piper, he led their way through the crowd of frolicking females.

The "barking" of the "babes" proved worse than their bite and we three Yanks finally joined each other in the hub of the hubbub where little Stephen Stein broke up the brouhaha when he started playing grab-ass down at his altitude. This caused T.S. to complain that Stein had a special talent as a "party-pooper" and told him, "Don't harass the girls."

"Well," Stein rebutted, "It's her ass that made me do it. It's a lovely ass. I was just complimenting it."

I could see from the Air Medal ribbons with three Oak Leaf Clusters that both T.S. and Stein wore that they had flown at least twenty combat missions. They must have also had numerous missions to London. So I asked them to brief me, since I was alone and that this was my "Virgin Visit" to London. So they invited me to join up with them and they would check me out on "Sin City".

I really looked forward to some needed change in my life, the most important being that nobody would be shooting at me for at least three days. The other change would be that life would be more metropolitan than the rural setting of our Air Station.

Unlike the established Royal Air Force Stations, our accommodations were rather primitive, having been built on some farms with plenty of mud. American criminal prisoners had better facilities than we did. Our billet was located right next to the farmyard through which we took a shortcut to the showers.

I joked that, "In London you could go to the privy and never wet your feet…They'd gone about as far as they could go," and Stein picked up on it by informing me that Sir Thomas Crapper had invented the flushing toilet in London in the 1800s.

"Right," T.S. said, "The British invented indoor plumbing and they haven't improved on it since."

I was glad they'd taken me in tow, because I would have been lost in getting a taxi and finding a hotel so quickly.

We *Yanks* appeared to be an oddity by the reaction of the residents in the family style hotel where we'd gotten lodging and where we'd decided to eat in the hotel's dining room.

An older couple kept glancing at us in a disapproving manner. So in an effort to invite some friendliness I caught them in mid-glance and said, "Howdy, neighbors," but it didn't win me any votes. Our presence was not appreciated, so I accepted the fact.

T.S. , on the other hand, was not so generous and purposely spoke to me loud enough to be overheard,"Now, Smithy" (deliberately giving my name an English flavor), "since this is your first visit to old London Town, you should be prepared to be accosted by some of the ladies. They will expect to be paid for their hospitality. So what you tell them is, I came over here to save your ass and not to buy it."

A tinkling of our neighbor's china pleased T.S. that he had hit a nerve. So what would be the reaction?

The elderly gentleman rose from his chair and addressed T.S. .

"Lieutenant, while I am out of uniform this evening, I am a Major in the Home Guard, having served God and country in World War One and at Dunkirk in this one. And, as you have offended both my wife and I and the ladies of our country, I must express my opinion of your improper behavior."

T.S. started to rise.

"No, no, Lieutenant, please keep your seat…I see by the ribbons on your tunic – more than I've received in two wars – that you are over-dressed; that you are obviously over-paid and, by your comment just made, that you are over-sexed and, unfortunately, you are over-here…Good evening.

The Major then escorted his wife from the dining room.

"That was good." T.S. said, "Not original, but damn well done."

T.S. and Stein had planned on an evening of pub-crawling, so I excused myself in hopes of getting to see a play . The small hotel did not have a concierge, but the desk clerk found that I could probably get a ticket to *Macbeth* at the Old Vic theater and gave me instructions on how to get there by bus.

There was an advantage to being alone, in that a single seat in the theatre was easier come by and I seemed to have gotten the best one in the house in the center stalls. On the other hand, however, it wasn't much fun being alone, not having someone to share the good as well as the bad.

Except – Good fortune appeared to have favored me. For seated next to me was an attractive lady, just a bit older than I. Well, she could not have been over thirty and I fancied that she could probably teach me a few things.

Was she alone? Would she care for my companionship? Was she really as stunning as my first impression of her?

Well, it was difficult to determine without obviously staring, so I tried to keep my focus on the stage.

Even so, just as the house lights dimmed, I sneaked a quick peek and confirmed that she was indeed a knockout. Also, there were three older women seated on the far side of her, which suggested that she didn't have a date. I would get a better look at intermission and just be content to sit next to her and appreciate her fragrance, which was much more gratifying than the odors I'd been living with.

Oh my gosh! Maybe my aroma offended her. I had gotten used to it and I was sure it was still with me: Royal Lyme. It wasn't even a favorite of mine, but my dad had gotten it to me for Christmas. I'd packed it in a side pocket of my B-4 bag. But in moving around somebody had tossed my bag out of the plane, it landed on its side and the bottle broke, soaking everything I owned. It was good cologne and had long staying power. Too good. I couldn't get rid of the scent.

Even so, it had served me well in the blackouts, which I discovered the night we departed Ireland for England in a large troop movement. A thousand of us on the docks and we were told to retrieve our personal luggage. All I had to do was follow my nose, while everyone else spent most of the night searching for their bags.

Well, that had been months ago and I could only hope that I didn't offend anyone with my Royal Lyme fragrance. But what the heck. Wasn't I in Lymy Land? And as a Yank, wasn't I expected to be overdone.

I watched the actors upon the stage, but I could not get into the play. It seemed to be going well with the players, but something was happening to me. Macbeth had his problems up there, but so did I. Mine were naturally greater than his, because he was play-acting and my life was REAL.

That's what bothered me and destroyed my ability to focus on my present condition: seated in a theatre next to a vivacious young lady with a fresh scent of lilac, with bursts of flak going off in my head, aircraft exploding, and men falling from the sky.

It was crazy…I was going – crazy.

The Germans had been shooting at me for six weeks and the fact I hadn't yet been hit was extraordinary. It was as sure as God made all-that-is that my time on earth would end shortly and I was wasting it in a goddamned theater watching play-actors instead of experiencing life. I had the urge to grab the girl next to me and to go live life. However, that would not be civilized.

I'd heard of falling in love with love, but it wasn't the same thing. I was in love with life, having experienced both too much of it and yet not enough of it. What was it all about anyway? What was going on?

Well, there was a WAR going on is what it was. Here I was trying to be civilized in appreciation of the Arts in a world that was UN-civilized. Yesterday I was dropping bombs on people and before the week was out I'd be back in the killing field over the Continent and could very likely end up dead. The End! It was crazy as Hell. That's what it was. It was HELL and it was crazy. Therefore, insanity was my ally in Hell.

"They call me Smitty."

"My name is Lee."

"You're very pretty."

"You smell nice, Smithy."

"Thanks Lee, but I am crazy."

It was intermission. Lee was my target and I started my *Run*.

"Can I get you a drink?"

"Kummel."

I made my way through the crowd to the bar and ordered two kummel, having no idea what it was, except it was served in small shot glasses.

"I guess I should have ordered a dozen. They're rather small."

"Maybe later," Lee said.

A gong was sounded and the crowd moved back to their seats.

This time as the houselights dimmed I took a longer and admiring look at Lee, which she accepted gracefully. She was petite and if she hadn't been a blonde she could have been mistaken for Scarlet O'Hara in *Gone With the Wind*. And thanks to a boost from the kummel, I was starting to feel like a twenty year old Rhett Butler.

For all of my interest, Macbeth could have been Othello or Hamlet, because my attention kept going to Lee. At least I wasn't thinking about the war anymore and that was a relief.

I thought I saw her pour a thimble or so of something from a small flask, but never caught her sipping it. Yet, it had to have gone somewhere or she wouldn't have needed the refills.

Before the end of the play her hand was, at first, lightly on my knee and then, warmly, on my thigh. (Ohh, my goodness). At one dramatic moment of the play I felt her long fingernails dig in slightly.

(Ohhh, mercy). Macbeth could not have been more excited up on the stage than I was in the darkened theatre.

Finally the last curtain call ended, the house lights went up and I slowly bowed my way out of the theater behind Lee, embarassed at the bulge in my trousers. So, bending forward, I asked if she would join me in an after-theater treat.

No, not at her place. She suggested we go to my place, not knowing that I didn't have a place – for what I hoped for. I could imagine what a disaster it would be for me to take her into the family hotel under the stare of the residents. Oh well, I'd think of something, because I knew that we were meant for each other. There was no question about it. It was going to be a wonderful night.

Unlike Broadway theatres, there were no taxis waiting. Would Lee mind waiting while I tried to find us a *cabby*? Of course not. She bundled up in her dark fur jacket and I took off into the wild black-out looking for a cab.

In my excitement I was almost run over three times, because I would naturally look to my left as I darted back and forth across the street through the traffic. This was wrong by English standards, since oncoming traffic didn't come from the left, but from the right and from behind. It was damn dangerous.

What an embarassment that would be to have the Ponca City News announce: "PONCA CITY PILOT KILLED IN LONDON BLACKOUT."

I had absolutely no luck in getting a taxi despite the distance that I traveled. At one point I chased what I thought was a sure thing up a narrow street and out of the main traffic, but he must have been taking a shortcut instead of letting off his fare.

Then I decided to take a shortcut back to the sure thing I'd left at the theater and damned if I didn't get lost in the blackout.

I remembered the lesson in navigational training about Daniel Boone. . . Had he ever been lost? "No," he replied, "Never lost, but I've been bewildered for months on end."

Well, it didn't take a month for me to find my way back to the theater, but it was long enough that my date had disappeared. I couldn't believe it, but I had lost a sure thing in the damned blackout.

It wasn't easy, but disappointed, I eventually found my way back to the hotel around midnight. I took the stairway to the second floor of the hotel where our rooms were located.

Being a family hotel there was no activity and most of the lighting had been turned off. But as I rounded the corner on the second floor I could see T.S. quite clearly in the hallway.

Of course in his condition he didn't know he was there, because he was blind drunk and was struggling to carry a nude woman.

"Where'ya going?" I whispered.

I'm gonna throw this woman outa the hotel!" he answered in a slurred but full voice.

"You can't do that!" I protested.

"The hell I can't!"

"Come on. Get back into your room."

After I get rid of this woman…I'm takin' her down to the desk and I'm gonna tell 'em that she forced herself into my room!"

"T.S. ," I said, "They won't believe you. They wouldn't believe you even if you had your clothes on. Now, get back into your room!"

He objected, so I went to the door of his room to open it, but it was locked. I bumped on it hoping that Stein was inside and would unlock it and help out. If not, the three of us were all going to be in big trouble.

But having turned my back on T.S. , I turned back around to see him waddling down the hallway bare-assed naked, carrying Lady Godiva – and just about to turn the corner for the stairway where he would descend and present his objections to the night clerk.

I almost yelled at him, but ran instead to turn him around and pushed him with his burden back toward his room. The closer we got the more he resisted until he lost his balance and the three of us ended up in a pile on the floor.

That's when Stein opened the door and staggered into the hallway, also nude. "What the fuck's going on?"

I told him that there was *no* fuckin' goin' on and for God's sake to not let the door –

Too late. The door to their room clicked shut behind him.

I untangled myself from the pile of nudity, found my room key and finally rounded up the three drunks into my room.

Now, my room, cozy enough for me alone, was standing room only with four people in it.

Conceding his battle lost, the big Tom Schneider collapsed onto my small single bed, and then there were the three of us standing: little Stein, the blond and myself. Stein was also nude and I couldn't help but notice that he was actually not so little, holding up the nude blonde next to him, and that she was really a brunette.

I grabbed T.S. 's feet and pulled him crosswise of the bed. He didn't fit that way, of course, but I was desperate. So with his head off the bed on one side and his legs off the other side, I pushed the wobbly couple over onto what little space remained.

It was obvious that there was no room for me, so I found my gas mask "purse," from which I'd removed the mask to make room for my toiletries and a change of underwear, and I left the trio in my room without looking back.

Piccadilly Circus is the theatrical and entertainment center of London. And what entertainment. Even in a blackout the music of Glenn Miller was recognizable and I followed its sound to the source, in the basement of the Red Cross RAINBOW CLUB.

Unfortunately, I discovered that I was a fish out of water and, as an officer, was considered an intruder. There was no sign posted that it was for "ENLISTED PERSONNEL ONLY," but it was made abundantly clear that I was not welcome in this happy place.

It reminded me of the reverse of Bill Mauldin's cartoon showing two officers admiring a sunset and wondering if the enlisted men's view was just as good. In this instance, the enlisted men had the best of it. Reluctantly I left the merriment and went back outside into the blackout.

Hard to tell in the blackout, but I guessed I was standing on a street corner and heard a man selling newspapers.

"PAIYPA, PAIYPA. Get-cha paipa here."

Then in a low voice, almost like an echo, he called, "Condoms, condoms, condoms."

I lit a cigarette and checked my watch with the light. It was a little past 2:00 in the morning and I was going to have to find me a room; which didn't appear to be that difficult from the offers I received.

I don't know how they did it, because I couldn't see a bloody thing in the blackout, but the "Piccadilly Commandos" had a special talent for identification in the dark.

"Aiyee, Yank, a Pound around the corner?"

"Aiyee, 'Ony. Five Pounds for the night?"

"Yea, Yea. I'll get him down!"

"CARMEN!" I called out to the familiar voice.

"Yea, Yea. Over here!"

Incredible! With thousands of people milling about, I couldn't – although I somehow could – believe I'd run into my own crew in Piccadilly Circus. Why not? That's where everybody went.

Appropriately, at the center of the Piccadilly Circus is the statue of Eros, the mythological son of Aphrodite who excites erotic love. To protect Eros from the ravages of war it had been sand-bagged. And appropriately or not, according to my crew, Herbie Hill had climbed the sand-bagged statue and Carmen was confident that he was the one to get Herbie back down. I was invited to assist before Herbie hurt himself – and whoever he might fall on.

Most everything had to be taken in faith, because I was blind in the blackout. So I joined the crew in trying to climb some sandbags and commented that I thought it was goin to rain, because I felt some sprinkles.

"Yea, Yea." Carmen said, "That's the problem. "Herbie's pissin' on us all. He doesn't wanta come down."

"In that case," I said, "Let him stay up there."

Did they have a place to stay?

"Yea, Yea."

They were in enlisted quarters. And if I didn't have a place, they'd sneak me in.

Had I tried the Reindeer Officers Club?

No, but I was sure I would be alright and that I'd take off, because they might be up until daylight getting Hill down.

Close by, I checked for a room at the Piccadilly Hotel. No luck and no suggestions as to where I might find a place at 3 a.m.. I was told the chances were not good at the Reindeer Club at such an hour.

Okay, I'd take a hike.

"Wanta spend the night with me, Dearie?"

The doormen worked at keeping the *Commandos* away from the hotel's clientele, but a bit away from the doorway there was just enough light to see the face of the lady of the night who had entreated me. Such features made me frigid; maybe for the rest of my life, I thought.

While I declined her proposal and tried to lose myself in the blackout, she latched onto me.

"You're a 'andsome young thing, Dearie."

"No deal. No way."

"I know ways that could put you in 'eaven."

"Look," I said, "I've spent almost every day this week in "heaven" and I'm content to be left alone. Please."

"No offense, Dearie." she said and pulled me up short. It was obvious she'd been drinking and was a bit melancholy. "I like you."

"Sure." I said.

"And I want to tell you something…You've got to be careful of the girlies around 'ere. A lot of 'em are diseased and I wouldn't want you to catch anything."

"Well, I appreciate that."

"So you remember, if you do decide to go to bed with somebody, be sure and protect yourself…Promise me?"

I promised and she vanished, but she was immediately replaced by others plying their trade.

Finally I made my way out of the hard core area to the front of a Never-Close newsreel theater where I considered spending what was left of the night. I'd done that before in New York City and in Hollywood when I was an aviation cadet and couldn't get lodging. However, I was a bit hungry and decided to get a bite before retiring in a theater seat for the night.

While the Grill was not as jam-packed as the streets outside, the counter and tables were all filled with the residue of the night. It was an eclectic crowd, mainly Yanks in uniform and a wide assortment of females. Back in the corner I was surprised to glimpse a single blonde head with a dark fur coat, alone at a table for two.

Grabbing the empty chair at the table I asked, "Do you mind?"

The woman who answered was not whom I'd expected. She barely glanced up from her plate and nodded an I-don't-really-care consent.

"It looks good." I commented and asked what she was having.

"Welsh rarebit."

"I don't see the rabbit."

She looked at me for the first time and I at her. Not bad. Not as good as the first fur coat; possibly older and a bit tired. She was at least in her thirties.

"It's cheese on toast."

"I thought you said, "Rabbit?""

"I did." she said, starting to smile. "Welsh rarebit is cheese on toast."

"What's Welsh cheese?" I asked.

We both chuckled a bit and a waiter asked my order. I pointed at the lady's plate and said, "One of those and – " with an attempted English accent, "A spot of tea."

"You're a pilot?"

I pointed at my wings, "That's what it says."

"You look too young to be a pilot."

"How do you know how old I am?"

"You're a pilot. Doesn't it take years to become a pilot?"

Dammit, I'd been thinking about growing a mustache to look older, but I didn't have enough hair on my face to make it work. I was just a kid and I looked like a kid. I wished I was at least twenty-five.

"You're right," I agreed. Then a thought flashed: what if it came to me performing like I was twenty-five? I couldn't let that happen.

"Will you want to go to bed with me?" she asked.

"No. . . ohhh, ahhh, no. No, not tonight. Ahhh. No offense, please. The truth is, ahhhh, I'm awfully tired. I've had a busy week. You know, fighting the war. It's pretty, ahhh, pretty tiring."

She smiled knowingly, saying she understood, because she too had had a pretty grueling week and added, "War is Hell."

During a long awkward pause in our conversation the waiter served my grilled cheese and poured us tea. The lady lit a cigarette while I fumbled for my lighter. Then she watched me eating self consciously as she smoked. Before I finished my snack she asked straight forwardly, "Do you have lodging for the night?"

I looked at my watch, then answered, "Well the night's practically over. It's after four."

"You know," she said, "Every few weeks I take off for a week and go visit my parents. I closed *shop* about an hour ago and I'm leaving this morning. You're certainly welcome to use my place for some shut-eye. You can have the couch and I promise not to disturb."

I t was almost noon when I awoke, quite alone. My hostess was gone and I'd not even thanked her for her hospitality, but I found a paper and pencil and jotted her a note of appreciation before leaving her "flat."

Big Ben, Houses of Parliament, Westminster Abbey, Buckingham Palace, Tower of London and St. Paul's Cathedral were the sights to see. It was dinner time when I finished and I took in a movie afterwards. It was *A GUY NAMED JOE* with Spencer Tracy, Irene Dunne and Van Johnson, a good "flick" that I'd already seen three times before.

Seated next to me in the theater, between two beautiful girls, was a Staff Sergeant. And since it seemed somewhat out of balance, I offered to help out and was, surprisingly, welcomed.

Afterwards the four of us stopped in a pub for a few drinks and to socialize and then – another pub and then…

It was peer pressure. I didn't even like the taste of alcohol, especially straight and without the sweetness of some kind of soda pop, but that's the way the girls ordered it and that's the way they drank it. And was the Lieutenant not going to match them drink for drink???

Some people were talking in what sounded like a cave or tunnel, because of the echo. They had a problem. They didn't know what to do with a drunken Lieutenant. They didn't know where he'd come from nor where to return him. I wanted to ask if I could help, but my face was numb and my voice didn't work. That's all I could recall.

I don't know what kind of a room it was. I was in a bed, but it wasn't a bedroom. It was as large as a warehouse or maybe a dance hall. It was empty and unfurnished, except for two beds: the one I was in and another at the far end of the room.

My clothes were laying on the bed and alongside on the floor. I definitely did not feel well, but forced myself to get up anyway and I got dressed. It was almost noon and I recalled I had to catch the train back to base, but I seemed to be moving in slow motion, had no idea where I was, nor how I was to get to the train station, wherever it was.

Out of curiosity, I walked to the opposite bed that was occupied by two beautiful girls. Oh, yeah. I recognized them from – last night. The way they were embraced I felt they must be in love. So, quietly, I left them in peace and headed back to war.

Flak Map.

PRE-D DAY
CHAPTER 8

In May of 1944 the press and public were preoccupied with the coming invasion of Europe. The German radio announced that if the Allies should be foolish enough to attempt such an impossible objective, that Germany was prepared to launch a counter-invasion of England.

Without the advantage of hindsight, other than the Germans making everything happen their way for the past five years, until the United States slowed things down a bit by getting involved, there was no assurance that the Allies – disadvantaged by being outside of the Heartland – could pull off an invasion and defeat the greatest proven Superpower in history.

Germany had certainly earned its reputation as being the Bad Guys. And the only way to beat the Bad Guys, was to be worse than they were. That's what it really boiled down to: GOOD GUYS DON'T WIN WARS!

Therefore, we would have to create more destruction and kill more people than had the Germans. Could we do that? We'd better, unless we wanted to learn to speak German and pay the consequences. The same went for the Japanese who were also out to take us.

This business of destruction and killing was really serious; especially to me, hauling my ass up over the Fatherland as an invitation to have it shot off.

Well, there was no way I could make it. It was an obvious conclusion. So the only questions were WHEN and HOW I was to die. Even so, there was no point in being suicidal and my instinct for survival was even greater. I would try and eat the entire elephant with just one bite at a time – and the next bite was a dandy: #13.

It was a bad omen for anyone who was superstitious. Some guys even called it Mission # 12-B. But then, our success so far was proof that we could nix any hex, as long as we didn't forget to kiss the props and to piss on the tent peg.

The TENT PEG! We'd lost our TENT PEG!! That was bad!

Yes. Whoever had flown *PRIDE OF THE YANKEES* in our absence had not brought it back from a mission. This meant that we would have to fly some other plane at a different revetment, with a another ground crew who had a separate tent with virgin and unqualified tent pegs. There was no proof or assurance that the magic would work with a pristine peg.

Therefore, with Mission #13 doomed, it could be the end of combat for me, along with everything else. So call it superstition, stupidity or plain desperation, facing death was a serious matter.

Well, it had to happen sometime. That was common knowledge. That was the business we were in. We knew that up front. That's why nobody had "graduated" for over a month that I knew of; even though the powers-that-be had increased our combat obligation, based on *their* opinion that our odds had improved from additional fighter support, of which I had personally not seen enough of.

Well, I'd at least had a couple of days to experience London. Maybe not everything it had to offer, but plenty for me for the time being, which was more than a lot of twenty-year-olds would get a shot at. I'd tried to behave myself, but morality was not any more of a real guarantee of survival than pissing on a tent peg.

Morality was for those who wanted to live with a clear conscience. However, dying was a different matter in the non-matter environment of death. So my real concern was to keep on living as long as I could. However, there was an overpowering feeling that Mission #13 was really to be my last mission.

MISSION #(13)"12-B"
Aachen, Germany, 20 May 1944
Saturday: 17 ships up   (5:40 Flying Time)

Eutrecht was back from the hospital and the rest of the crew all made it back from pass, except Dyer, who got back okay, but had a bicycle accident on the night of his return and ended up in the Infirmary with a broken arm. A replacement would fill in at his left-waistgun position.

Unable to sleep, the longer I laid in bed thinking about #13 being the one that we wouldn't complete, the more convinced I became, knowing for certain that this mission had to be avoided in order to survive. So when Gatt offered to put a cigarette between my lips I refused it, rolled over on my side and said, "I'm not going."

I heard him tell Moon that I wasn't going and I expected Moon to give me some sort of a pep-talk, but he and the others proceeded to dress in silence, ignoring me completely. He would have to report my absence and they would assign someone to replace me like they had for Dyer. But what would happen to me?

Would I be courtmartialed for refusing to fly? What did they do in such a case? I'd never heard of it. Would I be sentenced to a firing squad? If so, at least it wouldn't happen today when we were going to be killed anyway.

Moon and the others needed to know about my precognition, so I spoke up. "I've got to tell you guys something. I happen to know for certain that we won't survive today's mission."

Moon, Ears and Eut all looked at me without any kind of reaction. "Believe me. We won't make it today. I'm not going!"

"Okay," Moon said, "Goodbye."

The three of them just turned and left without an argument. They didn't threaten, blame nor shame me. They just left me. The word "coward," would have been convenient, but it wasn't used. But, then, it wouldn't have made any difference with me. Better to be a living coward than a dead hero. Right?

Funny I should think of it, but it was known that Clark Gable, the same age as my dad, had halted his acting career and volunteered to be a gunner in the Eighth Air Force. After only five missions he was reassigned to Public Relations, which caused me to think of him as a coward – until I flew my first mission.

There were also reporters and writers like Hemingway who had gone along on usually just one mission, who would describe the grim hardships and conditions of aerial combat, without flying more than just a sampling. For them I also had no respect. But after flying just one mission, I would never again brand anyone a coward who had voluntarily put his life on the line and flown at least one mission.

However, there were degrees of separation on the Coward/Hero scale, which ran from minus-1. to off-the-graph at Infinitely Crazy. So at #13, paranoia had to kick in to replace diminishing adrenaline, because it was illogical that – KNOWING YOU WERE GOING OUT TO DIE – you would go anyway.

Okay, so they were heroes all: Moon, Ears, Eut and the rest of the crew, but they were NUTS! I would sure miss them, especially on Memorial Days, or when I saw the American flag, or found the good life after the war with all of its freedoms and benefits for which they were actually willing to sacrifice their lives...Yep, I'd sure miss 'em, because they would be dead and I would still be alive for having not gone today.

But??????? What kind of a life would that be, knowing that I had told them they would be killed – and in their stupidity they went anyway – and they would be dead and I would be alive?????

Yes, alive I might become a successful businessman, raise a family and, who knew, I might even become President of the United States, because I would be alive. I sure couldn't do it by dying.

But could I live with that????? No...In that case I would have to consider myself a coward. They hadn't and wouldn't blame me, but *I* would – every day and night of my life – blame myself.

"HEY GUYS – WAIT FOR ME – I'M COMING – WAIT UP!!!"

The mission to Aachen wasn't really that bad. To Hell with intuition. It was proof positive that I was not tuned into the Source of All-That-Is like Turner had been the day he pulled out of formation and avoided the flak.

But what about that fortune teller in the penny arcade in London? It had been a way to kill a couple of minutes and spend a Pound for some assurance to know that I would survive the war.

Well, she'd given me my money's worth and told me what I wanted to hear; that I would live to a ripe old age. But what was it that she didn't tell me? Why was she crying after she thought I'd left?

She was crying because she knew I wasn't going to make it. But knowing the truth, was she going to tell me that the end was near? Of course not. That's why she was crying: lying to young soldiers, sailors and airmen, like myself, telling each one that they would live to a ripe old age, but knowing they were dying.

How could you have any faith in a fortune teller? They lied. But on the other hand??? She had told me that I would make it – and I did make it,so far.

Trying to live life could sure get confusing. I had been totally convinced that the day's mission would be my undoing, but it hadn't turned out that way at all.

There were no fighter attacks and the flak was nominal. My premonition of total disaster had been as far off course as *we were* after leaving the target!

"We're headed right straight for a heavy flak area." Ears said on the intercom.

Standard intercom procedure was to announce your position in the plane, then call the position you wished. Officially it should go like:

"Navigator to Copilot."

"This is the Copilot. Go ahead Navigator."

"Copilot, this is the Navigator. (Such and such and such)."

Adhering to protocol only added to the problem of communicating in conditions of crisis when a lot of information had to be exchanged between as many as ten crewmen on the party-line. So our crew had become more cryptic, since everyone knew each other's voice.

Ears, although still laid back and casual by nature, had improved his skill as a navigator in the past six weeks, the same as everyone else on the crew. He kept up on exactly where we were at all times, even suggesting what he considered to be the best escape routes in case we got shot down. The only exception to his precision would be when he would lose his pencil to man a machine gun during fighter attacks, which he did on occasions.

"Are you guys gonna let 'em lead us into that flak area?"

"Stand-by Ears."

As was our practice, Moon monitored the VHF Command Channel while I was on Intercom with the crew, calling for "CREW CHECK" about every fifteen minutes. Instead of breaking in on Moon with the CALL override I stuck my index finger in the air between us, circled it around to get his attention and dove it down to the VHF transmitter where I took hold of the TRANSMIT switch, which had been safetied with safety-wire.

I paused to give Moon time to stop me. Because, if I broke the safety, there would be some serious explaining to do. He didn't know why I was going to break the safety, but the look he gave me was one of trust. So I broke the safety and he heard me transmit:

"HOTSHOT YELLOW, (Not mentioning who was calling), My navigator tells me that we're headed straight for a large flak area."

"GET OFF THE AIR! MAINTAIN RADIO SILENCE!"

Someone else called, "HOTSHOT YELLOW, ditto on that transmission. My navigator confirms we are headed for a large flak area!"

"THIS IS HOTSHOT YELLOW! GET OFF THE AIR! THAT'S AN ORDER!"

Then another protester joined in, "Echo, Echo, HOTSHOT YELLOW. You're gonna get us into a buncha trouble. Better change course HOTSHOT."

"DAMMIT, THIS IS HOTSHOT YELLOW and..."

BLOOMP-BLOOMP-BLOOMP.

Flak started to burst around us and HOTSHOT YELLOW made a steep bank to the left to alter course.

Avoiding the worst of the flak – thanks to insubordination – we didn't lose anybody. We also didn't catch Hell for our defiance after we returned. Although, Captain Cerrone did ask why the safety wire on our transmitter had been broken. Moon replied innocently, "I don't know. Are you sure it was broken? I didn't notice." And that was the end of it.

S unday was a Stand Down. So with no mission to fly, I took the train up to Norwich to visit Paul Stout, a classmate through all of pilot training. For whatever reason, he'd ended up as a B-24 pilot.

Paul was over six feet tall. From Wichita, Kansas, he'd played varsity football and was a great guy, except for drinking, which turned him into a Frankenstein monster and made everyone run and hide.

We both had the same pre-service flying time of eighty hours and competed against each other, sneaking out of the Practice Area at Ryan Field in Tucson to dogfight on the other side of the Sierrita Mountains, almost into Mexico. What made it so much fun, with helmet, goggles and white scarves in the slipstream of our little open cockpit Ryan Primary Trainer PT-22's, was that we were so evenly matched in piloting skill. But one day I did manage to get one up on Paul.

Back when I'd been an aircraft dispatcher at #6 British Flying Training School in Ponca City, Oklahoma, Eddie Myron, one of the instructors, explained the Double-Dilly to me. "A beautiful maneuver," he said. Then he cautioned me to wait until I got into the Air Corps and got a good airplane stressed for aerobatics before I tried it.

Eddie explained, demonstrating with outstretched hand, "You go into a snap-roll with the stick back hard and rudder in. And just as you get inverted, shove the stick all the way forward and kick in the opposite rudder. This will give you an inverted snap and you'll pop right back into level flight where you started. It's a beautiful maneuver...Just don't try it in those Piper Cubs you fly!"

The flight instructors in Primary were civilians. Mr. Matheny (Heavy on the "MISTER") was my instructor. Three years my senior, at 21, he had 500 hours flying time, and I figured he knew all about it.

So after my military acceptance ride, as was customary, Mr. Matheny flew in the rear cockpit as the "Student" and I got to fly up front as "Instructor" for our final flight together. It was to be a friendly competition in aerobatics.

We started with the easy stuff: stalls, spins, Lazy 8's, then progressed to Cuban 8's, snaps and slow rolls; each one of us showing what we could do as a challenge for the other to try and do better, until we reached the limit. That's when my "Student" attempted an outside-spin from the inverted position in a slow-roll.

Well, it didn't work. The plane was too stable and refused to take it. So I gave my "Student" a second chance, while trying to think of how I could top him if he did make it work. What I needed was an impressive beautiful maneuver.

On the second try he pumped the flaps down – which was really up from our inverted position – and the little Ryan tucked her tail between her legs and sucked down into an outside-spin so hard that my feet were jerked off of the rudder peddles by negative "G's" and kicked the gas tank. And as tight as my seatbelt was fastened, I was still thrown outside of the cockpit enough that the slipstream slapped me in the face. We made three turns, Matheny recovered, shook the stick as an invitation for me to take over and to just try to do something more impressive.

I climbed us back up to altitude, made sure the airspace was clear and entered the Double-Dilly. It was easy enough, just a half-snap-roll. But when I kicked opposite rudder and shoved the stick forward, all Hell broke loose because the single low-wing Ryan did not have the same characteristics of the PT-17 Stearman biplane in which Eddy Myron claimed he had performed his "beautiful maneuver."

At the time I didn't understand that in pitching up from upside down, that forward airspeed was killed and we were no longer flying, but were at the mercy of the pitching momentum. And not flying, we naturally fell and tumbled earthward, jerking and banging about the cockpit enough to shake your brains and give a headache.

I was completely disoriented. My vision was so blurred that I couldn't find the horizon to know up from down. I didn't know how to recover. It didn't make any difference, because we weren't flying and the controls were out of control. All I could do was to wait for the crash, because bailing out would be to fall with the plane doing its diddoes. So I held the controls in a spin configuration and prayed we'd fall into a spin, because I knew how to get out of a spin, *if* there was enough altitude left.

Finally I was relieved when we settle down into a normal spin. I kicked opposite rudder and shoved the stick forward to gain some airspeed in a straight dive. Then I eased back on the stick to pull up into level flight and added engine power.

Just when I thought I had the problem solved, the power came off and it got awfully quiet, except for the sound of the wind, the puckity-puckity of the idled engine and – there was a helluva pounding noise! It was new to me and it sounded like the plane was coming apart. Then I heard Mr. Matheny screaming above the sound of the 80 mph wind.

It was Mr. Matheny who had shut down the power and pulled himself out of his cockpit to get as close to me as possible and was beating on the aluminum fuselage with his fist to get my attention!

"*MISTER SMITH!!! WHAT THAT MANEUVER WAS I'LL NEVER KNOW!!! BACK TO THE FIELD!!!*" Those were his last words to me even after we got back to the field and he left the plane to clean himself.

So when Paul started out to his plane to do some solo work, he asked what I'd been up to with my "Student."

"Ohhh," as casual as I could make it, "Some outside spins and a Double-Dilly."

When he asked what a Double-Dilly was I knew I had him. So I explained how it was to be performed and added, "It's a beautiful maneuver."

He landed about an hour later and I watched him get out of his plane and retrieve his parachute with a far-away look. He didn't even see me, nor much of anything else, because he appeared to be in a trance. I spoke to him and he asked me to wait for him to put up his chute, because he had a question.

He wanted me to explain again how a Double Dilly was performed. So I stuck my hand out and demonstrated how it was *supposed* to look as I flip-flopped my hand back and forth, like Eddy Myron had demonstrated to me and added, "It's a beautiful maneuver."

Paul stuck his hand out and tried to move it to match his description of the maneuver, but his hand seemed stuck.

"So I shoved the stick forward…" he said and gave a pensive pause, then, "Kicked the opposite rudder and – "

"And what happened?" I asked, watching him struggle with his mind for some sort of an explanation. It took quite awhile. He flip-flopped his hand a couple of times then used it to scratch his head.

"Well," I insisted, "What happened?"

"I don't really know." He pondered, "I must've hit a goddamned tornado???"

Had I laughed he could have killed me. Of course I almost killed myself from the strain of keeping from laughing. But I never dared tell him that I too had hit a "goddamned tornado."

Gee, Whizz...While I lived in what amounted to a shed next to a cow lot, Paul had a private room in what appeared to me as a "luxury hotel" on a former RAF Air Station. Such were the injustices in wartime.

We were naturally happy to see each other and he introduced me to his new associates, who were also happy to be in Paul's company: kidding him about the time he got drunk, hearing that women had been brought into the quarters and he ("Frankenstein") had broken down four doors in trying to get to the women, and how the women went crazy and screaming, and everybody hanging onto Paul trying to keep him away from the women and how the women would never come back...That was Paul.

"So how's the flying?" I asked, and Paul's fans told him to tell me about shooting down the barrage balloon (?).

"Shooting down a barrage balloon?" It made no sense. Everyone laughed, except Paul, who shook his head and refused to explain what had happened. So everyone else volunteered to tell the story.

Coming back from a mission, just as they neared the English coastline, Paul's tailgunner called in, "Bogey, six o'clock low!"

"What's he doing?" Paul asked.

After time to study it, the tailgunner reported, "He's following us."

"Is he closing in?" Paul asked.

"No – He's just trailing us."

"Well," Paul asked, "What the Hell is it?"

What it was was their trailing antennae, being held out and down behind them by the weight of the lead "Bull's Nut."

After awhile Paul asked, "Can you make an identification on that Bogey?"

"I don't know," the tailgunner replied, "But it looks like a barrage balloon."

"Well, what's it doing now?" Paul asked.

"It just keeps following us," the tailgunner said and asked, "What do you want me to do?"

"Well, shoot the sonovabitch down!" Paul ordered.

We all went into convulsive laughter with the image of the tailgunner trying to shoot off their own trailing antennae, thinking they were being chased by a barrage balloon. But there was even more to it.

Other ships in the formation, seeing Paul's tailgunner blasting away, thought they were under attack, but could not see the phantom barrage balloon. Nobody else on Paul's crew could see it either, so everyone pitched in with a bucket-brigade to pass ammunition back to the tailgunner, the only one with hindsight.

It made me feel good to be with Paul, if only for a day, and I returned to base. It was the last time I would see him. I later heard that Paul finished his combat tour and was on a night practice mission when an engine caught fire in the traffic pattern prior to landing. He'd fought to keep his ship from rolling over and onto its back, but he lost the fight and crashed upside down in a ball of fire. Flying was so "flighty" and capricious – and DANGEROUS.

When I got back to base I found that we'd gotten another three-day pass and the rest of the crew had already left for London. Well, why not. So I went back to London Town. This time, however, I made sure to get me a room first. It was in the KPM, the Kensington Palace Mansion, a hotel for American officers. I also took my dress tunic that I'd burnt a hole in to hopefully have it mended.

No, it couldn't be mended, but the tailor suggested he could cut off the skirt of the tunic and alter it into a jacket, which would be styled similar to a British battle jacket, but dressier of course, yet not quite as formal as a dinner jacket.

Well, he sold me on the idea, if he would also reline it with bright red satin. If it was to look like an original design, which in fact would put me *out of uniform*, I might as well go all the way with a whorehouse lining.

In the afternoon I went to the theater to see WHILE THE SUN SHINES, about an American officer and his relationship with the British. It was a lighthearted and enjoyable production with Hugh McDermot as the American, Lt. Mulvaney. So after the performance I went backstage and met Hugh, who invited me to join him and his wife for an early meal before his evening performance.

His wife was a stunning lady. Since Hugh would be working, he suggested that his wife and I might wish to have an evening together on the town.

Hmmmm? While the idea surprised me and it was a most tempting offer, which I couldn't quite understand, I made the excuse of having made other plans, because her sophistication and maturity over me was intimidating.

I felt like a freak. Combat was making me into an old man on the inside and on the outside I seemed to be treated like a kid.

"Live it up today for tomorrow we die" was just a bunch of bravado, which I was told could get you sympathy and sometimes a *piece of ass*, as they said. But I was really in a quandary: not willing to die, yet not knowing how to live. I didn't want a piece of anything. I wanted the whole thing. But what did that mean? Fall in love, get married and live happily ever after?

No. Under the conditions I was living, there could be no "ever-after." There could be no permanency in my life until I reached the "ever-after," unless I reached the "here-after" first.

Did that mean celibacy? It did if the only choice was the Piccadilly Commandos. Maybe there was something between the extremes.

I met a Lt. Walter Furia back at the KPM. He was a high energy hotshot bombardier asking in the lobby if anybody wanted to join him for a steak dinner.

Now that was something I could relate to, even though I couldn't remember how long it had been since I'd had a steak. With wartime restrictions and rationing, steak was a rarity.

I'd really not eaten much at the early dinner with Hugh McDermot and his wife, so I asked Furia where we were going to get the steaks. He produced a business card someone had given him that gave the address and we went for it.

It was a respectable little restaurant and steak was on the menu. I thought it unusual that the clientele was only American, but then we Americans do have an appetite for steak. So we ordered and while waiting, went to the washroom down the hallway and near the kitchen.

I asked Furia, "What stinks so bad back here?"

"I hate to tell you Smitty, but I think we made a mistake."

"How so?"

"You obviously have never experienced it, 'cause you could never forget it if you had."

"What's that?" I asked.

"Horse meat. That's what they're cooking in the kitchen. We're going to have horse steaks."

"Maybe *you're* going to have a horse steak," I said, "But this cowboy from Oklahoma ain't gonna eat no horse."

I don't know what they did with the steaks we didn't eat, because we left, concluding that with all of the shortages that they wouldn't even be serving *good* horse meat, but probably some nag that had died from old age or disease and had been rerouted from the glue factory. Boy, it sure did *stink*.

So, having lost our appetites, we took a long hike and I introduced Furia to welsh rare-bit, or rabbit without the rabbit, in the same grill where I'd been introduced to it. I couldn't help glancing around to perchance see a dark fur coat, but without success.

Still walking, walking, walking after we ate, we came to a Turkish bath house where Furia suggested we purge ourselves with a steam bath and the luxury of a rub-down. Why not?

On my stop-over in New York City I'd met a couple of other Lieutenants at Leon and Eddy's club and a businessman, saying he wanted to "do something for the boys in the service," gave each of us his card and invited us to use his membership at the New York Athletic Club. I'd presented his card at the Club the next day, they called him and he okayed my use of his privileges: swim, steam and a great rub-down.

Well, the Turkish Bath House in London did not compare well with the New York Athletic Club, but it was still a large leap from the showers back at the base, so we checked in and exchanged our clothes for large Turkish towels and went into the steam room.

There were other guys in the room and after awhile the steam cleared a bit and whom did I recognize?

"MACBETH!" I said. "You're Macbeth and you're Macduff and – I've seen you guys on the stage."

Furia looked at me strangely, because Macbeth's steam room voice was at least an octave higher than his stage voice and he thought it was "sso ssweet" that I had recognized them – and Furia was looking at me, his new acquaintance, with doubt in his eyes.

"Look, goddamit," I told Furia, "It was your idea to come in here, not mine."

"Well, you can stay in here if you want," Furia told me, "But this kid from Los Angeles ain't stayin'."

"Oh, merrrcy." Macbeth said. "It looks like s-s-somebody is going to have a s-s-spat. Now maybe we can watch you perform for us-s-s."

Furia and I left immediately and headed for Piccadilly Circus.

Maybe? Just maybe that's the reason McDermot had offered me his wife, suspecting that I had formed some kind of a homosexual attraction to him, since there seemed to be an inclination for that sort of thing in the theatrical clique. If so, he couldn't have been more off course. And if only I could have found his wife, I would have proved his judgment of me to be in error. If only I could have found his wife I would have enjoyed proving my point to her.

M eanwhile, back at the base, the 385th Bomb Group was targeted for attack by the Luftwaffe while I was still in London. It was before dawn on the 23rd of May, 1944, when the crews were being briefed and the ships were being loaded, that a German sneak raider dropped seven 500 pound bombs onto Great Ashfield.

While most of the bombs landed around the perimeter of the field without too much damage, one bomb hit the old #1 hanger, which had previously been accidentally damaged by our own bombs.

Accidents did happen, especially with the newer "RDX" explosive. The older explosive meant that bombs could be handled roughly, which they were. But the "RDX" bombs could go off without a fuse by low order detonation from a strong bump, like rolling off of an ordinance trailer or being dropped from the bomb-bay accidentally while loading. Yes, those accidents did happen. So those who didn't fly missions were also in harm's way.

MISSION #14
Liege, Belgium, 25 May 1944
Thursday: 24 ships up   (7:00 Flying Time)

I asked the Corporal for my parachute in the Equipment Room. It was #91, a back-pack, which I had managed to get just after I discovered over Stettin that a pilot couldn't pilot very well while wearing a chest-pack.

A plane flew overhead, but I hardly noticed, since we were, after all, on an air base. However, the Corporal dove under the counter at the sound of the plane.

"Hey, where'd you go?" I asked.

Cautiously coming out from under the counter, the Corporal suggested I look at the ceiling. I looked up and saw a huge hole in the ceiling and in the roof that opened to the night sky, as it was about four o'clock in the morning.

"Lieutenant," he said, "If yesterday you had been standing where you're standing right now, you wouldn't be standing where you're standing right now. We got bombed!

I don't know who was flying around up there but, from what I'd heard from those who'd experienced the raid, it wasn't a good idea, since the attack had made everyone jumpy and a defensive gun battery had done more damage to a pursuing P-51 than to the intruder he was pursuing.

When Moon and I got to the revetment we found the plane alright, but we couldn't find the aircrew nor the groundcrew, so we started calling out in the darkness.

"Yeh, Yeh, we're over here!"

Yelling back and forth we followed the sound of their voices as they detailed how they'd all taken cover, since the place had been shot up just yesterday and they thought they were in for it when that plane came buzzing around a little bit ago.

"So you figured this ditch was a good place to hide?" I asked when we found them all in a ditch.

Burnell said, "It's a helluva lot better'n the Chief's tent."

"Yeah," Hill drawled, "That tent sure wouldn't stop much."

"So you figured," I asked, "That this ditch you're in would be a lot safer, because it's right under the fuel truck?"

"Ohhhh SHIT!" Corky said, "We didn't see that truck in the dark."

"And the Chief didn't tell you it was there?"

The Crew Chief was with the rest of them in the ditch and spoke up in his defense, "Well, it wasn't there last night."

After the fiasco of blowing up the brussel sprouts instead of the target at Brussels on the 11th of May, the order was to bring our bombs back if we couldn't put them where they were supposed to go.

So it was, now two weeks later, that the target was obscured by bad weather. And flying around to try and skirt the weather, the mission was made even longer. Even so, we could not drop and we had to take our bombs all the way back to England.

The only thing positive about landing with three tons of high explosives was that the weight of the bombs overcame any tendency of bouncing on landing. When you hit the runway you stuck to it.

On the flip side, however, any number of things could go wrong from a flat tire to a loose bomb. And as far as I was concerned, nothing could be more wrong than blowing up in a B-17.

As we approached the English coastline and got down to 10,000 feet where oxygen was no longer needed, Eutrecht left the nose and went back into the bomb-bay to safety the bombs. He would also check all racks and shackles that held the bombs.

We were carrying twelve 500# H.E.'s (6,000 pounds of high explosive bombs). This was about the same size and weight of twelve filled 60 gallon hotwater heaters.

Each bomb had a fuse in its nose and tail. Each fuse was safetied with a small propeller or "vane," designed to keep the fuse from activating the bomb until the vane was removed. The vane was prevented from moving (coming unscrewed) by a cotter pin. When the pin was removed by the Bombardier, the bomb was considered to be "armed" and dangerous.

However, there was a secondary safety, which was an arming wire that still kept the vane from turning and coming unscrewed. The opposite end of the arming wire for each fuse was fastened securely to the bomb rack, so that the wire would remain fastened to the bomb rack when the bombs were dropped. Thus, the arming wire was pulled out of the vane when the bombs fell, leaving the vane to unscrew itself from the fuse by the force of air pressure turning the little propeller: bomb falls, arming wire remains on bomb rack, allowing the propeller to unscrew the vane. When the vane comes off, any bump to the fuse and – BOOOM!

Eutrecht came back from the bomb-bay and stood between Moon and myself. His complexion was ashen and he looked sick, weak and frightened.

"An *arming vane came unscrewed!*" he said.

"Well," I said, "Go screw it back on."

"SCREW YOU!" he replied. "DROP THESE GODDAMNED BOMBS RIGHT NOW!!!"

Ohhh Shittt! We had a live one! It was HOT! The slightest bump and we were goners. It had to be the reason some ships blew up without a clue.

Easy, Moon, don't hit any propwash.

Moon carefully banked left out of formation. Eut went down to his station in the nose. I made one of those many little, quick and urgent prayers.

"BOMBS AWAY," and they dropped for the sea below.

Free of the bombs, we diddly-pooped around making a half-assed Lazy-Eight to try and see our bombs hit the water, but we couldn't manage it. Unlike in the movies, it was not possible to see your own bombs strike from the cockpit and we were naturally curious. This is not to say that we couldn't see the effects of the bombs dropped by others. But unlike painting, or other work, you could not see what you might have accomplished.

Well, all of this playing around to get rid of our "hot" bomb took us out of formation. So we didn't know till later that when we left the formation, neglecting to break the safety of the VHF transmitter and tell anyone what we were doing, that most in the Group thought we were a Nazi B-17 and everyone had trained their guns on us.

The Germans naturally had a large collection of B-17's that hadn't returned to England. We'd been told that they were assigned to join into our bomb groups to call off altitude, course and speed of the formation to assist the **FLegerAbwehrKanonen** batteries to fire on us more accurately. And with their mission accomplished, they would leave the formation – as we had done – on the approach to England and return to Germany.

So when we pulled out of formation just before the English coast, we were later told, all guns in our Group lined up on us, thinking we were a German "Pirate." And the reason given for everyone holding their fire was that the intruders were supposed to be armed with 20 mm cannons, which would allow them to stay out of range and fire back.

It was just as well that we didn't know what the rest of the Group was thinking, because we were in pretty good spirits, having left the Group, tooling around all alone on what had turned out to be a beautiful day for flying just off the coast of England. The freedom of not flying in formation was refreshing.

Finally it was time to go home.

RADAR (Radio Detection and Ranging), while experimented with by the U.S. Naval Research Labratory as early as 1922, was developed into a fine art by the British who had installed a chain of radar-warning stations on their shores prior to the war in September of 1939. It contributed greatly to the survival of Britain through the Blitz.

You could not fly over England without being tracked by RADAR. If for example you became lost, all you had to do was to fly a triangular course and "DARKY" would contact you and give you directions -- even if you didn't have a transmitter and were unable to contact them.

All of our aircraft were equipped with I.F.F. (Identification Friend or Foe). So if you approached England, all you had to do was to turn on the IFF and you would not be intercepted and shot down.

Wellll – people sometimes forget things, because there is so much to be remembered. Flying within our Group we didn't have to think about IFF, since the Group Leader took care of such details. Besides, Intelligence kept track of which groups were leaving and returning to England.

Carmen called, "Barrage Balloons, three o'clock low. They're coming our way."

Shit, he was hallucinating as badly as Paul Stout's tail-gunner had when he'd tried to shoot off their own trailing antennae, thinking it was a barrage balloon chasing them.

I took a look out to the right at three o'clock low.

While I saw some barrage balloons that were tethered in place on cables and not coming our way, what grabbed my attention was the – FLAK!

Just as we flew over the coast, British Ack-Ack was exploded and its puffs walked their way down the coastline toward us!

I reported what I saw over the intercom and reached for the IFF switch above the instrument panel, where I met Moon's hand doing the same. We flipped on the IFF and both saw, at the same time, an RAF Beaufighter approaching to challenge us.

Not any too soon, he got the message, broke away and the Ack-Ack ceased.

Now wouldn't that have been something to write home about, getting shot down over England after returning from a mission?

Jake McNiece, far right.

Members of the 506th Regimental Demolition Section of the 101st Airborne.

JAKE
CHAPTER 9

Saturday, a day off, and what a nice day it was. I checked with the Motor Pool to see if I could get a Jeep to drive over to Cambridge and visit Bud Bishop for the day instead of hitchhiking a ride in an ambulance.

"Sorry, Lieutenant," the Dispatcher said, "We don't have any drivers available. We're usually short on Saturday."

"Oh, I don't need a driver." I said, "I started driving my uncle's tractor in the plowing season when I was ten. I was driving wheat trucks when I was twelve. I think I can handle a Jeep all by myself."

"Do you have a G.I. Drivers License?"

"Well, no, but I've got a "G.I. Pilot License" and I'm sure I can handle a Jeep okay."

"You'd also have to have an authorization for a vehicle," he said, and proceeded to lecture me about a war going on and the need to conserve fuel, tires and equipment.

I told him that I was well aware of the problem and that I was trying to conserve. He didn't know what I was talking about, so I thanked him and left him satisfied that he'd been able to put a Second Lieutenant in his place.

I found Moon back at the billet and suggested we go for a little flight on such a beautiful day. He agreed, we rounded up the crew, got a B-17 and spent about 500 gallons of 100 Octane fuel, oil and enough rubber on three landings to re-tread a half a dozen Jeeps in what we used in our flight over to Bud's fighter base.

Bud and his buddies welcomed us, because it was almost a week before payday and they were sort of stuck on the base without funds and nothing to do.

"How'd you guys like to go for an airplane ride?" Moon asked, and morale shot up.

"Your only 'ticket' is that you've got to have a parachute," I said. "That's regulation. The only problem is, we don't have any spare chutes on board."

It was no problem for Bud and his buddies. While I had not been allowed to have a Jeep, these guys had one. So we piled on and into their jeep and they dropped us off at our ship. Then they raced around the perimeter "borrowing" parachutes out of the Mustang fighter planes.

Being on a fighter base, they did not have the opportunity to go along on any flights and their excitement got in the way of their not knowing what they were doing. They didn't even know how to put on a parachute.

Bud located himself between Moon, the top turret and myself. Since there was little room, Bud was having a devil of a time banging himself on the turret and all sorts of protrusions in trying to nervously and awkwardly strap himself into a parachute.

"Bud...Bud," I said trying to get his attention and calm him down. "You don't have to put the chute on. Regulations only require that everyone on board must have a parachute. It doesn't mean you're required to wear it at all times."

He stopped his rigorous calisthenics with the seat of the chute up around his neck instead of the other way around and studied Moon and myself seated comfortably in our seats, then asked, "Are you guys gonna wear your parachutes?"

"Well, sure," I said, "We always sit with our chutes on. That way we don't have to put them on before we jump."

"Okay." he said, "If the pilots are going to wear their parachutes, then you can bet that I'm going to wear mine." He then went back to knocking himself out to get his chute on.

All things considered, it really turned out to be a very good day-off for everyone. We had a wonderful low-level flight around the countryside. It served as a needed intermission to the missions after the ACT II curtain and the finality of the upcoming ACT III.

A lot had happened in just the last seven weeks of my life. Would it get better or worse?

MISSION #15
Konigsborn, Germany, 28 May 1944
Sunday: 22 ships up, one down   (8:30 Flying Time)

Konnigsborn was a routine mission with the expectant flak; no fighters (theirs or ours) and we destroyed the railroad marshaling yard with accurate bombing.

As it was the fifteenth mission, I was awarded another Air Medal for meritorious achievement. Actually, it was another Oak Leaf Cluster to the original Air Medal, which gave me a total of an Air Medal with two Oak Leaf Clusters, signifying 15 missions.

MISSION #16
Leipzig / Mockau, Germany, 29 May 1944
Monday: 27 planes up   (8:00 Flying Time)

Leipzig, not far from Berlin, was well defended by antiaircraft guns.

We were assigned a new aircraft, BARBARA "B": Call Sign "ALFREK "C" Charley, Serial # 42-32078. That is, it was a brand new airplane when we left in the morning. However, by the time we got home in the evening it was well "broken" in.

In addition to the customary and assorted flak holes, there were two noteworthy scars. The electrical harness on #3 Engine was broken from a flak burst, but BARBARA "B" performed well on three engines. The explosion of the other burst destroyed the plexiglass nose, giving Eutrecht his second Purple Heart.

Eut appeared to be our "flak-magnet." Again, most of the damage was done by shards of plexiglass going into his eyes. This time, however, the Medics located and removed small pieces of flak with their own medical magnet. The physical damage to him was not great, but it was unknown how much mental damage Eut had suffered. So, "Have another drink and forget it."

MISSION #17
Watten-Stracourt, France, 30 May 1944
Tuesday: 30 ships up   (4:45 Flying Time)

The ground crew worked all night to have BARBARA "B" ready for the "NO BALL" mission the next morning. The meaning of "NO BALL" was never explained to me. And since it's meaning was evidently Classified, and restricted information was on a need-to-know basis, I had to guess at its definition. Therefore, I assumed it referred to the idea that it took "no balls" to fly a short mission across the English Channel.

However, the truth is that airplanes could blow up just sitting on the ground and you didn't have to be shot at to have a crash. So I was probably wrong about the origination of a "NO BALL." Anyhow, it took a lot of male hormones to fly any mission in a combat environment.

Even so, judged not needing-to-know in order to fly over it and blow it up, we did know that "NO BALL" missions had something to do with destroying launch sites for weapons.

According to Lord Haw Haw, broadcasting and boasting with his English accent on the radio from Germany, Britain would soon be experiencing a new "Blitz" from pilotless bombers. It was a new "Vengeance" weapon designated the "V-1"; implying that V-2's and V-3's would be forthcoming in the war of vengeance that had evolved.

The Allies were bombing cities and other civilian targets, so the Germans would retaliate in like manner, although *they* had started it.

MISSION #18
Hamm, Germany, 31 May 1944
Wednesday: 24 ships up   (7:00 Flying Time)

Hamm, Germany is in the industrial Ruhr Valley, "Flak Alley" or "Happy Valley." Any trip to "Happy Valley" is hostile and sardonically not a "happy" experience, because the industrial complex of Germany was heavily defended. The only good thing about all of the bad was that they had so many antiaircraft guns there that even the Luftwaffe seemed to keep clear of it.

This was the fourth mission in a row and a diet that did not agree with me. I felt that the Air Force, the United States and England were all getting their money's worth, since I figured I was being paid about $10.67 a mission before taxes.

However, as the month of May became history, I was still alive and I had only seven missions left to complete my combat tour of 25 missions.

Well, at least I had finally passed the halfway mark to finishing this terrible business.

MISSION #19
Equihen-Wimereux, France, 2 June 1944
Thursday: 29 ships up   (5:00 Flying Time)

Railroad marshaling yards, like Equihen, and launching sites for V-1's were what strategic bombing was about: to cripple the enemy from fighting back. It was being done in preparation for the coming battle: the invasion of Europe. There was no question that it would be the most monumental invasion in history. But, exactly when it was going to take place? That was the SECRET.

THE BEGINNING? THE MIDDLE? OR THE ENDING?

I knew I had made a Beginning by having personally invaded Nazi occupied Europe nineteen times. However, I had not yet reached the ending of my war. By my calculations I was past the Middle with only 24 percent left to the end.

So, grateful for a three-day pass, I did not concern myself with the Big Picture, leaving that to General Eisenhower, and I went back to London Town to get away from the "farm" and to take a break from the war.

While I had a "rare bit" on my mind, the first thing I did when I hit town was to get a room at the KPM and then I struck out for a Welsh rarebit, or "rabbit," which represented a bit of luxury for me.

A Welsh rarebit wasn't that much of a meal, but its association seemed to take me out of the war mood and connect me to a more civilized world.

I'd gotten away from the base rather late without lunch or dinner and it was well into the blackout when I felt I was approaching my target, the S & F Grill, about a block from Piccadilly Circus.

I say "felt," because the blackout eliminated the sense of sight, leaving touch, smell, taste and sound.

"PAIYPA, PAIYPA. . . ." Turn left here.

It was crowded. I could feel the bodies and they felt me as everyone jostled and groped each other. Then I finally felt a non-body.

What in hell was it? It wasn't soft, yet it was moving along in the flow. It kind of rattled like a Coke truck full of bottles – and it felt like a bunch of bottles – in a canvas sack.

A little bit of light came from between the blackout curtains in the doorway of a bistro and I saw that it was a G. I. carrying a duffel bag and – I recognized him.

"JAKE!" It was Jake McNiece from my home town.

"Friend or enemy?" Jake challenged in the dark, having not recognized me.

"Truman Smith, from Ponca City, Oklahoma."

"Well, howdy boy," Jake responded in a little cheerier tone. "I'd like ta say its good to see ya, but I can't see a bloody thing in this blackout."

Having reached the S & F Grill, I steered him inside where we could see each other.

Jake was about four years older than I and had been one of my idols when he played high school football. And senior to me, I was pleased that he even recognized me.

"Well, son, it's good to see ya, even though you're wearin' a Lieutenant's uniform. I don't like Lieutenants…Good thing I didn't see that uniform in the blackout, or I'd-a knocked the hell outa ya just for the fun of it."

He was smiling and I hoped he was kidding, because Jake was known as a fighter and a hell-raiser. That was his character and his charm: friendly, smiling, easy-going, one-hundred and seventy-five pounds of impulsive "dynamite." It was no wonder he was in the 101st Airborne. Although I was a bit puzzled that he was still a Buck Private.

In high school Jake was a little below average size. However, the unusual thing was – at 140 pounds back then – he was not only on the "A" string, but he was Captain of the team. And if that wasn't different enough, he called the plays while playing the center position. He was formidable. In fact, he was a "professional" football player in high school.

Jake was so good at football that it was arranged for him to work for the city fire department so that he could be paid for his football skills, year after year. And Jake gave them their money's worth, because he needed the job to help support his parents and a younger sister after his father had lost their farm in the Depression of the thirties and could not get a job.

Jake was a holy terror; often playing without padding. Sometimes, even in bitter cold he played barefoot. To help make the match even, he chewed tobacco and when necessary he would spit it into his opponent's face – usually a 200 pound tackle. This of course, besides blinding his opponent, made him crazy, which gave Jake the advantage in "Putting some 'ugly' on 'em," as Jake would say.

Jake played by his own rules, which meant, playing to WIN! Even if it meant swallowing the chewing tobacco when questioned by the referee – and then throwing it up the rest of the night.

McNiece played to win...I was glad we were on the same side in the war. Especially since Good Guys don't win wars and Jake could be as tough as they came. He'd left town the night he almost killed a bootlegger who had cheated him.

One of Jake's older brothers, Jack McNiece, had been a flight instructor and was the one who checked me out for my solo flight on my 16th birthday in January 1940. He then sold out to his partner Tommy Smyer and became a flight instructor for fighter pilots in Texas. Afterwards he became a transport pilot and was flying the "Hump" from India and Burma over the mountains into China at the same time that Jake and I visited on the other side of the world.

Jake had some flying experience, but said he preferred jumping out of airplanes instead of landing inside of them. "Probably," he said, "Because I tend to get impatient and I like to be in control of the situation."

We took a booth and ordered food. Jake sat his heavy duffel bag down gingerly next to him, explaining that it was his "loot."

"If that whole bag is full of what I think it is," I said, "I can't believe it, because no one person could come by that much hooch."

"Good guess," Jake said, "But this is only one of four bags full."

Knowing the demand for whiskey exceeded the supply in England, which was overpopulated by a million American GI's, I asked Jake if he had gone into bootlegging.

No. He was on a "Mission of Mercy." The 101st Airborne had sent him for enough "sauce" for a special pre-jump party.

This meant to me that, if the 101st was going to jump, D-Day was imminent.

"So what have you been doing, Jake?"

"Ohh, I been keepin' busy; shootin' the King's deer an' dynamitin' the King's fish...Ya know, ya gotta help out the Army chow, otherwise we'd starve on just Brussel sprouts and tomatoes."

I asked him to explain it to me, because I wasn't understanding.

"Well, we're stationed on royal property, which they say belongs to the 'Crown' and it's run by some Lord or Count and it's got a lotta deer on the place. Then there's this little lake full of fish. So the other day my buddy Hen-gut an' I were hunting an' came by the lake. I tossed a grenade into the pond an' all these fish floated to the top and I told Hen-gut to get in the water an' toss 'em out on the bank. Well, he objected, sayin' it was too cold, so I warmed him up. I unholstered my .45 pistol, charged a round into the chamber an' said, "Hen-gut, get in there an' get them goddamned fish up here onto the bank!"

"Or you'd've shot him?" I asked, regretting I'd asked, because Jake looked at me sternly for even questioning him.

I was pleased when his face mellowed and he smiled with his reply. "I guess I don't have to answer that question, because ol' Hen-gut jumped right into that cold water an' got all the fish we could carry. At least there was no question in his mind what I'd do."

Special paratrooper training had also taught Jake to operate every type of vehicle from tanks to even a locomotive. But why did he have to know how to operate a locomotive?

"Well, I'm in the sabotage business," Jake said. "Besides, it sure came in handy one night back in South Carolina when I'd missed the Liberty Run truck back to camp."

"You mean you stole – 'borrowed' a train locomotive to get back to camp?" I asked.

"Well, I was already AWOL, but I had to get back to ship out or they would've put me in the brig if I had missed the departure of my unit."

Didn't it bother him to be AWOL?

"If it did, I wouldn't be here right now."

"You're AWOL?" I asked, "I thought you said they sent you in to pick up the booze?"

"Well," Jake chuckled, "Yes and no; or no and yes they did."

Jake then explained to me that a week ago he had rigged a booby trap with a trip wire for practice. His specialty was demolition-sabotage and his life depended on the highest level of skill. So he was in bed in the middle of the night when a sentry tripped the explosive charge he'd planted under the corner of a building.

"It wasn't a big charge," he said, "I wasn't out to hurt anyone – and I didn't. But immediately the Lieutenant was standing over me and accusing me of the deed."

Well, Jake had defended himself pretty well, inviting the Lieutenant to bring charges in a Court Martial.

"I believe that I'm the best there is in my business," Jake told the Lieutenant. "At least I'd better be, because I get to jump in before the rest of you follow me in. So if you can prove I did what you claim I did, I'll take the punishment. But if you try me and can't prove it, I want a transfer out of this chicken-shit outfit."

The outcome was that they put him under house arrest to wait for D-Day, because they obviously needed him. So when it came time to get the booze, the unit had collected 2,000 Pounds and the Lieutenant came to Jake for information on how to get the booze, because that was another of Jake's specialties.

"Oh, I couldn't do that Lieutenant," Jake had told him, "But if you'd give me the 2,000 Pounds and cut orders for me to go to London, I'll get the hooch."

"McNiece," the Lieutenant told him, "I can't even get you to the mess hall, let alone giving you 2,000 Pounds to go to London!"

So what they finally worked out, at Jake's suggestion, was to put him on orders to Northern England, where he was to give a lecture on Sabotage Demolitions and he promised, with no questions asked, and given the 2,000 Pounds, that he would return with an adequate supply of 'rations'.

Yes, he *was* actually Absent With-Out Leave as we sat in the S&F Grill in London and he really had to be getting back.

As a Lieutenant, and Jake as a Buck Private, I started to pay our check, but he stopped me and pulled out a roll of pound notes as large as two fists, and *ordered me* to put my money back into my pocket.

"You mean you've got that much money left over from what they gave you for the booze?" I asked.

"Ohh, this is *my* money here." he said.

"Even Generals don't have *that* much money, Jake."

I wasn't about to ask him where he, a Buck Private, had gotten so much money…It was better I didn't know.

"Oh, it's legal," he said, "It's the treasury of a little club I've founded. It's called the "Dirty Dozen." Well, that's the way it started out. It's now called the "Filthy Thirteen." I'm the president and treasurer."

The "Dirty Dozen?" I had to know more.

Jake explained that his little band of blood-brothers, who had accepted his ritual of mixing their blood with each other, had vowed not to bathe and to remain dirty and filthy until D-Day when they – demolition saboteurs – would be jumping ahead of the invasion and behind enemy lines.

While Jake McNiece had a talent for being a permanent Private – perhaps the record-holder in all of history for time-in-grade – his skill in demolition, sabotage and plain old destruction, as well as his natural flair for leadership, and despite his inability to take orders or to follow anyone else; McNiece was, nevertheless, always made *Temporary* Sergeant when it came to JUMP TIME.

So who else could be more qualified to be the President of the *DIRTY DOZEN/FILTHY THIRTEEN* than Jake McNiece? And who else would be a better treasurer and keeper-of-the-money? Nobody, because those who knew Jake McNiece best would trust him with their lives.

Jake made it a point to tell me that, while his troops had some pretty rough edges and were definitely not model garrison soldiers, that they were not hardened criminals and that they, like himself, had committed themselves to each other and to the United States.

I told him that I understood. He smiled, we shook hands and Jake shouldered his booty. I wished him "Good Hunting" and he faded away into the blackout.

MISSION #20
Niorte, France, 7 June 1944
Wednesday: 36 ships up   (9:00 Flying Time)

The English Channel was loaded with Allied ships in support of the Invasion, which had started the day before: D-Day, 6 June 1944. And, as promised by General Eisenhower, thanks to the Eighth Air Force, the only aircraft were Allied, except for two ME 109's that made only one pass over Normandy.

Looking down onto the panorama of the historical event, I wondered how many of my friends from high school were participating. I also thought about Jake, who should be somewhere beyond the beach and hiding behind the enemy line; if he'd been lucky and survived his jump during the night before D-Day.

Then, as usual, we too penetrated enemy airspace, but maintained our margin of safety of three miles above the ongoing spectacle of the Allied invasion of the Continent.

Our target for the day was the railroad marshaling yard at Niorte, France. The strategy was to cut off all enemy supplies from the beachhead. However, we discovered on our arrival that someone else had beaten us to it. Therefore, we flew to the alternate target and found that it, too, had been destroyed.

Thus began the Grande Tour de France in search of a target in need of destruction. So it was that what should have been a relatively short mission turned out to be an all day event.

The target finally selected was a bridge that was far from Normandy. While it was not a bridge too far, it did screw us up pretty well, because it put us back over England after dark, which took us out of our standard operational environment.

This brought to mind some advice given to me by an RAF pilot in a pub one evening.

"I know you chaps don't operate at nighttime," he said, "But if ever you should find yourself caught in the dark with *Jerry* on your tail, here's a bit of advice."

He then went on to explain how all pilots learned to fly by coordination of the flight controls. That in the unlikelihood event that I should find *Jerry* on my tail at night and he was about to "bugger" me, I should enter a turn with *Jerry* following me. But once established in the bank, I must un-coordinate. That is, kick either top or bottom rudder and un-coordinate my bank.

"*Jerry* will naturally be flying a coordinated turn and when you skid or slip out of the norm, he will momentarily lose you from his sight. And at night, once lost, it's not likely he can re-find you. So just remember to *un*-coordinate."

His advice was not lost on me, because I was a sponge when it came to survival techniques; even though he was right, we didn't fly night combat. True, this was a mission and it was nighttime, but it was hardly combat, because we had made it back over England.

Our Group formation had reformed into *Trail*, one ship after the other. We followed our leader back to our base in East Anglia. It had been a very long day. How nice it would be to finally land, have dinner and get some rest.

Moon was listening to the Command Channel while I was on the intercom and doing the flying. We were down at 7,000 feet and no longer on oxygen. I wasn't cold and the drone of the engines almost put me to sleep. Moon too was relaxed and sprawled out as best he could while still in his seat. Then, without any extra effort he spoke casually across the cockpit to me, repeating what he heard from Command.

"Bandits in the area...Steer a heading of two-seven-zero degrees...Turn out all lights and shoot at anything with lights on."

"Look Moon," I said, "We're tired and we're practically back home. Let's just go on in."

"No," he said, "Look down there. They're firing red-red flares at us."

I banked us over, took a look, then banked hard toward a western heading, yelling to "TURN OUT ALL LIGHTS!" because the red-red flares were actually 20 mm tracers coming up at us!! My adrenaline kicked in and I was no longer weary.

It was good that somebody had figured out what to do in case *Intruders* jumped into the middle of 2,000 bombers at night.

First of all, get all traffic going in the same direction to avoid collisions. For that I was grateful, because it seemed to me that most of the aircraft that had been going down had collided into each other.

Then there was the neat idea to have everyone turn out their lights and shoot at anything with lights on, because it was likely that Jerry would be the only ones with lights on.

"Bogey, six o'clock level," Hill called. "He's got his lights on and he's closing in...What do I do?"

"Shoot the sonovabitch down!" I said over the intercom, as I immediately started a left turn and said aloud – not over the intercom – "DOUBLE DILLY, HERE WE COME!!!"

Of course Moon, not on the intercom to know that a Bandit was closing in on our tail, nor having any idea of the meaning of Double Dilly, must have thought that I'd gone "crackers" when I went into my act: left aileron, wheel back, left rudder. Just before we dropped off on the left wing into a spin or snap roll (who knew in a B-17?), I pushed forward with all of my strength, gave it right aileron and kicked in the right rudder.

HOLY SHIT!

Talk about *un*-coordinated? Old BARBARA "B" protested with a shudder as she started to break to the left out of the bottom of the turn and then she shook and groaned when I forced her into negative "G"s in the opposite direction out of the top of the turn.

Exactly what this maneuver might have looked like I had no idea, but I was sure it gave Moon and the rest of the crew some wonderment. It amazed and frightened me, and I thought I knew what I was trying to do.

The gyro of the artificial horizon tumbled and went crazy. I don't really know what happened, but it had to have been a first for a B-17. So I can't say that it was a "beautiful maneuver," only that it was definitely *un*-coordinated.

All I knew was that it took me 6,000 feet of altitude before I could get everything unwrapped from around the axle and wrestle BARBARA "B" back to straight and level flight, because we were down to a bit less than 1,000 feet above ground level (and even less if we happened to be over hills). The main thing on my mind was wondering if the Bandit was still on our tail, so I asked Hill over the intercom and his reply was immediate.

"JESUS CHRIST ALMIGHTY!!"

It sort of sounded like Hill, but he was usually not so expressive. So I asked again, "Herby, is that guy still back there?"

"JESUS CHRIST ALMIGHTY!!"

"YEH, YEH," Carmen came on, "I'm still back here, but I think I broke my fuckin' nose!"

"The BANDIT?" I asked. "Hill, is that Bandit still behind us?"

"HELL NO!" he replied, "There ain't NOBODY back here, but ME – and I'm not even sure of that!"

Moon was so intent on monitoring the radio that it didn't seem to bother him – not as much as it bothered me – and he said, "We can go back in now. They say the base is clear."

I called Moody for a QDM, heading for home, but he didn't have one. "I'VE LOST ALL OF MY FUCKING PENCILS!" he complained.

I called our radio operator to see if he could get us a QDM. He said that everything on the radio was all jammed up, because it seemed that everyone was lost and everybody was short of fuel, but that he would try.

I missed Rudy. He'd been taken off of flying status and had been replaced by a young twenty-year-old kid whom I didn't have much confidence in. But to my surprise, he quickly gave me a QDM, which allowed us to be among the first to land.

How had he gotten us a QDM when the airwaves were so crowded?

"I Just screwed my key down and blocked everybody off of the air," he said, "After a bit I unscrewed my key, they were all off, since they couldn't get through, and I got us a QDM."

There was much excitement on the base, because from the ground looking up they could see the silhouettes of JU-88's in the formation of B-24's that had passed overhead on the way to their base north of us. The JU-88's had their running lights on just like the B-24's. The report was that when the B-24's had turned on their landing lights, the German Junker 88's blew up three of them on final approach before anyone knew what was going on.

Before I'd gotten to the Eighth Air Force I'd read that this was an old trick the RAF had used on the Germans early in the war. And when I read it, I thought it had been a clever idea.

Reading and listening to the experiences of others seemed to be a good idea and I was grateful to the RAF pilot who had shared his knowledge with me about un-coordination.

"You're more dangerous than the enemy!" Carmen complained, "You damned near broke my nose! So watch it, will ya?"

"Yea, yea." I kidded him.

"Yea, yea, my ass," he said, finding no humor in it.

"Do you want me to cite you for insubordination to an officer?" I asked.

"Yea, yea, yea, yea, yea, yea, yea," he mumbled away.

There was never any anger between the members of our crew, because everyone respected what we were all going through. We were *all* in it together and cooperation was essential to our survival. We would each do what we had to do to endure our tour.

This had been my twentieth mission, for which I was awarded a third Oak Leaf Cluster to my Air Medal and a second Battle Star to the European Theater of Operations medal. The first Battle Star was for the Air War over Europe and the second was for the Invasion of Europe. This was average for our crew, except for Eutrecht and Dyer who had lost time in the hospital and for Rudy, who had been transferred out of the Group.

So with twenty missions accomplished there was at least a bit of hope for completing only five more. ONLY FIVE MORE? Yet it could all end on just one mission.

I could tell from Moon's low spirit when he entered the billet that something was not right.

"They've increased the tour to thirty missions," he said. "Don't wait up for me. I'm going to the Club...Wanta go and have a drink?"

"No," I said, "I think I'm gonna have a cigarette and a puke."

I wished I could have cried, but found that I had no emotions for it. With the sentence of thirty missions, I felt as if I were somehow dead. There was to be no future.

Then, unable to understand why, a feeling of relief came over me. It was strange. It had to be that the certainty of death freed me from the worry of losing my life. I wouldn't have to worry so hard anymore. What the Hell, I might as well relax a bit; take a shower and read a book. Well??? Make that a short story.

Ears and Eut didn't even make it back to the billet. I figured they'd first stopped at the club. However, most of the other crews straggled in: Turner's, McDonald's and Borns'.

The name of the game we played was BITCH AND MOAN AT THE BRASS; who had figured that the war would be going easier now after the invasion and, therefore, it was they who had increased our missions.

Flying their desks, they were willing to bet our lives that a mission to Germany would be easier now, because the Allies were on the beaches in France. Their speculation had to be that, even if we won the war, it wouldn't be over for a year or more and that they had better stretch the air combat tour out to 30 missions in order to have enough fliers.

Well, that might be okay in theory, but with 20 missions to my credit, I didn't personally know anyone who had more than that. Therefore, my chances of completing 30 missions was ZIP – a big fat ZERO.

I jumped up onto my footlocker to be a part of the growing clamor of discontent, raised my arm in a "Heil Hitler" pose to gain attention, pulled my elbow down with my palm still extended and said with my best imitation of a German accent, "Chust in case vee lose."

The majority thought it was funny and took turns giving each other the Nazi salute with, "Chust in case vee lose."

For whatever reason, probably a guilty conscience for upping the missions, the Brass gave us off a few days to go to London – just in time to be there for the arrival of the first "BUZZ BOMBS"!

V-1 rockets, or "buzz bombs," were filled with a measured amount of jet fuel to fly to a predetermined target. When the fuel was exhausted, it fell straight down and exploded on impact.

BUZZ BOMBS
CHAPTER 10

The "Blitzkrieg" (Lightning War) on London was from September 1940 through May 1941 and the ruins from 190,000 tons of bombs were still quite prevalent in 1944. The "Baby Blitz" was between January and the middle of March 1944, and some Londoners continued sleeping on the platforms of the subway stations down in the "Tubes" where they still maintained their dignity and, somehow through necessity and strong character, were able to preserve their privacy in the midst of public activity.

Then came a third "Blitz" at 3:00 a.m. on the 13th of June 1944 when the first V-1 "VENGEANCE WEAPON" (*Die Vergeltungswaffen*) hit London and started the "Buzz-Bomb Blitz," as Lord Haw Haw had forecast.

British Prime Minister Winston Churchill, in a radio broadcast a few days after D-Day, warned of the serious times ahead with the hardest battles yet to be fought, because he was well informed about the German's development of a pilotless robot flying bomb and the many launching sites that had been established in northern France, all aimed at London.

These were the "NO BALL" targets that both the Royal Air Force and the Eighth Air Force had been hammering on intermittently for many months. The fact that the Allied invasion, delayed in breaking out from the beaches and not capturing the launching sites of the V-1's as hoped for, was a guarantee that London would once again catch Hell.

In fact, the Germans could have destroyed the Allied invasion force with the V-1 "Flying Bombs," if the 6 June invasion had not gone when it did. That, of course, would have made a major change in history. Thus, due to the arbitrary nature of warfare, victory for the Allies was far from certain – and all that that implies.

Even before Hitler had come to power in the 1930's, Germany had started the development of rocket weaponry in an effort to get around the limitations placed on it by the Versailles Treaty of World War One.

So after more than ten years in the making, and motivated by the desperation created by the stalemate on the Eastern Front by the Russians and the invasion of France in the west, the Flying Bombs were still committed to the defense of the Third Reich.

The V-1 Flying Bomb was in effect a pilotless airplane guided by aiming its launching rails in the direction of the target and controlling its flight with gyros. It was 25 feet long with a wingspan of $17^1/2$ feet and carried one ton of high explosives. Driven by a ram-jet engine using 80 octane gasoline it cruised about 300 mph. The bombs were manufactured at the Volkswagen plant in Fallersleben near Hamburg: 1,000 in April; 1,500 in May and 2,500 in June of 1944.

I t was the last day of a three-day pass in London that I stopped in to pick up my customized "Smitty Jacket" from the tailor, who mentioned that he was also making one for a general who liked the idea of it.

Hmmm? This was probably just a sales pitch to keep me from refusing delivery of the odd-ball garment, because he knew I was concerned about being out of uniform, since a one-of-a-kind could hardly be considered "uniform."

While we discussed my acceptance of, and payment for, the short-waist tunic, the air-raid sirens began to wail, which stopped everything. I followed the tailor out of the shop and into the street and did what he did in looking up to the sky between the buildings that lined the street. If he knew what he was looking for, I didn't.

Maybe I'd learn something. I'd heard air raid warnings before, but nothing bad had ever happened to me by doing nothing.

If in a movie theater, a notice would appear on the screen that an Air Raid Alert had been given, in case you wished to go to a shelter. I never went to a shelter. Rather, I just did nothing, except to watch the movie. This had worked for me.

So I did nothing except to observe nothing happening in the sky, except scattered low clouds, when I followed the tailor into the street. We were joined by many people coming out of the buildings to do the same as the tailor and I.

"It'll be a 'Doodlebug," the tailor said. "It'll be coming from that way." He pointed to the top of the building above his shop.

"Buzz Bomb?" I asked, just to make sure I knew what I was looking for, since the new secret weapon already was being referred to by various names.

The tailor acknowledged that it was the V-1 he was talking about. So I fixed my attention on the location from where he said it would make its appearance, because I was very curious to see one of the damn things fly by.

The sirens continued to wail and then an electric alarm bell started ringing, which was joined by – I presumed – local air-raid wardens tooting whistles, which must have meant that they could see one of the flying bombs from their positions atop the roofs. And sure enough, I began to hear the god-awful-est noise increasing above all other sounds as the "monster" approached.

It was a deep throbbing growl like nothing I'd ever heard before: B-R-G-A-A-A-A-A-A-W-W-W-W-W-W!

It was fast approaching and it sounded very mean and dangerous! It's rumbling, like an approaching tornado, reached an almost unbearable crescendo. And then it was quiet?

Quiet!!!

By contrast to the racket it had made, there was an absolute absence of any kind of sound. I turned to the tailor.

He was gone!

What had been a street full of people was, to my greatest surprise, EMPTY, except for ME!!!

I ran my hardest for the tailor shop and, bursting through the door, I heard, "OVER HERE!!!"

It was the tailor under a table and I hit the wooden floor in a running hook-slide, as if stealing second base, and joined him.

We waited, staring at each other and listening.

K-R-A-K-K-H-H-A-A-A-B-B-O-O-O-O-O-O-M-M-M-M-M!!!

Even though the damn thing hit and exploded a block away and the buildings absorbed most of the shock, it was, nevertheless, one Hell of a blast!

I promptly paid the tailor, took my jacket and returned to base in order to get out of harm's way.

MISSION #21
Florennes, France, 14 June 1944
Wednesday: 38 ships up   (6:15 Flying Time)

The Buzz Bomb launching sites, such as Florennes, and the supply lines in France and Belgium, were well defended by the same guns and flak used in Germany. And even though it was June and the coming of summer, it was still 40 degrees below zero up at 27,000 feet and the air was just as thin as it had been before.

Therefore, nature was allied with the Germans and could even strike over England after returning from a mission.

DAMN!!! Oh, GOD!!! I was blinded with pain from what felt like an icepick jammed right between my eyeballs! Water shot from my eyes. And even though we were in the middle of a thirty-plane formation, I let loose of the controls and grabbed at the pain in my head.

Moon was immediately on the controls and, detecting the problem at once, pulled back and up out of formation for higher altitude and thinner air to equalize the pressure in my sinuses.

We had completed the "average" mission without any great mishaps; normal flak over the target and a long four hour ride through enemy territory. We'd gotten back to the English coast and were letting down – rather rapidly – to keep the formation out of the clouds and in the clear when, without warning, a simple thing like my sinus cavities became blocked, which prevented the equalization of the greater airpressure at a lower altitude.

The normal airpressure at sea level is 14.7 pounds per square inch. I don't know how many square inches there are in my sinus cavities, and there couldn't have been 15 pounds of differential, but I know that a bullet fired into my brain could not have hurt any more.

Besides that, I was having pains in my knees, especially my right knee. And as young as I was, I physically felt like I must be over a hundred years old. I was definitely not well.

The Flight Surgeon checked me after debriefing and diagnosed the problems as aerosinitis and aeroembolism, which sometimes crop up from high altitude flying.

"It might never happen again," the Doc said, "Don't worry about it."

Sure, easy for him to say. He'd never been hit between the eyes with an icepick and blinded while holding ten people in his hands in the midst of another 300 troops and a large amount of flying hardware.

And as far as nitrogen bubbles boiling in my blood, which had caused the pain in my knees, the Doc did not consider it lethal and that it was a normal occurrence among deep sea divers and sometimes high flying airmen.

"Maybe some aspirin?" I asked.

"It doesn't hurt now does it?" he questioned.

"No."

"Well, see. Nothing to worry about."

"Thanks, Doc."

The Doctor was Captain William C. Huff, who was above my social level, but still known and discussed by us "fly-boys." His reputation had been one of congeniality and sympathy.

However, he had volunteered for duty with the ground troops on D-Day and it was rumored that the experience had changed him, because he had considered that to be a "real war" and fly-boys who complained to him about head colds and minor discomforts were somehow less worthy of compassion than "real" soldiers.

After all, we had clean sheets to sleep between at night. And even though we couldn't sleep – not knowing were we'd be the next night – we fly-boys "had it made" and were spoiled by the good life.

MISSION #22
Hannover, Germany, 15 June 1944
Thursday: 29 ships up   (8:30 Flying Time)

What happened before the mission was more impressive than the mission.

The fire started at 03:44 hours. Being very dark at that time in the morning called attention to any kind of light. So the silhouette of a cockpit with the glare of red/orange flames dancing from inside the plane grabbed my attention.

We were seated in BARBARA "B" at our revetment near the beginning of the northwest runway awaiting the order and the signal-flares to "START ENGINES" when I noticed the fire from my side of the cockpit only about the length of a football field away from us and I pointed it out to Moon.

Other ships in other squadrons had already started engines and some were taxiing into position for takeoff and they, too, obviously saw the fire.

It was the proper assumption that the fire was burning inside of a mission aircraft. This meant it would be loaded with ten 500 pound H.E., High Explosive bombs, and 2,700 gallons of gasoline.

Therefore, safety was in direct proportion to the distance away from the fire. And since B-17's taxi rather slowly and there were so many of them, there was a traffic jam on the taxi strip in front of the burning ship, which just happened to be parked in closely to the AMMUNITION AREA!

So, unable to get past the jammed traffic and wanting to distance themselves from what was about to be one gigantic explosion, crews started bailing out of their ships and onto the ground and running like hell in the blackout.

With engines running and brakes not set, it was a miracle that there were no collisions and that bodies were not shredded by whirling propeller blades.

The explosion came within about one minute after I first noticed it. And – my seat belt not yet fastened – the concussion of the blast almost knocked me out of my seat.

Entire engines were catapulted across the field from the bomber, the hardstand was cratered, the armament and bomb-fuse buildings were totally destroyed, gasoline flames and the blast damaged two other B-17's, yet nobody was killed!

At the time we didn't know if there were any casualties or the extent of the damage. All we knew was what we heard on the radio: "Alfreck "C" Charley (That was us), this is Hardlife. You are Number One for Takeoff."

A green-green flare arched up into the night sky and we took off on the northwest runway that was in front of us and we were on our way to Hannover, Germany.

While the flak was heavy and accurate over the target, it was not quite as impressive as the nighttime fireworks at the beginning of the mission when the bomber blew up. The excitement of the exploding B-17, plus bad weather made it a long day. And since our work had been unsatisfactory, we were rescheduled to go back to Hannover three days later and do the job properly.

MISSION #23
Hannover, Germany, 18 June 1944
Sunday: 35 ships up   (6:45 Flying Time)

The mission was predictable with heavy accurate flak, but otherwise uneventful, except for a personal problem.

It was not my sinuses, nor the diver's bends in my knees,which the Doc had told me not to worry about. It was my own stupidity.

Ralph Cooley had told me back when I first started to fly that, "If you get in a hurry around airplanes and don't pay attention to what you're doing, you can expect to get into trouble."

For sheer comfort I enjoyed wearing my cowboy boots on my own time, which of course was strictly out of uniform. But in the shared privacy of our billet, everybody was out of uniform.

I wasn't fully awake when I dressed for the mission, my cowboy boots were handy and I was in a hurry; which made me *stupid*.

By the time I drew my parachute from the equipment room and started to put on my flying garb after the briefing, I discovered that my sheeplined flying boots would not accommodate the higher heels of my cowboy boots. They wouldn't work so I tossed my flying boots back into my locker and went forth on the mission to Hannover, Germany in my cowboy boots. It was an act that I would regret.

One of the Escapees had lectured us on the importance of details in evading capture, should we be shot down and survive.

For instance, assuming you're on the run and have disguised yourself with clothing you've stolen from a closeline and are brave enough to go public by eating in a German cafe, be sure and eat European style with the fork in the left hand and the knife in the right hand.

That part of the lecture we had all taken seriously and even practiced eating European style in the mess hall so as to make it a habit and to not be awkward about it.

As to passing yourself off as a German in a restaurant, he related how he, a pilot, was fortunate that he had become fluent in German, as he grew up in a German family in a German community.

So, having avoided capture after being shot down, he and his copilot managed to steal some native clothing, and having money from their escape kits, and being hungry, he suggested they go into a village for dinner.

"Not me!" said the copilot, "You speak the language and even look like a damn Kraut, but not me!"

Well, the pilot convinced the copilot that they could pull it off if the copilot acted like he was the deaf and dumb brother of the pilot. That way the pilot would do all of the talking and take care of him and they could satisfy their hunger.

However, they almost blew their cover when the copilot, so frightened of being discovered, over-acted by exaggerating his role as a *super*-idiot; slobbering food out of his mouth and getting potato up his nose. It was not done to be comical, but out of the utter terror of being detected as a downed American airman.

This of course was the funniest thing the pilot had ever seen his copilot do and he could not contain himself. So the more he laughed, the more it scared the copilot into believing that they would be discovered. And the more frightened the copilot became the more he over-acted and the funnier it got to be for the pilot.

The only end to it was to pay their bill and get the copilot out of the restaurant even though they were both still hungry.

However, that was not the end of their misadventures.

Instead of carrying his Government Issue Colt .45, the copilot carried his grandfather's old single action "thumb-buster" Colt .45 Peacemaker that his grandfather had brought with him to Texas.

After leaving the restaurant the two pilots were walking down the street of the village. It was nighttime and they were going to try and find a place to sleep, when around the corner came two SS officers.

About to pass the SS, the pilot gave a salutation in German. When the SS returned the greeting, the copilot pulled out his grandfather's Colt .45 and pointed it at the two SS officers!

It was so unexpected that all four of them stood still in shock, wondering what happened and what was going to happen…It was all up to the "idiot" with the gun.

There was no way the copilot could take prisoners. What could he do with them? If he did nothing and ran, they would shoot him. So he did the only thing that came to him. He pulled the trigger on the old Colt .45.

In the frozen silence, the hammer on the .45 made a loud "SNAP!"but the gun didn't fire!

He clicked it again, but it didn't fire!

The two SS officers cut and ran for their lives, as did the pilot, leaving the copilot standing on the sidewalk snapping and clicking the old Colt .45 that wouldn't fire.

Finally the copilot dropped the pistol and caught up with the pilot who was running in the opposite direction from the SS officers.

Eventually, they actually made it all the way back to England, with the help of the Underground. Exactly what took place with the Underground was not disclosed, since the underground operations had to be protected.

"One other thing," the pilot had told us, "Don't ever wear rubber heeled shoes, if you don't want to be discovered as an American. They're a dead giveaway, because only Americans wear rubber heeled shoes."

He then told us how some airmen had been doing well in their escape until, in a railway station, someone had spotted their rubber heels and they were captured.

This information was not wasted on Carmen, who even managed to get a pair of leather-heeled shoes that he'd dyed black, inserted a hacksaw blade into the sole and carried them tied to his parachute.

So it was on my mind, as we flew toward Hannover, Germany, that if I got shot down and anybody saw me trying to buy a ticket in a train station, calling a taxi, or doing anything else while wearing my cowboy boots, they would immediately know that I was not one of the local boys.

How could I have been so stupid?

Yep, and if this wasn't enough for me to worry about, this was the day that the heater malfunctioned and it was as cold inside our ship as it was outside.

Thin skin-tight cowboy boots are no protection at forty degrees below zero, so for at least four hours without any place to warm my feet, I tried sitting on my feet – one at a time, of course, because I needed at least one foot at a time on a rudder pedal to fly formation.

Just like he'd asked Ears on the Stettin mission, Moon, observing me trying to keep my feet warm by trying to sit on them and fly at the same time, and knowing the answer, asked me, "You cold?"

It was a mistake I would not repeat.

MISSION #24
Konigsborn, Germany, 20 June 1944
Tuesday: 38 ships up, one down   (8:00 Flying Time)
Target: V-1 (Volkswagen) factory

I was disappointed that this was not the next to the last of my missions, as was promised in the beginning. Yet I would not have traded places with the "Groundpounders" in the Infantry who were fighting for the peninsula and port of Cherbourg.

Their war was just starting, while mine was more than half finished; unless, of course, they changed the rules again or – ? Oh, well, we were all expendable, weren't we.

Well, they *did* change the rules!

After twenty-four missions over enemy occupied Europe, the required 25 missions had been extended to 35.

Eutrecht was used up. He had two Purple Hearts from flak tearing holes through his "greenhouse" in the nose and into him: no armor plating to protect him, just plexiglass and thin aluminum.

Some bombardiers would collect extra flak vests to put under and over themselves like a turtle in a shell. Some, I was told, would even tie a string to the toggle switch so they could toggle the bombs away without leaving their shelter, which might well have saved a number of bombardiers. However, it was not Eutrecht's style.

At least you think you've got some protection in the cockpit behind a bullet proof (?) windshield. But sitting in the clear plastic bubble of the nose, where there is virtually no protection, the bombardier is ALONE IN SPACE, because there is not even a reference to the airplane, which is behind him.

There are other planes around him, but he alone is in a space-bubble sliding between the dancing puffs of flak in a state of rapture.

At least that was Eut, who sat unflinching on his perch, his mind off in some other dimension, when it came time to release our bombs.

I happened to be flying the Bomb Run and I knew that something was WRONG when all of the ships in our Group jumped up fifty feet or so on "BOMBS AWAY!" except for us!

There are three cues for release of bombs: "BOMBS AWAY," over the radio; Signal Flares fired upward and Smoke trailing from the falling bombs.

Ears said that Eut did not react to anything. Not even the bursting flak about him. He just sat bravely upright in the midst of everything; not flinching or attempting to take cover, just sitting there with his hand on the toggle switch.

The fact that all of the other ships jumping up and making a steep turn to the right to head for the R.P. (Rally Point), and out of the flak, while we continued to plow our way through the flak alone and still loaded with three tons of bombs, was of no concern to Eut. He was "Out to lunch."

Ears went forward, touched Eut on the back. Our bombs dropped and we played catch-up to the Group.

Eutrecht's subconscious had shut him down. I knew from my own feelings that everyone of us on our crew, who had been exposed to this same terrible virus, were all fighting our own demons and it was only time before it would take each of us, because there had to be a limit to the amount of abuse that can be taken.

Our Group Air Executive Officer had been heard to comment that it would be of great help if there was, in addition to physical doctors, a *mind doctor* who could detect, diagnose and treat any mental disorders, because such afflictions were manifesting themselves in our Group.

One excellent pilot, while he could fly, could not manage to button his clothes. Bedwetting, not an accidental release while sleeping, but standing up in bed and urinating onto the pillow had also been reported. Such were a few symptoms of combat fatigue that were apparent.

The only conspicuous abnormal behavior in our barracks was by Lt. McDonald's bombardier, Lt. Henry, who built a wooden frame around the head of his bed and covered it with a blanket to isolate himself from the rest of us, because he considered the rest of us abnormal and evidently didn't want to catch whatever it was that we had.

What we had was only a desire to have a little fun like inflating condoms, heating the air inside of them over our stove, so, like hot air balloons, they would float over the neighboring village; or dropping colored flares down the chimneys of other billets; or putting lighter fluid in condoms and igniting them to simulate flak – without the iron.

We also had playthings and props that added to our amusement. Things that had been brought back from leave or pass. There was a a Bobby's helmet and a pair of lady's under-knickers. There were no questions nor answers as to how they had been acquired.

The knickers had been made crotchless, which gave cause for discussion and presumptions. The fact that the Bobby's helmet had been knocked about a bit also created a mystery that remained unanswered.

The important thing was that both items served well as costumes and excuses for extemporaneous acts of *dumb show* and playing the fool(s).

Could such behavior be considered abnormal, or was Henry abnormal in his quest for solitude in his "tent?"

Eventually, someone was bound to make a study of men or boys under the stresses of aerial combat in order to better deal with it in future wars. However, I had already come up with my own conclusion that anyone who had volunteered to fight a war in a flying machine had to be nuts to begin with. Therefore, it could not be surprising if they went a bit "bonkers" when the shooting started.

The point was that everyone had to be overloaded with woes. And who knew when, like Eutrecht, any one of us would slip or be pushed over that unknown boundary of sanity?

What was WRONG in the wrongness of aerial warfare, which itself was WRONG and abnormal? Well, things were starting to go right in the sense of behavior. Which is to say, abnormal behavior – dropping bombs on other humans – can lead to abnormal personal behavior. For when you do this, it should be no surprise that your subconscious, knowing right from wrong, would shut down the system.

There is also the opinion that it is not right for people to try to kill you for trying to kill them for their effort to kill you in the first place. Therefore, fight or flee comes into play when the shooting starts.

And when it comes to a *hot stove*, which you can't fight, the only choice is to flee; if not outwardly, then inwardly, as manifested in Eut's behavior.

Mark Twain had said that a cat that sits on a hot stove will not only never sit on a hot stove again; he will not sit on *any* stove again, hot or cold. However, the military does not offer the options, nor the nine lives, of a cat. So we're stuck.

MISSION #25
Berlin, Germany, 21 June 1944
Wednesday: 37 ships up, two down   (9:30 Flying Time)

What a stinking rotten lousy day it was – instrument flying for three of the nine-and-a-half hours to get to the target and back. Hours of aching boredom; crunching ice to keep it from forming in my *suck-sack* and the damn thing paralyzing the muscles of my face; cold feet; electric heated suit giving me the sweats around the chest and chills in the thighs; the monotonous drone of engines – interrupted by moments of total terror – vertigo and disorientation; prop wash; near collisions; fighters and flak.

GOD DAMN IT ALL!!! It made a fellow want to quit.

However, it did give me time to think along the way and I thought about the court martial that was going on back at the base.

The Group had held a dance. Local girls and American nurses had been trucked in for the party. I'd missed it, because I'd been in London.

Some young copilot like myself had agreed to take an older nurse for a walk. They'd ended up in the haystack on the farm behind our billet.

Witnesses at the court martial, every one of them biased for the copilot, accused the nurse of getting the "youngster" turned on and not being able to get him turned off. So he boffed her.

Spectators at the court martial expressed their opinion that the nurse had not objected to playing *Hide the Wiennie*, and had most likely even enjoyed it. However, her main objection and cause for bringing the charges was that when he had finished, he'd pulled his trench coat from under her and just left her alone and that she was frightened, inebriated, lost and had trouble finding her way back to the Officers Club.

Well, why hadn't I thought of that?

Wouldn't I rather be the copilot back at the base at the court martial instead of flying this stinking mission? They might even send him to serve time in prison at Fort Leavenworth in Kansas, not far from Oklahoma.

At least he wouldn't get a death sentence by flying missions. The suspense in flying missions was certainly cruel and unusual punishment.

But, NO! As bad as it was, flying combat would have to count for something, even if I might not understand what that might be until sometime in the future.

But how much future was there for me? There was *always* that question which was eating me up.

There was one thing for sure. Combat had to be the *ULTIMATE TEST FOR COURAGE.*

Certainly there would be better pilots than I would ever be. But would they ever have enough courage to perform their skill under the stress of combat?

Well, there was only one way to find out and that was in combat.

Such strength had to count for something in the living of one's life, no matter how little time might be allotted. One thing for sure, this would be an unforgettable benchmark against which I should be able to measure any other living experience.

Hopefully it would remind me that sometimes – when you think you can't possibly continue – you just have to keep reaching down into the depths of your soul until you can get a hold of something called *COURAGE.*

The main mystery seemed to be, just how much time would each of us be allocated before life ended?

BANDITS! THREE O'CLOCK HIGH!!!

Damned interruptions!

At least they had waited until Burnell had taken a shit.

About an hour before the fighters attacked us some amoebae had attacked Burnell's intestines. He'd asked me what he could do about it.

Hell, I didn't have an answer, so I asked Moon.

"Use your brain-bucket," Moon said.

"Brain?" Burnell responded in agony, "Use my brain(?)-bucket? I don't understand."

"Shit in your FLAK HELMET," I clarified.

So that's what Burnell did, frostbiting his butt a bit in the process.

When finished he'd stored his "bucket" with its contents in a corner; taking care to prop it up with some flares to prevent it from turning over and spilling. He needn't have bothered, because it naturally froze solid almost immediately.

What a humiliating experience it was to have Nature call in the midst of a combat mission at 27,000 feet.

It doesn't matter what rank or station in life, it is humbling to be reminded that we human beings are ALL, each of us, tied to the earth by our ass-holes.

Poor Burnell. He had to take off his flak vest; parachute harness; Mae West; flight suit; electric flying suit and long underwear just to prepare for the task – of what? Trying to balance a steel helmet upside down and catch his droppings. And when finished, the subzero temperature hastened him to reverse the entire process, while making sure to not dislodge his oxygen mask.

Fortunately there was no problem with the odor of it, since we were all breathing oxygen.

So as bad as it was for Burnell, it worsened for him when the fighters started their attack.

Instinctively, Burnell retrieved his helmet to protect his head.

However, when his head temperature went up from the excitement of battle, his frozen waste thawed out and dribbled down out of his helmet and soiled him badly.

So what had started out as a stinking rotten day did not change.

The unusual had become the usual. We got back from the mission and, as usual, *BARBARA "B"* had battle damage.

This time, however, we decided to count the holes we'd picked up during the day.

When we reached a count of two-hundred we stopped.

A quarter-inch bolt under the left wing had backed itself out of its hole about two inches. I was able to reach it, gave it a quarter turn and it came out and into my hand.

Back at the tail there was a hole large enough to pass a football through it on the left side of the ship. I examined it and saw through it that there was another hole in the other side, just across Hill's seat at the tail guns.

So I called him over and asked, "Herby, where were you today?"

Surprised at my question he answered, "I was in the tail. I'm the tailgunner, remember?" Patting the tail he reminded me of his motto, "This is tail. Come and get it."

"Look through those two holes." I told him and he did.

"Now if you were sitting on your seat and a blast big enough to make those two holes came across your seat, and you were there, you wouldn't be here now."

"It wasn't a single blast," he pointed out. "There were two blasts, one on each side."

That was possible, but unlikely that he'd not been hit by either one of them.

Then I remembered when at one point he'd called on the intercom, "I think I've been hit in the back, but I'm afraid to look!" I'd sent Carmen back to check on him and Carmen had reported back that Hill was okay.

But that didn't figure, because the holes in both sides of the tail were from flak and he'd called during a fighter attack when there was no flak, and he thought he'd been hit in the *back*. It was a mystery.

Hill was too honest for me to be skeptical, yet the pieces didn't fit. For how could he, in the tail, have been hit in his back during a head-on attack? The slugs would have had to come in through the nose and travel all the way through the plane to have hit him in the back. Even so, the back of his flak vest showed that he had been hit by something.

Finally, I found the answer and called Herby over to show him the holes from machine gun slugs in the fuselage. It was a deflection shot that had not gone directly through the ship, but had entered the fuselage just above the right horizontal stabilizer where it was attached to the fuselage. Three rounds had creased and cut their way through the metal and lined up perfectly on Hill's back. It was fortunate that he'd been wearing his flak-vest.

Since the guess was that we would be flying again tomorrow, for three days in a row, we hurried through debriefing, a meal and back to the billet for some welcome rest, only to discover that Captain Stern, our Squadron Executive Officer, had given us an extra-duty assignment.

On each of our beds was a large stack of mail. Sergeant Gatt informed us that it was our turn to censor the Squadron's mail.

Shit! It was just what we needed after a long hard day in the "office" of a B-17.

Since it was our lives that were on line, we should know better than anyone else what was sensitive information that should not be written about in letters home, but we didn't really. However, we got our razor blades and went to work cutting out whatever we thought might be classified information.

"Look what I did," Eutrecht exclaimed, holding up what looked like a white paper frame of what had been a letter. At the top was the greeting, "Dear Betty." At the bottom was "Love Sam." Eut had cut out everything in between as being "too sensitive."

Soon, despite our negative attitude, we were involved in intimate family details, no longer thinking about our own woes. How terrible it had to be for those who were separated from their wives, children and parents and attempting to communicate to their loved ones with pencil and paper.

I was grateful that I didn't have a close relationship with anyone, except my parents and my 15 year old younger brother, who disliked flying, claiming that even birds frightened him.

I did have friends, who were all in the service and scattered around the world with whom I occasionally scratched a note to. Like Jay Lee "Hog" Forney who was at West Point.

Jay Lee and I had gone to Citizens Military Training Camp at Fort Sill in the summer of 1939 when he was sixteen and I, at fifteen, had fibbed about being sixteen. Jay Lee trained in the Infantry and I was trained in Field Artillery in the Citizens Military Training Camp: CMTC.

When Jay Lee had gotten his appointment to West Point and wrote that he was going to take pilot training.I sent him my "Good Luck" silk scarf, guaranteed to make him a "Hot Pilot." He'd written back that I would surely need it more than he, but I insisted he keep it.

Well, so much for "Good Luck."

Jay Lee was killed on a training flight when flying instruments under the hood and another AT-6 Trainer had spun down from above and crashed into him; proving that you don't have to be in combat to be killed.

If there was some Master's Plan for survival, it was beyond my comprehension, because Jay Lee Forney was a better person than I was, or would ever be. Yet, he was no more.

Why didn't God let the *good ones* live?

I couldn't understand it.

Where Tons of Bombs Rain on Hitlerland

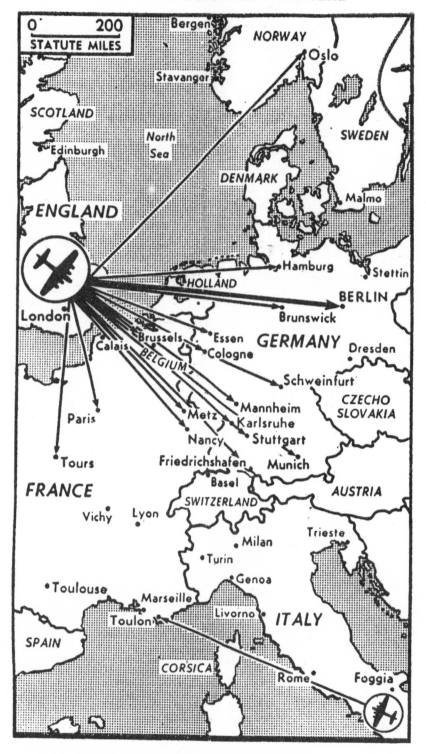

From the **Ponca City News**, Ponca City, Oklahoma
Tuesday, May 2, 1944

UP AND DOWN
CHAPTER 11

P ractice! Practice! Practice! When not flying actual combat we
flew practice missions, because good formation flying was our
best protection against enemy attack. So with a steady loss of
crews, it was necessary for the replacement crews to become
proficient in flying good formation. Stateside training took care of
the basics, but the basics would not take care of all the skills needed
in combat.

Within the first eight weeks, I'd seen as many ships go down from
collisions as having been shot down. So it was that you could never
get too much practice.

In addition to improving piloting skills, everyone drilled in their
respective specialties: pilots in the Link Trainer; radio operators
practicing code and everyone polishing their shooting skills. This had
paid off in allowing us to survive and well enough for the gunners of
our crew to have confirmed seven "kills" against the Luftwaffe. So,
having shot down more than five enemy aircraft, we had what
amounted to an Ace Crew.

While it was not official policy, Moon had insisted that everyone
on the crew be qualified in landing our ship in case we, the pilots, were
knocked out of the game. And of course, the main objective of our
enemy was to shoot down the American bombers by killing the pilots.

It wasn't necessary that our non-pilot crewmembers know how to
take off and do a lot of the aviating stuff, so our "Private Flying School"
focused on steering and landing. And so as not to take a chance of
busting up a B-17 on a hard asphalt runway, we used a layer of clouds
as an imaginary runway. But while a cloud would not damage the plane,
neither would it support a B-17.

So the training consisted of each one of the non-pilots on the
crew being able to steer the plane; line up for a landing on the mock

(cloud) runway; slow the ship down without stalling out; get the wheels and flaps down and make a landing-stall on the cloud. At which point we fell through the cloud.

WHHEEEeeeee!!!

It was against my desires to stall out, except when the actual runway was there to catch us. Otherwise, my millions of years of evolution fell away and my "monkey-tail," which I no longer had, tried to grab a tree limb to save me. Thus, I got a tingle up my butt from where my tail was no longer attached.

WHHEEEeeee!!!

Even strapped into my own familiar seat, I didn't like stalling and falling. But then, I wasn't in my own seat, having given it up so that our non-pilots could practice.

Therefore, while Moon instructed the crew, I roamed about the ship to become familiar with everyone's gun position. And from time to time when one of our non-pilots stalled out to land on the non-runway and we fell through the clouds, I grabbed whatever I could for the freefall.

The worst place for me during the stalls was in the tailgunner's position. So it was in the tail that I got sick as hell and tried racing through the ship for security in the cockpit when I ran into Hill in the radio room. He was headed for his position in the tail. Because, like me, he was also sick from the unfamiliar motions to him in my position.

The lesson learned seemed to be that everyone was content with their own position and not envious of anyone else, except for me. I felt I had enough copilot time and I had a desire to move from the right seat to the left seat and become the Aircraft Commander.

It's not that I was envious of Moon. He was a damn good pilot and I bore him no resentment. It was just that I wanted to be the Commander. Nor did Moon resent my ambitions. For, as my mentor, he made sure that I got plenty of firsthand experience at the controls.

Of course I had not gone through transition school and been taught everything I should know about a B-17 like Moon had been.

"No," Moon corrected me. "I learned just like you; flying copilot back in the States. I didn't go through transition training either."

That really surprised me, because it meant that *neither one of us had been officially trained in flying the B-17*. It was a case of "Monkey-see-monkey-do" and "The blind leading the blind." There was no way of knowing how many bad habits Moon had picked up from flying with – only God knew who. It was more like a social disease where I had picked up every mistake that Moon had learned and that we were both most likely flying the Fortress the *wrong* way.

Well, what difference did it make?

All I could do was to go on ahead with what I'd learned from Moon. This included kissing the props and pissing on the tent peg. After all, it had worked for us so far. Right?

I'd completed 25 missions; been awarded the Air Medal five times; shared in earning the Presidential Unit Citation for the Bomb Group at Zwickau; received three Battle Stars for battles before, during and after the invasion of enemy occupied Europe and I even got to tour such memorable places as Berlin yesterday and – Paris today.

MISSION #26
Paris, France, 22 June 1944
Thursday: 26 ships up   (6:25 Flying Time)

Ears got up from his chair at his navigation table in the nose and leaned forward to look through one of the windows in the nose section and down onto Paris, just before he was shot.

The shortest distance between two points is supposed to be near a straight line, but the highest priority of the bombing business turned out to be not flying the shortest distance.

It was WRONG to assume that the purpose of the Eighth Air Force Bomber Command was to bomb the targets. No, the objective of the U.S. military was to destroy the enemy and the Eighth's participation was to prevent Germany from defending itself by demolishing its shield.

In other words, the highest priority was to destroy Germany's protection, which was the Luftwaffe. For it was the Luftwaffe that had made possible Germany's success in annexing Europe. So how was the greatest air force in history to be destroyed?

The strategy was that of American football, different than soccer or any other sport. It was the "MOUSETRAP." Bait the trap and SNAP!!! And the bait? It would be the bombers.

It had not started out that way and many participants never knew that it had evolved into what amounted to suicide missions:

(1) FLY AMERICAN BOMBERS INTO ENEMY OCCUPIED EUROPE TO BAIT THE GERMANS;

(2) WHEN THE LUFTWAFFE RESPONDED TO SHOOT THE BOMBERS, AMERICAN FIGHTERS WOULD SHOOT DOWN THE LUFTWAFFE.

Well, that was the PLAN.

However, even the best plans don't always work. The fallacy of the design was, after the bombers attracted the German fighters, there weren't enough American fighters to destroy them. This then resulted in the Eighth Air Force having the greatest casualties of all American military forces in World War Two. It also resulted in the Eighth Bomber Command destroying more German aircraft than the Fighter Command.

Thus, we did not fly directly to Paris, drop the load and try to return for home. No, no, no. We flew south, past the west side of Paris toward southern France; then turned east, flying past the south side of Paris toward Germany; then turned north and flew up along the east side of Paris to the I.P. , the Initial Point. Then we were to turn to a west heading for the Bomb Run – all of which was a grand invitation for the Luftwaffe to come and get us.

Heading north toward the I.P.,a British Spitfire came up along our right flank and out of range of our guns, flipping up on his side to show his silhouette to make sure that we didn't misidentify him as a bandit and shoot him down.

In the contest for survival it is natural to be concerned about one's SELF and to think that you are the only show in town. In fact, however, there is a great war taking place and you are really only a very small part of many individual battles.

This thought was brought to me as we flew on the northerly course just east of Paris and a British Spitfire slowly pulled into our formation.

He must have assumed that we were heading back to England and he sought refuge in our midst, suffering the bad effects of some other battle in which he'd been. It was a reversal of roles, since it was the fighters who were supposed to protect us, the bombers, but this poor guy really needed help. Unfortunately, it was more than we could provide.

As he came up closer alongside I could see that his leather helmet was covered with blood and he had difficulty holding up his head. He was also slowly losing altitude. So much blood from a head wound suggested that he must be mortally wounded.

What a disappointment it must have been for him then when we turned away from him on a westerly heading at the I.P. and entered the flak to begin our bomb run.

So alone, he continued to the north bobbing his head and losing altitude.

My guess was that he would not make it.

"I've got a P-51 closing in at six o'clock," Hill called over the intercom. "What do I do?"

The basic rule of survival is that *nobody* can be allowed to point their weapons at you. Fighters should know this better than anyone. That's why they would sidle up alongside cautiously out of range and flip over on their side to profile themselves before moving in like the Spit had done. But not this guy.

"Shoot him down!" I said.

The Mustang must have really been screwed up to begin with, because fighters always avoid flying in flak. Not even enemy fighters followed us into the flak over the target, because there was simply no future in it. But this guy came busting in to follow us in over the target, pointing his guns at us – until Hill opened up on him to warn him to break away.

There must have been a real battle going on someplace for us to have picked up two friendly fighters wanting desperately to join the Bomber Command.

The flak over Paris was no less than that over Berlin. And once we turned on the I.P. we were locked into a tight formation without any evasive action, because the Lead Bombardier needed a steady platform to synchronize his Norden bombsight onto the target. And the bombsight – lacking any human instinct for survival – controlled the autopilot along a *straight* track regardless of circumstances.

Today, for whatever insane reason, our bombing altitude was only 22,000 feet; a mile lower and closer to the ground than our normal 27,000 feet.

Thus, we caught hell from the relentless flak in holding a tight formation to concentrate the bombs onto the target in an effort to keep them from falling on the non-military civilians.

But what was "non-military" anyway?

The target was the Standard Oil Company on the bank of the Seine river within the city of Paris, and the French were our Allies. Or were they?

The flak coming up from Paris was certainly not friendly. The captured American and British airmen who had been marched down the Champs E'lyse'es and were beaten by civilians was certainly not a display of friendship. The Frenchmen who voluntarily joined and served in the Nazi SS, and the Informers who turned in their own countrymen to the Nazis, were not sympathetic to the Allied effort to defeat the Third Reich.

No. The demarcation between Friend or Enemy in warfare is not clearly defined. Even your own fighter escorts could not be trusted. And, as far as the French?

The Vichy government had pledged total collaboration with the Third Reich to obtain favored status with the Hitler's ambition for a New European Order. However, there was no "Order." Certainly not in France, which was really a mixed bag: Communists, Christians, Jews, Resistance, Nazis. etc. . They couldn't even get their own act together. Such were the French.

Even so, our job remained to try and defeat the Third Reich, which France and the rest of Europe had failed to do. This, of course, included destroying targets, even inside of Paris.

I had met a Lt. Bill Shannon when we first got to England. He was a navigator who had told me that his ambition was to be awarded every medal possible.

I looked down on the ship in which Shannon was flying and I was certain that he had finally gotten his wish to receive the Purple Heart when I saw that the nose of his plane, in which he worked, was opened with a multitude of flak holes. There was no way he could have escaped the damage.

Ears never wore his parachute because it was impractical, getting in his way when working at his navigation table. But for some unknown reason, however, he had snapped his chute onto his chest when he got up to look out and down onto Paris.

BOOOOM!

The blast came through the thin aluminum skin of the ship, hit him in his chest-pack-parachute and knocked him backward and across the nose compartment onto the floor!

The thing about it was that when he got slammed by the flak burst he reacted in typical Ear's fashion and he just lay on the floor studying the problem until Eut discovered him. But then, that had not been right away, because Eut was playing his own role as the stoic bombardier-statue in the plexiglass nose awaiting –

"BOMBS AWAY!!!"

Eut then called over the intercom: "Ears got hit!"

"How bad?" I asked.

It took a few moments before he replied. "He seems to be okay. Most of the blast caught him in his chute."

As general information to the crew, I said, "Get him the spare chute."

It was an unnecessary order, because the crew was already on the move.

That was the beauty of our crew. Rank-wise it was micromanaged from the bottom up instead from the top down. It was a credit to Moon that he had given full authority to the crew to do whatever was necessary to get any job done.

Carmen and Burnell had decided that it was to our advantage to have an emergency bag on board. Left to their own means they filled it with a spare parachute, a couple of blankets to protect against shock and some of our own first aid packets, since the first aid kits on board had usually been robbed of their morphine syrettes by some addict.

So hearing on the intercom that Ears had been hit, the crew went into its own first-aid-drill: Carmen grabbed the bag in the waist and passed it to the radio operator; who carried it into the bomb-bay where he met Burnell coming aft from his top turret. Burnell then took the bag forward to the nose to help Eut tend to the needs of Ears.

However, this was not as simple as it sounds. In fact, it was a pretty exciting performance of two guys doing a "high-wire" act four miles above Paris on a narrow catwalk through the bomb-bay. They had to work at poking an overstuffed parachute bag through the narrow space between the bomb racks while making sure to keep from exposing any bare skin to the hazard of freezing, as well as managing their critical source of oxygen from their individual and awkward walk-around bottles.

"BOOM, PUFF, PRUMPHF!"

We danced through the flak over the target. And for some ungodly reason, we made a sweeping reverse turn back over the target after Bombs Away, instead of breaking away to an R. P. that would allow us to rally at a point out of harm's way. But not today. After dropping our bombs onto the Standard Oil Company refinery our route away from the target was in reverse to our approach!

This meant a hundred and eighty degree turn after the drop – turning inside of the flak area – and retracing our way from west to east back over Paris for plenty of *deja vu*; which should have meant: *Jesus Christ! Once is enough!*

Who knew the why of such folly?

Maybe it was some idiot's idea for a show of force to intimidate the Germans into thinking that the U.S. Air Force was taking Paris. If so, it was a bit premature, because the gunners on the ground were the ones doing the intimidating with a second chance to hit us with their damned flak.

Forget the flak. What about Ears?

Burnell had returned to his top turret, but Eut must have his hands full in trying to help Ears, because he hadn't reported back. Something was definitely wrong. So I called for a report from Eut.

The stress in Eut's voice expressed more than his words.

"He stole my goddamned candy bar!"

"What?"

"Ears stole my goddamned candy bar!" Eut complained.

"It's mine!" Ears said, "I found it on the floor."

"It's *mine*!" Eut said. "He found it where I hid it."

"Are you talking about a candy bar?" I asked.

"Yeah." Eut said. "MY candy bar!"

"No." Ears said. "It's MY candy bar, cause I found it."

"Fuck the candy bar!" I said. "Did you get wounded?"

"All he's got," Eut explained, "is a little tiny hole in his leg and – *MY CANDY BAR!*"

"Listen you guys – both of you." I said sternly, "Forget the goddamned candy bar. Just *DROP IT*! Get to your guns and watch for Bandits. They're starting to fire Red flak. That could be a signal that they're about to stop shooting and an invitation for the Bandits to come in an get us. So just DROP IT!!!"

Ears dropped the candy bar on his navigation table. Eut started to make a grab for it. Ears grabbed Eut to restrain him – and it was a good thing. For as they struggled, a burst of flak stole the candy bar from the both of them.

When we got back to base, Ears refused to go to hospital for the wound in his thigh. He was afraid the Medics would ground him. If he was grounded, he would lose out on flying with our crew and "OUR CREW" was the only security that any of us had.

Considering how badly things could have gone, I felt great that we'd made it as well as we had. It was that basic euphoria of surviving a roller-coaster ride. So we all shared Ears' happiness about the flak burst mainly hitting his chute instead of his chest and marveling over the fact that it had been the first and only time he had put his chute on.

Shannon, however, was less fortunate. Flak had driven aluminum from the plane into his left eye. If they removed the metal, he would lose the fluid from his eyeball and, therefore, he would lose his eye. The decision was to get him to a specialist in London. It was the last time I saw Shannon.

What made it so bad was the fact that he had volunteered, "Which you never do," he'd said. Except, it was Bill's nature to volunteer. That's why he'd completed 29 missions in only 78 days. He was an "Eager Beaver." I'd not known anyone who had done so many missions in such a short time. I thought I was moving through my tour pretty fast, but he was three missions ahead of me.

Since the number of missions were being prorated up from 25, his quota had been set at 29, which he had completed. He was "Home Free" without further obligations. However, Paris, the "Sex Capitol of the World" was a personal attraction – even though he would be no closer than four miles above it, unless he got shot down. So when he was "invited" to go, because there was a shortage of navigators, Shannon eagerly chose to make one mission extra.

Well, that was the story of Bill Shannon, who knew beforehand that you "Never volunteer."

In the billet we gathered around, popped open Ears' chute and dug the shrapnel from it.

Ears was lucky as hell. The wound to his leg seemed insignificant compared to what it had done to the *silk*. The thought of what it could have done to him was sobering. His life had actually been saved by a fluke; putting his chute on, which he never wore…Why had he put it on this one time?

Jagged pieces of steel, like assorted hooks, had torn into and snagged the nylon, knotting it into clumps of metal and cloth. The heat of the exploded round was evident in its having melted the nylon. It was proof that flak was certainly damaging stuff.

Even so, it was history and everyone was jubilant. I offered my switchblade knife to Ears and he did the honors of *carving* up the parachute to give everyone a piece of it for a souvenir as a memento to what-might-have-been.

But while it was now history, it could also be a prediction. It was just another reminder of that damned *sword* hanging over everyone's head. The feeling is best described as the agony of untreatable *Emotional Constipation*.

Oh well, look at the bright side. I'd gotten mail from home. At least part of it was from home.

My mother, whom my dad called his "Chin-up Girl," and my little brother were doing their best to keep the family Boys' and Men's store going despite the difficulty of getting merchandise. Besides, most of the men customers were in the military and not buying clothes.

However, dad subsidized the business by sending home most of his Captain's pay.

Private Herman J. Smith had not gotten overseas in World War One. So when World War Two came he had joined the Army Air Force before I had. Again he was not sent overseas. He was made a Post Exchange Officer and stationed at Sedalia, Missouri, just fifteen miles from where he'd been born.

Mother sent me a *Reader's Digest* that had an article: "It's Grim Hardship All The Way In The Big Bombers." She had flagged it and wrote: "Be sure and read this," as if I were unacquainted with the subject.

I'd been so busy and worried about survival that I had not allowed myself the luxury of dreaming about the "Good Life" back home. Besides, homesickness was a pain that I didn't need and that I'd tried to ignore. However, it seemed to be catching up to me, reminding me of how vulnerable I really was.

There was no question about it. I was definitely HOMESICK and I was going into depression, so I changed the subject.

"Hey guys!" I announced, "I got a package from home!"

The package was from my grandparents Smith and that meant cookies for sure. Delicious oatmeal cookies from Grandma Smith.

Grandma Schneider, who had come from Germany about 60 years ago and was staying at home with mother and brother John, always sent her popular German sugar-cookies – whenever she could save up enough sugar ration coupons.

The invitation to share my gift brought almost everyone to my bunk while I opened the package. The entire contents seemed to be covered with powdered sugar.

No...It wasn't powdered sugar...It was FOOT POWDER! What?

Packed with the oatmeal cookies were thoughtful little gifts like a toothbrush, fountain pen, writing tablet and a can of FOOTPOWDER?! Why would they send me a can of footpowder?

Why, for that matter, would they send me a toothbrush? I could get those things easier than they could. But they didn't know that. They were doing their best to send what was difficult for them to get and thought it would cheer me up.

It was unfortunate, therefore, that the lid had come off of the footpowder and dusted everything in the package including the cookies...Wonderful homemade oatmeal cookies – dusted with footpowder!

What a rotten disappointment. I would still write and thank them for their thoughtfulness; keeping the accident a secret.

Even so, the cookies all disappeared from the box and everyone walked around with footpowder-cookies trying to figure out a way to salvage something edible. It was an unintentional cruel joke and all spirits took a nose dive.

I picked up my toilet kit and a towel and left through the far door of the billet to hike across the farmyard to the ablution area for a shower. However, I didn't get very far.

It was just turning twilight and my intentions left me as I crawled through the fence and had to steady myself on a fencepost.

Leaning on the post, I had no desire to go any farther. Alone, I just wanted to think things out.

Had Jake McNiece survived his jump into enemy territory as a demolition saboteur?

That had been a couple of weeks ago. The odds were against him making it. But if he had somehow survived and was lying in the weeds or woods to avoid capture, it wasn't likely that he had the luxury of a bath – nor much of anything else. He was maybe envious of me and my shower and clean sheets and was probably thinking that I was running around London with a blonde on each arm.

What the hell? I was twenty years old. I would have trouble with just one girl…Jake would know what to do…If ever I got to be as old as Jake, maybe twenty-three or four, then I'd know what to do, but I had enough problems without getting emotionally involved with a girlfriend. No, to know me would not be doing anybody a favor.

Twenty-year-olds, whose total life experience is focused on Self, should not get emotionally involved with anyone; especially others who were also young and selfish…No, this was not a time for love – while at the same time there was a deep craving to be loved.

So what was wrong with a little romance along the way?

Well, there were three-hundred-thousand members of the Eighth Air Force in England. Maybe a million American G.I.s on a little island so overloaded it would have sunk if it didn't have the barrage balloons to hold it up. There was hardly a girl for every guy despite their apparent spirit of cooperation.

However, it was discovered by one G.I. in the Motor Pool, after he'd gotten married to a girl in London, that she was already married to two other G.I.s and was collecting an allotment from each of her three husbands.

The words from some wedding came to me: "Love is giving and not taking."

So don't get any ideas about falling in love with anybody, because I was not prepared to give my life to someone. Right now I was giving my life, bit by bit, to my country. The good old U.S. of A. Why?

My country was my extended family...My country would protect my family...I would protect my family by protecting my country.

That's what all of us were doing, weren't we?

I guess that's what patriotism is. If so, then I was patriotic – along with millions of others...And if we got real lucky, we might even be able to keep our country a bit longer. If not for us, at least for the survivors, who would forget the sacrifices as we had forgotten those before us.

There was so much uncertainty. The only thing I knew for sure was that it had gotten dark and I was still with the fencepost.

Why was that? Was the post a pulpit from which to preach to myself, or was it the foot of a cross at which I was praying for help?

Evidently it was neither. It was just a goddamned fencepost and something to hang onto for support and I was grabbing for whatever I could get. This might be my last opportunity to get to know myself. Wasn't that okay?

God knows I was frustrated and I had a lot of questions. But mainly, how in hell had I ended up like this anyway?

Why was I born?

My parents had no business having me...What stupid kids they had been...Well, it had sure put me in a helluva position. If only I had been aborted it would certainly have saved me a lot of grief. But then, who knew it was going to turn out this way?

Now, if only Hitler had been aborted.

"That SONOVABITCH!" I called aloud.

"Who's the sonovabitch callin' me a sonovabitch?"

I could tell by the slur in his speech that it was some drunk who was wandering around the compound, probably on his way back from the Club and maybe looking for someone to pick a fight with. I'd better hold it down.

Although, maybe getting physical would make me feel a bit better? I was about ready to kick the shit out of somebody! Anybody would do.

No. I'd been in too many fights to know differently. There was no point in adding physical pain to my mental anguish. Better I save any fight in me for Hitler.

Besides, whoever the somebody was, he was drunk. I would have the advantage. There was no honor in that. Anyone who pressed their advantage would plague themself with unkown demons and would, themself, be disadvantaged. Anyone who abuses a child, a spouse – a drunk, or someone over which they have an advantage will ultimately be made to suffer the consequences. Thus, the real challenge is in overcoming one's own disadvantages.

S ince we were not scheduled for a mission, Moon went with Ears to the Infirmary where his wound was examined and bandaged professionally and Moon persuaded them to release Ears for duty. Ears was also given a Purple Heart for injuries from enemy action.

Injuries from enemy action?

You got a medal for physical injuries, but what about mental injuries? Surely there were unseen wounds in our heads.

Just how beat up inside were we all? It was something that nobody talked about. Sure, I could talk to myself about it, but what about the other guys on the crew. Were they also talking to themselves and wondering, not so much *IF*, but, *WHEN* their minds might just give out during this unknown experiment of so-called strategic daylight bombing?

Well, It could be a problem. I'd better watch for any clues, because I had a strong feeling that the time was near for something to start coming unraveled. Yep, something was going to happen. As sure as God made little green apples, something was going to happen.

MISSION # 27
Wessermunde, Germany, 24 June 1944
Saturday: 16 ships up   (7:15 Flying Time)

Moon was either tired or confident with my piloting, or both, because he was willing for me to do most of the flying.

So far the duties had been shared about equally, but I figured he was grooming me to eventually check out as a First Pilot and I began to have a greater appreciation of his burdens as Aircraft Commander (AC). It was a great deal more than just knowing how to fly the airplane.

At twenty-four years of age, like most pilots in command, Moon was responsible for ten crew members, which included himself.

It was much more burdensome than my job. While I was an apprentice, I had the luxury of being an observer, free of the obligations of command. However, I began to understand that, even riding side by side through the same experiences, the Aircraft Commander has a different perspective.

It was more like Moon was on the inside looking out, while I was on the outside looking in. He was concerned with the *moment* of things happening and everything was in the *NOW*. Now we fly. Now we eat. Now we drink. Now we make merry. I doubt he could have recalled what happened yesterday or the night before.

Maybe that was his talent for dealing with the stresses, because he didn't appear to be carrying any problems around with him. He was well tempered, unflappable and equally dedicated to duty and pleasure – depending on the Now he was in.

"You take it now," Moon said as we turned onto the runway for takeoff.

Takeoffs for missions, fully loaded with fuel and bombs with a gross weight of over 60,000 pounds, usually belonged to Moon with me backing him up on the throttles and extra musclepower when the old *battlewagon* would sometimes want to go astray.

Since Moon weighed only about 145 pounds, the machine had him outweighed by more than 400 to 1 and there was no hydraulic or electric boost on the controls to help equalize the score. That's what a copilot was for, besides being a *Wheel-and-Flap-Man*, he was there for musclepower.

This time Moon backed me up. And while I had experienced many takeoffs, each time was always a physical as well as an emotional *uplifting* occasion.

Moon and I traded shifts along the way and as we turned onto the I.P. to start the bomb run, again, he said, "Now you take it." Then he seemed to relax into the role of spectator, allowing me to become more familiar with the feeling of responsibility.

As badly as I had always wanted to be First Pilot, I felt a flicker of doubt and my ambition slacked. After all, nobody had demanded that I be the Pilot in Command...Who needed the burden of such responsibility?

BOOM – BOOMITY – BOOM!!!

Wessermunde gave it to us and we gave it to Wessermunde. It was all in a day's work and no casualties.

Only eight more missions to go.

We'd flown six missions in April; twelve in May and nine so far in June. It would soon be July and, for better or worse, it should shortly all be over for us.

So as far as counting our eggs before they hatched; just how were things shaping up so far?

Excerpts from the Associated Press
& the *London Sunday Chronicle*

• 24 April 1944 •
*"TWO-WAY ATTACK TAKES SKY FIGHT
INTO ITS 10TH DAY"*
In a two-way blow, an American sky force approaching 2,000 heavy
bombers and fighters from Britain and about1,000 more from Italy
attacked targets in Germany, Rumania, France, Yugoslavia and
Belgium. This was the greatest aerial offensive of all times.

• 29 April 1944 •
"77 U. S. WARPLANES LOST"
*"2,000 U. S. Warplanes Blast Heart of Reich
at a Loss of 77 Craft"*
Two-thousand U. S. warplanes smashing through box-like stacks of
hundreds of German fighters in the greatest daylight battle of the
war cast a 2,500-ton torrent of exploding steel and incendiaries on
invasion-skittery Berlin today at a cost of 63 bombers and 14
fighters.

• 30 April 1944 •
"1,000 DAY BOMBERS STUN BERLIN"
"Heart of City Blazing in Worst-Ever Raids" Say Nazis"
One-thousand day bombers stunned Berlin yesterday in what the
Nazis say was one of the worst raids of the war.

• 2 May 1944 •
"AIR FLEETS POUNDING INVASION BEACHES"
"Pre-Invasion Air Activity Against Reich in 18th Day"
The U. S. strategic air force based in Britain hurled more than
43,500 tons of bombs on Germany and German-occupied Europe
during April. This was a new daylight record. American losses were
537 American bombers and 191 fighters.

• 8 May 1944 •
"FORTRESS FLEET HITS BERLIN SECOND TIME; BRUNSWICK POUNDED"
"Today's pre-invasion offensive is into its 24 consecutive day"
After the big fellows carried out what the German communique
called "terror attacks" on Berlin and Bucharest, approximately 200
Ninth Air Force Marauders (B-26's) struck at military objectives in
France.

• 20 May 1944 •
"6,000 PLANES HAMMER ATLANTIC WALL"
"Greatest Mass Raid of Air War Thrown Over Invasion Strip"
150-mile path from Brittany to Belgium blasted by at least 8,000
tons of bombs in the greatest mass air attack of the war against
Hitler's west wall defenses.

• 29 May 1944 •
"ALL OF GERMANY BLASTED IN FIERCE, DAY-LONG RAID"
"Fleet of 8,000 Allied Planes Taken Part In Crushing Blow"
The predominately American fleets of warplanes scourged the face
of Europe, bombed the invasion coasts of France and Belgium,
strafed the front lines in Italy and reached deep inside of Germany,
Poland and Austria to tear up hideaway plants of the German
aircraft industry.

• 31 May 1944 •
Stockholm Sweden
"NAZI LYNCHING OF FLYER RELATED BY WAR WRITER"
"Eyewitness Account Of American's Death Told in Stockholm"
A German broadcast denied a story published by Aftonbladet from
its Berlin correspondent that five American airmen had been
lynched by agitated Germans and stated that no lynchings could be
confirmed.

• 2 June 1944 •
"AMERICAN RAIDS DIRECTLY SUPPORT RUSSIAN ARMIES"
"Five Railway Yards in Axis Transylvania, Hungary Pounded"
Allied fliers struck over 2,000 miles of airways from Scandinavia to France and from Crete in the Mediterranean to Hungary. Fliers of the U.S. strategic air force in Europe during May loosened more than 63,000 tons of bombs on targets in Nazi-held Europe and destroyed 1,268 enemy aircraft in the air. Striking points from the shell-pocked invasion coast to the Balkans almost daily, the planes from Britain and Italy amassed 49,811 sorties with 30,106 bombers and 19,705 fighters.

• 6 June 1944 •
"AVENGERS LAND!!"
"INVASION FORCES STRIKE HITLER'S FORTRESS EUROPE"

• 7 June 1944 •
"ALLIED PLANES FLY 13,000 MISSIONS ON INVASION DAY"

• 15 June1944 •
"HEAVY FORCE OF U. S. BOMBERS, FIGHTERS SWEEPS OVER EUROPE"

• 21 June 1944 •
"SHUTTLE RAIDERS HAMMER BERLIN, HEAD EASTWARD"
"German Radio Indicated Some Planes Flew On Eastward – Possibly In The First Shuttle Raid From Britain To New American Bases In Russia"

"LUFTWAFFE STAGES SURPRISE NIGHT RAID ON 8th AF BASE IN UKRAINE"
"44 Flying Fortresses destroyed; 26 men killed"
Shuttle raids to Russia subsequently abandoned.

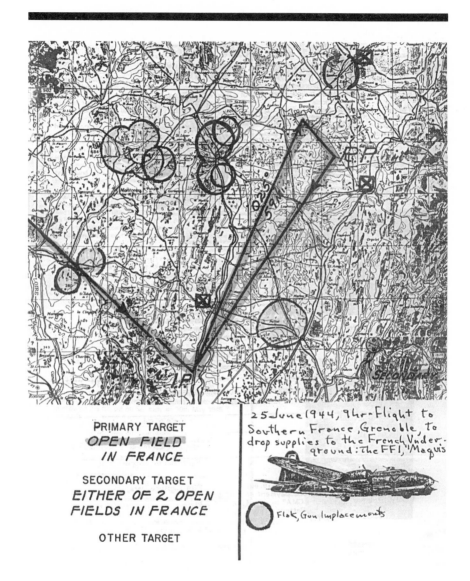

PRIMARY TARGET
*OPEN FIELD
IN FRANCE*

SECONDARY TARGET
*EITHER OF 2 OPEN
FIELDS IN FRANCE*

OTHER TARGET

25 June 1944, 9 hr. Flight to
Southern France, Grenoble, to
drop supplies to the French Underground: The FFI, "Maquis"

Flak, Gun Implacements

*Target map from mission on 25 June 1944 – a 9 hour flight to Southern France
(Grenoble) to drop supplies to the French Underground, the FFI "Maquis."*

TOP SECRET
CHAPTER 12

"IN VILLAGE OF USSEL"
PORT BOU, Spain: June 26, (AP – Monday)

German troops who blasted their way back into the guerrilla held French village of Ussel Tuesday night climaxed by hanging 100 Frenchmen in the town square, a Paris dispatch reported today.

A Spanish correspondent of the Barcelona newspaper Vanguardia, writing under German censorship, said that after "liquidation of the 100 partisans" calm was "again imposed" in the town, located in the Correze province at the foot of the Plateau de Mallevache, a stronghold of the French maquis.

Frenchmen expressed belief that those hanged were probably chosen at random from Ussel's civilian population.

Some Frenchmen said the Germans might be trying to provoke premature attack by the maquis, who are reported building a strong force in the adjoining hills for use at a time and place to be chosen by the allied supreme command.

It did occur to me that my life was certainly not boring. Within the past eleven weeks I was involved in the greatest air-war in history; the largest invasion ever and, now, the attempted defeat of the Third Reich. And as a *suspense-thriller*, I could not anticipate the next change of events.

MISSION # 28
"FRENCH SPECIAL" 25 JUNE 1944
(9:00 Flying Time)

Major Tesla, our Squadron Commander, identified each of us personally as we entered the briefing room. Other squadron C.O.s did the same with their men. Such security was a first.

Therefore, being briefed for a TOP SECRET mission was unsettling for guys who didn't want to tempt fate with change; who clung to eccentric rituals like kissing propellers and pissing on tent pegs.

The briefing began with Colonel Van introducing an RAF Wing Commander, who in turn introduced a French Colonel who gave us a brief background on the "FFI" Free French of the Interior; with whom we would be dealing before the day ended.

The FFI, having started as the independent and fragmented Resistance, or partisan freedom fighters, against the Nazi occupation of France; had evolved into the FFI. In the southern and more mountainous region of France, these saboteurs were referred to as the "Maquis." Tens of thousands of them had been shot, hanged, tortured and sent to prison. Entire villages were destroyed. They needed help!

The FIELD ORDER #289, June 15, 1944 stated:

"The French Maquis (Partisans) in southern France have been rendering far more assistance to the Allied invasion than was ever thought possible. Not only did their activities delay for several days the movement of the 2nd SS Panzer Division from Toulouse to Normandy, but it now appears likely that both the 9th and 11th Panzer Division will be pinned down in south France in an attempt to restore the situation for the Germans. In addition to this enemy armor, the Maquis are also tying up substantial numbers of German infantry troops.

To cope with the situation, the Germans have recently launched a large scale offensive against the Maquis. Several areas controlled by the French Maquis have already been lost to the enemy, necessitating several changes in plan for this operation.

On JUNE 20TH (just five days prior) This message was received:

"We are being attacked by two divisions coming on all roads…we ask urgently for assistance!

Unless weapons and ammunition reach them soon, thousands of these allies of ours will be slaughtered and this diversion of German strength will be ended!"

TOP SECRET

USLIST SB-SC V OITHE NR 28 -P-
FROM OITHE 24/2130B
TO USLIST SB-SC

SECRET 3 B.D. U-386-E

INTELLIGENCE ANNEX TO 3 B.D. FIELD ORDER 289

ALL TARGETS
The French Maquis (Partisans) in Southern France have been rendering far more assistance to the Allied Invasion than was ever thought possible. Not only did their activities delay for several days the movement of the 2nd SS Panzer Division from Toulouse to Normandy, but it now appears likely that both the 9th and the 11th Panzer Divisions will be pinned down in south France in an attempt to restore the situation for the Germans. In addition to this enemy armor, the Maquis are also tying up substantial numbers of German infantry troops.

To cope with the situation the Germans have recently launched a large scale offensive against the Maquis. Several of the areas controlled by the French have already been lost to the enemy, necessitating several changes in plans for this operation. On June 20th this message was received: "We are being attacked by two divisions coming on all roads...We ask urgently for assistance..." Unless weapons and ammunition reach them soon, thousands of these Allies of ours will be slaughtered and this diversion of German strength will be ended.

Crews will be briefed that all details concerning this mission will be treated with the utmost secrecy. The purpose of the mission, the type "bomb load" carried, route, target areas, and all similar details will remain secret after the mission has been completed, and crews will not discuss the mission even on their own bases. Public Relations Officers will be instructed that this mission is to be given no publicity whatsoever.

NOTE:
It is desired that all containers hit within 1000 yards of aiming point. However, containers dropped anywhere within the area outlined on the respective maps will be recovered. Any containers that drop outside of this controlled area very probably will fall into enemy hands.

LOCKSMITH (AREA NO. 11)
No definite confirmation has yet been received from this site and it is not known whether it will be ready to receive the supplies. Consequently, crews will be especially careful not to drop here unless the site signifies its readiness by lighted bonfires or by having men on the field waving flags.

MARKSMAN (AREA NO. 1)
It will be noted that this area is comprised of two sites:
Marksman Alvis and Marksman Austin, which are located only a short distance from one another. The containers are to be dropped at whichever field gives the proper signals.

Above and on following page, Field Order 289.

NOTE:
Tactical reporting system and time limits will apply for this mission. In all reports, targets will be referred to by area numbers only. Groups will report manner in which target area was marked or whether supplies were observed to have been recovered.

FLAK:
For information of light flak defenses when approaching target areas, suggest groups refer to MI 15, 1:500,000, flak maps. Pertinent sheets are Nantes, Dijon, Lyon, and Bordeaux. These sheets also give some locations of possible heavy defenses. Light flak defenses should be considered as dangerous below altitudes of 3000 feet, and as having an effective radius of about two miles. In addition to normal flak defenses, there are enemy troop concentrations in vicinity of targets. These should also be avoided as small arms fire can be effective at altitudes involved. Troop concentrations in the vicinity of Salesman are at La Courtine (4542N/0217E) and at Tulle (4517N/0147E). In the vicinity of Trainer there is a division of ground troops located in the area northeast of the target, roughly including Grenoble, Chambery and Chambarand A/D, and there is another concentration at Vienne (4532N/0455E).

In the vicinity of Director "A" and Marksman there are troop concentrations at Macon (4618N-0450E), at Lons LE S. (4641N-0533E), and at Dole (4705N-0530E).

The area, free of known flak and troops, that is suggested for possible circling or second runs in the vicinity of Salesman is south and southeast of the target: for Director A, east of target; for Marksman, east of target; for Trainer (Crayon) south and southeast of target.

Director "A" – there are heavy gun defenses nearby at Chalon sur S., Dijon and Tavaux A/D.

Marksman – There is a heavy battery nearby at Bourg and light guns to the southwest at Amberieu.

Trainer (Crayon) – There is a heavy battery to the west at Valence (PA A/D) and possible battery at Grenoble to the northeast. Lyon should be avoided enroute.

Salesman – There are no known heavy guns in the area. See MI 15 map for several locations of light guns near target. Balloons may be present at the light gun positions at La Courtine and St. Julien.

– PARTRIDGE –

TOD 24/2150B AGF
AS FOR CHECK

The drapery was drawn away from the briefing map at the center of the stage and the red ribbon indicated the courseline was as long as a mission to Berlin; except it went South instead of East. I guessed the flying time to be over eight hours – if everything went okay...But what did the man say?

"This is the first time that such an effort has ever been *attempted*.."

So what did he mean by that?

Well, the plan called for at least thirty-five ships from our Bomb Group to fly supplies and arms into the midst of enemy occupied territory in the *middle of daylight*! And there was more.

Climbing for our traditional 27,000 feet high-level bombing altitude over the Channel, we were to deceive the enemy by changing procedure by letting down to less than 1,000 feet! Actually it was less than 700 feet above the ground!

Heavy bombers operating at less than 700 feet – in a valley – that was naturally surrounded by hills and mountains? If we got into trouble and unable to climb, we wouldn't even be able to get up and into nearby Switzerland...Even our standard landing pattern was was up at 800 feet!

The 385th Bomb Group had developed the eight-foot long metal canisters with parachutes that held the supplies and arms. We, and other groups, would be dropping them from less than 700 feet – *deep behind enemy lines!*

The briefing continued:

"Light flak defenses should be considered dangerous below 3,000 feet. There are enemy troop concentrations in the vicinity of the targets. These should also be avoided as small arms fire can be effective at altitudes involved."

It made no more sense than moths flying into a flame, but damned if it didn't sound like an exciting adventure. Maybe it was as close as I would ever get to Errol Flynn playing in a spy thriller. Maybe it was the relief of getting away from high-altitude bombing. And maybe, it might even help the Maquis who were also trying to shorten the war. All I knew was that I was actually pleased to be going on this one.

"The Drop Zone will be in a meadow marked by three smoke bombs."

The idea that we would be "going up *Shit Creek* without a paddle" behind enemy lines, at less than 700 feet, and looking for three smoke bombs reminded me of a joke and I giggled.

Moon, who was not in a humorous mood, jabbed me and gave me a stern look. It tickled me even more, because I knew he knew the joke and if I gave him the punch line he would laugh.

The joke was about the paratrooper who was told that if his main chute failed to open, he was to open his reserve chute and when he landed a Jeep would pick him up. When his main chute failed he pulled the reserve, but it didn't open either. His comment was, "I'll bet that damn Jeep won't be there either."

So when the French Colonel said, "If the smoke bombs aren't there, there will be three men waving flags." I whispered to Moon, "And, I'll bet that damned jeep won't be there either."

Moon burst out with a guffaw that was as startling as a loud fart in church and Colonel Van scowled at the both of us from the stage.

At 13,000 feet above the English Channel all gunners were given the standard order to clear their guns and puffs of smoke choked out of more than 400 barrels of 50 Caliber machineguns.

With that done the group formation slowly started a descent over the Channel from the Normandy coastline toward the south of France.

The sea traffic in the Channel that supplied the ongoing invasion, now two weeks later, was still very heavy.

However, the ground war did not seem to be getting anyplace. For if the plan was to push the Germans back to Berlin, there was certainly a long way to go.

Some had said that the Invasion was the "Beginning of the End," but my appraisal of the campaign so far was that it didn't even appear to be the "Beginning of the Beginning."

Measured in flying time, the ground troops had occupied only three minutes into Europe; which left Berlin over fifty two times farther to go.

That meant, by my simple calculations, that it would take at least 26 weeks, or six months to reach Berlin – if the Germans didn't push us back into the sea where we would have to start all over again – if we could.

No. Despite the effort and sacrifices going on below us, there was no assurance that the Germans – who had machine guns that fired three times faster than ours, heavier tanks and bigger guns – would be the losers in the coming battles and the total war to follow.

Therefore, I revised my estimate. The war, now begun, would most certainly not be over by Christmas. In fact, I doubted we would even be in Germany by then, if at all.

As I looked down I wondered just how many of my friends from home were involved, since practically everyone I'd known in high school had gone to war...And what about Jake McNiece?

If Jake had beaten the odds and survived his intended night-jump behind the lines before the main assault, would he still be alive? I wished him well...God bless us all.

T he surprise did not announce itself loudly with an explosion of shot and shell. Rather, it was more sinister and it took my attention away from the fighting below to the mission at hand – not going as planned, because something was WRONG.

While we had started out as a spare in "Coffin Corner" we climbed up to the tail of the High Squadron and replaced Mc Donald when he had to abort.

What was very wrong and obviously out of place was a lone B-17, perhaps a mile away to our right, flying parallel and very slowly moving toward us, as if it intended to join into our Group. I bumped Moon's arm and pointed it out to him.

There was no need to discuss it, because it was such a glaring mistake. We were on a TOP SECRET and very special mission to drop supplies into the arms of the Maquis, while all other bombers were, naturally, *loaded with bombs!*

It was policy that, if you could not locate your bomb group, you were to join up with any group so as not to waste the effort and risk of bringing your bombs back to base.

So it was fair to assume that this lone B-17, like an abandoned calf out on the prairie, had gotten lost and was going to join our herd.

The problem was that today we were a herd of milk cows and not the traditional herd of wild buffalo. Therefore instead of dropping manna from heaven, this intruder was going to cause us to *rain on the parade.*

Since we were in the top slot of the High Squadron and closest to the approaching problem, I broke the safety wire on the transmitter for the Command Channel: "Hotshot Yellow, this is Alfrek "C" Charley. We've got an Intruder joining us at 3 o'clock level."

Because different bomb groups operate on different frequencies, the Intruder could not be contacted by radio, so I called Herby in the tail and told him to put a red lens on the Aldus Lamp and to start flashing it at the ship joining in on us.

With no real way to communicate, I tried to get my thinking into the head of the pilot joining up with us. He'd gotten lost from his group to begin with. He'd done what he thought was right by joining another bomb group, but was surprised to find that, instead of climbing up for bombing altitude, the group was letting down – over enemy territory!!!

Therefore, now just west of Paris on a southerly course, and still letting down, would he likely leave the group over enemy territory and go it alone?

HELL NO!

Given the choice of being alone in the killing field or joining *birds of a feather* – even if you didn't understand what they were doing or where they were going – you were in for the ride.

But what about the Maquis who were expecting to catch those supplies – who would CATCH HELL when the bombs were dropped?

It was good that it was a long mission, which would allow time to figure out a solution. But still inside of his head, I knew the guy had a real battle going on by the time we were down to within a thousand feet of the ground around Lyon and headed for the Alps – unless – ? What if it was one of those captured B-17's used by the Germans? God knows, they had plenty of them to pick from.

Ohhh, Boy! Even if the Intruder didn't know our mission, he was able to track our course and knew our position, to which he could call for fighters to try and shoot us down before we got to the target.

Well, this was a mystery that our leader would have to solve.

It didn't seem any too soon that Hotshot Yellow executed the remedy. Unable to verbally communicate with the Intruder, two of our ships were assigned to escort him away from our Group to prevent him from approaching the Drop Zone. Then after our Group dropped, two of the empty ships would hold the Intruder away from the D. Z. , Drop Zone, to allow the escorts to drop their loads.

Such was the *fiddle-farting* that was going on as we jockeyed into position for the drop.

Down around Grenoble we finally turned on the I.P. and started our run from the Initial Point flying back toward the north on a heading of 025 degrees for 59 miles to the D.Z..

What would it be, three smoke bombs or three men waving flags?

It was a fairytale fantasy. In the green and peaceful valley amidst the foothills of the Alps were three columns of lazy black smoke drifting upward from and empty meadow. On the road alongside was the only individual in sight: a farmer driving a gray horse that pulled a two-wheel cart.

By extreme contrast to the pastoral and serene setting from the farmer's perspective, thirty-five American Flying Fortresses, just 700 feet overhead, overtook the valley like a giant metallic avalanche, with the roar of 168,000 horsepower; beating the air with 420 colossal saber-like propellers!!!

Such a fury could hardly be kept SECRET – especially in the midst of enemy territory.

God, it was strange; like no other mission I'd ever flown. In fact it was a special low-level mission that nobody had ever flown.

Our Group passed over the three smoke pots in the empty meadow and made a sweeping turn to the right at only 700 feet above the ground. Incredible!

It was a beautiful Sunday afternoon in the south of France. It was the beginning of summer and warm. I slid open my window and recalled the joy of flying in an open cockpit on such days as this and I felt grateful that we were not up at 27 Angels, but forty times lower, not freezing off our asses; grateful that there was no flak; grateful to be twenty years old and very much alive.

It was – FANTASTIC!

Moon, too, was feeling great. For as we circled to the right – the last ship in the formation to come around before the drop – Moon spotted two young ladies waving from a second story window of the tallest-two story building in the small village – and he couldn't resist having a closer look. To heck with 700 feet.

As the last in the formation, nobody was flying on us, so we went down on the two girls in the window where we were at eyeball-level. We could see their expressions change from smiles to – Ohhhhhhh!

Seeing a B-17 coming straight at you did that.

Corky, in the ball turret on our belly, got an even closer look, because the ship was loaded and heavy and it did not respond so quickly when Moon and I both hauled back on the controls to lift us up and over the building. This, of course, almost put Corky through the girl's window.

"Goddammit-you-guys!!!" Corky called, "Stay away from the hard stuff! Putting me through that tree in Florida was bad enough!!"

By the time we got straightened around and back into the trail of our Group the scene on the meadow had changed. It looked like a colossal Easter-egg-hunt…No, it looked more like the Oklahoma land-run scene in the movie "CIMARRON". Grandma and all of the kids;

hundreds of people flooded onto the meadow from the forest along the western side of the field.

Silver canisters fell from the bellies of the bombers, arrested by parachutes and lowered to earth. But not all of them!

Some chutes failed to open and the canisters plummeted earthward into the crowd, thumping into the ground. As best I could tell, there were miraculously no casualties.

The farmer drove his horse and cart onto the field where it was loaded. Two black autos arrived from somewhere and they too were loaded. The smoke pots were extinguished and, after dropping the vital supplies, our Group exited the uncommon scene in a climbing right turn toward the R.P. where we rallied and reformed for our long trip home. Except, Moon and I had some fixing to do.

Our Tail End Charley position allowed us to tag along behind, giving us plenty of slack to play around, like showing off to the gals in the second story window.

Well, it turned out that the horseplay made us tardy over the target, which created no problem for anyone – except us.

For as the Group climbed away from the D. Z., there was no way for us to catch up and to climb up on top of the Group and back onto the tail of the High Squadron... What to do?

Since the escape route retraced the approach route by heading south – before eventually turning back north toward home – we cut our turn sharply and managed to catch up to the Low Squadron and back to our original position in *Coffin Corner*.

Better there than out in the cold as a straggler.

The order of flight out of the valley was: Lead Squadron; which was followed by the Low Squadron, with us in the tail; followed by the High Squadron. And since everyone had dropped from the same 700 feet, it took awhile to reform the Group and we were strung out in a line.

As we slowly gained altitude, reaching only a bit over 1,000 feet, Herby called in from the tail, "Bandits, six o'clock high!"

SHIT! I hated to hear that. It could mess up a perfectly good Sunday outing. We were practically sitting ducks, out of our element down on the deck.

I bumped Moon and signaled him to switch from listening to command to hear what Herby had to report over the intercom.

"Talk to me Herby," I invited.

"Wellll," he drawled, "It looks to be six Messerchmitts and they are way-to-hell up there."

Since there was no way that we could see them from the cockpit, I told him to let us know what the bandits decided to do.

"They're commin' down!" Herby said. "They've rolled over and they're COMIN' DOWN!"

We'd never had an overhead attack and I didn't understand why not, since we were more vulnerable from overhead than head on, because each Seventeen had only three guns that could point straight up…The odds were definitely against us.

Damn! Had the B-17 been a German "*Shadow*" and called the fighters in on us to catch us out of position and down on the deck with our pants down?

Great. This historical first-of-its-kind-mission was turning into a last-of-its-kind.

"Hot-diggity-dog!" Herby called. "They're gonna take the squadron behind us."

We waited for him to tell us more…

"I can't believe it," Herby said.

"You can't believe *WHAT*?" I asked impatiently.

"I've never seen anything like this," he replied.

"Talk to me Herby," I insisted.

"Sonovabitch!"

"WHAT?"

"Bad luck," Herby said, and I could feel the hairs on the back of my neck coming to attention.

"What happened?" I asked.

"Every one of those damned Bandits dove right through the formation!" Herby said.

"*AND*," I prompted.

"Well," Herby drawled, "Those Bandit-boys must be short of experience, 'cause they found out too late that there wasn't enough room under the bombers to pull out."

"You mean – "

"Yep." Herby concluded, "Every one of 'em smacked right into the ground."

No SHIT! I could imagine their surprise just before they died. It was bad luck for them, but good luck for us.

Returning safely from the tour to Southern France, we all agreed that it had been an interesting nine hour Sunday outing. Now, the nine hours is only the flying time. However, a time-clock would log it at least a sixteen hour workday, since more than flying was involved; such as transportation, briefing, preflight and debriefing.

So along with the factor of stress, the job was both physically and emotionally wearing. And while this day had been a positive experience, I did share that sick feeling of fatigue with the others of our crew, as well as the other crews. It wasn't that anyone's hands were shaking or that anyone's reflexes seemed to be off. It was simply a general feeling that everyone was just running down.

In 79 days I had flown 28 missions. But even if I had been paid more than $20. 00 a mission, it could not replenish my supply of energy and enthusiasm. I just felt that I was not the same lad that I had been at the beginning of April. But there was good news…Our crew was given a couple of weeks off for R&R.

Somebody knew it was time for us to have some Rest and Recuperation. The officers were given orders to report to a "Flak House" southwest of London and the enlisted men were sent to a different one.

These "Flak Houses" of which there were several, were also called "Flak Farms" because they were English manor houses that were located on estates.

We were given two days travel time to get there and another two days to return. And since hitchhiking was rather dependable with the large amount of military transportation in England, I decided to vacation on my way down to the "Flak Farm" southwest of London.

I stopped by Bottisham to visit Bud Bishop at Cambridge, then went over to Bedford to look up C. L. Halliday, with whom I'd gone through pilot training in our Class of 43-I.

Of all coincidences, it turned out that a close friend of C.L. 's had been the pilot of the B-17 that had intruded on us on the trip to Southern France, so we exchanged perspectives.

He had naturally been baffled when everybody started letting down into enemy territory. And since the two bombers had escorted him away from the target, followed by two more, he still didn't know what the target had been and he had to bring his bombs all the way back to base and land with them. Apparently it had been a tight squeeze on fuel.

After saying goodbye to C.L. and his buddy, the pilot of the "Phantom Bomber," I was fortunate to catch a ride to London in the last of three 6x6 trucks, which were hauling the Glenn Miller band. It was nothing like a concert, but visiting along the way did make for an enjoyable trip.

The *"FLAK FARM"* was a country estate of perhaps forty acres in the southwestern part of England. The purpose of this country manor, regardless of why it had originally been built, was to help war-weary aerial combatants rest and recuperate. And while the program had been started by the Air Force, these "resorts," of which there were several, were turned over to the Red Cross in an attempt to remove the stigma of a military operation. As such, they would create a casual homey atmosphere.

The Old World charm of stained glass windows, and other works of artisans, like antique paneling and stone and ironwork, did not take me back home to the west side of the railroad tracks in Ponca City, Oklahoma. While it was aristocratic and non-military, it was not "home."

In fact, the moment I stepped inside and signed in on the military roster, I had the feeling of *forced relaxation*.

An American Red Cross "girl," who reminded me of my aunt Marie, hosted me on a tour of the place; introducing me to perhaps a dozen other fly-boys from assorted bases and to some of the staff members. It struck me as if it was the cast and setting for an English stage play.

Jeeves, answering to his stereotypical stage name, was the senior in age. A large man, he was proper English and a butler or a gentleman's gentleman. As such, his dress was more formal than we "guests."

"Cooky" was an American Mess Sergeant in disguise. That is, he was evidently supposed to be kept away from us and in the kitchen so as not to remind us of our military status. However, Cooky was the most important asset to the place, since he cooked "American."

The rest of the housekeeping staff was English and for the most part, like stagehands, were mainly behind the scenes, leaving any drama to be played out by "Aunt Marie" and her two…?

No, the play was more like *CINDERELLA* – without Ella. This left a dozen of us "Prince Charmings" with the Stepmother, "Aunt Marie" and Two Stepsisters who represented the Red Cross.

Which is to say, that any sexual intrigue at the Flak Farm had been taken off of the menu. This, of course, destroyed any hope of a plot, because the Air Force was not about to sponsor a situation in which any of us would get caught with our pants down. Thus, we might as well have been sent to a monastery.

The Stepmother, who's name was Edith, gave me a choice of some simulated civilian casual clothing. I picked a pair of tweedy slacks, hightopped tennis shoes and a khaki turtle-neck woolen sweater, probably hand-knitted by a Red Cross volunteer.

Jeeves showed me my room on the second floor, where I changed into my casual dress. I then went back downstairs and into the library where I picked up the London Chronicle newspaper.

Moon, having come a different way with Ears, finally arrived – without Ears.

"I lost him in London," Moon said. "Goddamned buzz bomb!"

"Is he dead or in the hospital?" I asked.

"How would I know? He just left in the middle of the night when that damn bomb exploded…We were both a little tipsy. I got out of bed, stumbled to the window – and damn near fell through it, *'cause there was no more window left!* Hell, we were up seven stories on the top floor…I could have fallen to my death!"

"And Ears just left?" I asked.

"Yeah," Moon responded. "You know how he's sometimes afraid of heights. He was afraid he might walk in his sleep and fall out of where the window was supposed to be…I don't know where he went."

I asked about Eut and Moon told me that they'd sent him back to the hospital for an evaluation after he'd reported to Sick Call before the French Special mission.

Edith arrived and took Moon to wardrobe for his leisure costume while I read the paper:

- The Americans had captured General Schlieben, Commander of the Cherbourg fortress; as well as Rear Admiral Henneke, Commander of German naval operations Cherbourg.
- The British 2nd Army was still hung up at Caen – twenty days after their arrival, because they had met "fierce resistance" – as if nobody else had "fierce resistance."
- Princess Elizabeth's 18th birthday, although in April, was officially recognized and celebrated on the 18th of June by Trooping of the Colors. Serving in the Auxiliary Territorial Service, she had even exchanged a punctured pneumatic tire on a lorry by herself.
- General Koenig is to command the Free French Forces of

the Interior.
- American B-25s and P-47s make constant attack on Japanese supply lines in the Pacific.
- The Russians were moving in on Germany and theAllies were progressing up the boot of Italy.

"Would the Lieutenant care for orange juice, coffee, tea or cocoa?"

I squinted open my eyes and saw Jeeves standing a respectable distance from my bed. I had a headache, my mouth was dry and I mumbled, "Orange juice." Jeeves served me immediately from a tray near him and I tried to organize my mind.

"Breakfast is being served until eleven in the dining room, Sir." Jeeves announced formally.

The aroma of bacon and eggs accompanied his announcement.

Reeves then excused himself and I wondered what had happened to dinner. Never mind. I sat in bed drinking chilled orange juice and marveled at the fact that somebody in England had finally found some ice.

Come to think of it, there had also been ice in the bar last night. The bar?

It started coming back to me. Moon had kept me well supplied with Kentucky bourbon and Coca Cola. Maybe that had something to do with my dehydration and confusion.

Moon, my mentor, was still working at making a man of me.

Bless his heart. He'd gotten me hooked on cigarettes, had always tried to fix me up with female companionship and last night had me chug-a-lugging whiskey along with the other guests until…?

Well, that's where my memory ended.

When I saw Moon at breakfast I told him that I must be coming down with something terrible, because I felt shaky all over.

"That," he announced proudly, "Is a hangover. Here, have a Bloody Mary with the rest of us. It'll pick you up for the skeet shoot."

Everybody else had a glass and held them up in a salute: "Cheers!"

Well, the tomato juice tasted so good that I had three of them *instead* of eating breakfast. And before I realized it, everyone else had left the table and the staff started preparing it for lunch.

It was a happy and helpful staff. They laughed a lot and tried teaching me how to say "Worester – Wusterchester – Worse-ter-chester-ches-tire-shire," the sauce that made the "tomawh-toe juice" so tasty.

Jeeves accompanied me up to my room for a nap. . .

As much as I had wanted to check out as First Pilot, I was having regrets, because I couldn't find the switch – or – was it a lever? Or some kind of a knob? I didn't even know what it was that I was looking for. Whatever it was, it was important, because we were all going to die if I didn't find it, push it – pull it – or whatever it was that I was supposed to do with it.

I was in big trouble. I also had to take a piss at the same time and couldn't find the relief tube. I looked back over my shoulder for Burnell, but he wasn't there. His top turret wasn't there either. I wasn't even flying a Seventeen...I was flying a transport. It was a C-54...I'd never even been inside of a C-54, but I was the Pilot in Command!

Of course, I had hoped to be assigned to the Air Transport Command after graduation from pilot training in order to gain experience to become an airline pilot, but it hadn't happened.

DAMN, I had to piss in the worst way!

Thank God, the door was open to the cabin behind me. I'd go back to the toilet. It sure would beat pissing in the bomb-bay.

But what a shock! Seated in the bucket seats along the sides of the cabin were paratroopers. *GERMAN PARATROOPERS!!*

"Can I be of assistance, Sir?" It was Jeeves.

I turned to see Jeeves sitting in the copilot seat. But when he spoke again, his lips didn't move and his voice came from behind me.

"May I help you sir?"

I was laying across my bed with my knees on the floor.

Jeeves was above and behind me.

"Yes," I said, "I've gotta take a pee."

Jeeves bent down and pulled a chamber mug from under the bed.

"This should do, Sir," he said, leaving it on the floor next to me. "If you need me, Sir, I'll be just outside the door."

I was saved just in the nick of time; relieving myself into the pot while still on my knees.

Man! What a weird dream.

"BANG!" – "BANG!"

I went to the window and looked down onto Moon and the five other guys from breakfast out in back of the manor house.

They were warming up for the skeet shoot.

I'd never shot skeet before. Rabbits, squirrels, snakes, birds and qualified Expert with the Thompson sub-machine gun, pistol, the carbine and the 30 Caliber machine gun; but I had never shot skeet, especially in competition.

"We'll put a limit on the betting so you won't lose too much," said one of my competitors, whom they called Milford.

So there was Moon and myself, not feeling too well anyway, and we were going to compete in shooting with these fighter jocks who were noted for their large egos. The sport was to their advantage, because they, like our gunners, had been trained in shooting skeet.

However, Moon encouraged me, saying nobody had to win, "It's just a friendly contest. We're supposed to be having fun here."

Then he went too far by admiring the large wrist watches a couple of them were wearing and I knew where he was headed.

He was going to try and psych them out.

"You know what they say, Smitty, about these guys with big clocks and small cocks," he said. "They couldn't hit a bull in the ass with a shovel."

It could have gone badly right there, but Moon offered everyone some ice cold lemonade from a thermos along with sandwiches he'd gotten Cooky to make up by sharing some of the vodka he'd brought with him from London. Of course, most of the vodka had gone into the lemonade.

It sure tasted good in my condition, especially on an unusually warm afternoon in England. I was glad I had brought along my sunglasses, because the sun was especially bothersome to me in my poor condition.

"BANG!" – "BANG!" – "BANG!" I couldn't miss.

Milford, the fighter-jock, who was going to make it easy for me, got a bit tense when his fighter-jock buddies started joking him about almost being a double Ace, with 9 "kills" and letting a B-17 copilot outshoot him.

I thought to put him at ease and offered him some of Moon's lemonade, but he refused.

One of his buddies almost pushed too far when he said, "Smitty's not even sober an' he's out-shootin' you."

That's when the contest really started, because it occurred to me that if I wasn't completely sober, then I was not really in control of myself. And if I had to go through life depending on alcohol to put me ahead of my competition – well; I'd stop that right now. I drank no more lemonade. I left that and the betting up to Moon.

We were into shooting doubles. Everyone except Milford and I had missed at least one target by the time we got to 15. And like bowling or golf, for me, the greatest control is needed *between* shots when waiting to have a go at it.

So by the time Milford and I had reached 20, without either of us missing; my main effort was in the fight for the control of every muscle in my body. The delays and small talk of the others did not help.

"Hey, Smitty. When you finish your tour in the big-assed birds why don't you come and fly with us?"

"Yeah. Volunteer for a second tour and they'll give you your choice of aircraft."

Hmmmm? Volunteer for another tour? Go fly fighters?

I did have a tendency to be a loner, but it was an act of choice. I was afraid to make friends, because losing them was so painful.

We were down to 23. Only two more tries remained for Milford and myself. I was in a hurry to finish it off, but everyone was still in competition and – Man! Didn't they enjoy talking and wasting time.

"If you'd like to fly Mustangs, why don't you ask Milford here for a job."

"I don't even know Milford's last name." I said.

"That is his last name: Colonel Milford."

Shit! If ever I was to ask Colonel Milford to fly one of his P-51s, this was not the time, because I seemed to be doing a heck of a good job of shooting myself in the foot by outshooting him on the skeet range. However, I had not yet done that, had I.

Well, I was up for my last chance of hitting 25 out of 25 in a row. Milford – "Colonel Milford" would follow me...Damn civy attire, anyway. How could I have known he was a Colonel?

How could I have guessed that I would even have hit five out of ten – shooting doubles? I felt the pressure.

"Smitty."

I turned and Milford was smiling at me. "Show us what you've got, boy."

"Boy"?

That did it. He was working on my mind and was trying to talk me out of my victory – if he could. So I had to try and give it back to him.

As cocky as I could make it, I strutted to my position, told him "Watch this," turned, prepared myself and called "PULL!"

"BANG" – "BANG"!!

The two clay pigeons exploded into black puffs of smoke. I knew it was luck. Plain LUCK! I had never and would never again dare try to shoot 25 out of 25. Any boasting I might have had left me.

Milford, smiling, took his position, readied himself and called, "PULL!"

"BANG!" – "BANG!"!!

"One pigeon changed to a black puff of smoke and the other one sailed away – until "BANG!" A third shot and it died in place.

It was a cheap shot, not allowed and a foul. The victory was mine. No question about it. Yet, as far as the get-away pigeon was concerned, it didn't really get away. I was glad that we were only shooting clay pigeons.

Milford turned with a smile on his face, laid his shotgun back over his shoulder, strolled over to me and shook my hand.

"Congratulations 'Champ.' We got 'em all, didn't we?"

It was the pauses in between the actual shooting that I had trouble with. The contest is scored by the results, but the results depend greatly on how the *pauses* are handled. And right now – pausing at the Flak Farm – my life was on HOLD, awaiting the final moments of the game – and I was having trouble dealing with it. I wanted two things: to be away from it all and, yet, I didn't want to miss a single moment of it.

Patience. That was the trick: Being able *to live through the "pauses,"* because "patience" was hard to come by.

Coombe House, a typical "flak farm."

FLAK FARM
CHAPTER 13

The Red Cross gals were making me crazy…Ohhh, they were trying to do what they were supposed to do, I guess, but it all seemed to be so false and like so much "play-acting." They were faking it, and not doing it very well either.

Around nine in the evening everyone was invited to roast marshmallows in the large fireplace and drink hot chocolate while Jeeves told some ghost stories… Jesus Christ, a goddamned teenage slumber party.

I decided to stay in the library and read a story I'd found in the *Saturday Evening Post* that seemed to be pretty good. Unfortunately it turned out to be a continued story. And since the issue was five months old, the following issue – the one in which the story had been continued – was not to be found.

So not reading, but just thinking, I realized how my life, like the story in the magazine that I couldn't find, had also been Continued. Except I didn't know for how long, nor even how to continue. I felt that I too had been misplaced.

There was no doubt that I was depressed. I had a strong feeling of GUILT, which I thought was strange.

Hadn't I volunteered myself to my country? No guilt there.

Hadn't I done what was expected of me? No guilt there.

The newspapers caught my attention. They were full of the war.

There had been a slaughter at Normandy. Our own Flight Surgeon had volunteered and returned with a changed attitude; we fly-boys had it easy compared to the ground-pounders.

Well, that was his opinion. At least they had some medical attention on the ground, but in the air it could take hours to get back from a mission before there was help, which could be fatal. Down on

It was often a long way home.

the ground it was also not fifty degrees below zero and there was no worry about not having any oxygen to keep you alive. The ground-pounders also had fox holes for protection. There was no place to hide in the sky.

Well, I'd volunteered like everyone on flying status. There was no one to blame but me.

No, I didn't feel guilty doing my fighting in the sky. In fact, the Eighth Air Force had already lost four times more people than had been lost at Normandy; and that didn't count the losses of the Fifteenth Air Force coming all the way up from Italy to help. There was also the Ninth Air Force with their tactical ground support.

My God, the German ground forces had smaller losses than we did.

So why did I feel so guilty?

I guessed that God must have built us that way. That if you lived while other humans died, you had to feel guilty. It had to be one of those "Platinum Rules" for the preservation of humankind. It was probably under the heading of DOING UNTO OTHERS AS YOU WOULD HAVE OTHERS DO UNTO YOU. And God knew, as did I, that I was certainly DOING UNTO OTHERS.

Yes, I was.

It would have helped my conscience and also saved the victims of my bombing much pain and suffering if they had never been born, or if they had been aborted.

That was it. That was why I was feeling guilty. At least that was a big part of it. Like Lady Mac Beth, I couldn't get the stain of blood off of my hands. So what could I do about it?

Quit?

No. Others had quit early on before the war. They didn't want to get involved. They didn't want any blood on their hands. They would do nothing and remain insulated and isolated from world affairs.

Well, it didn't go away. It only encouraged the "bullies" to DO UNTO OTHERS, confident that nobody was going to DO UNTO THEM.

So that was how I had gotten into this terrible business of DOING UNTO THEM – BEFORE THEY DID UNTO ME…Too bad about the children, women and older folks, but that's the way it was. There were no other options.

At least that was the way it came to me sitting in a Flak House full of guilt and self pity.

Would my life change anything? Probably not a damn thing. However, the war was sure changing me.

"God," I prayed under my breath, "Don't let me forget any of this. I never again want to go through such an experience as WAR!!! Please help me in some way to contribute to the prevention of any future wars…Please, God, help us all."

Help was waiting – IF you got back.

"P.S., I would sure appreciate it if You could cut me a little slack here so I can have some peace of mind, at least for a little while…I'm awfully tired…But then, You already know that, don't You. Amen."

What I needed to relax my mind was to get physical. I'd seen that they had some bicycles at the Flak Farm and decided it would do me good to go for a ride.

My personal bike back at the base was better than those made available to us, because mine had a Coaster Brake. The Flak Farm bicycles were not so designed. The only coasting with them was with feet off of the pedals. And God forbid, don't stick your feet in the way of the rotating pedals, because momentum and the gear ratio would destroy you.

On level terrain the cycling was a pleasure and dreamlike as one mile followed the next through the wooded countryside.

But then, after several miles, everything changed to one of those out-of-control nightmares where you're going too fast and are helpless to stop.

I was headed down a lengthy and too steep decline, at the bottom of which was a stone bridge across a good-sized stream.

If I missed the approach and hit the stone bridge, it would do me real damage; like Dyer, who'd broken his arm riding a bicycle in a blackout. So I gambled on getting off of the road and onto the grassy right-of-way…Or was it called a "left-of-way" with the left-handed British traffic? In any case, it was the WRONG way.

No matter! Better to bail out on the grass than to slam into the stones.

Oh, Nooo! I couldn't synchronize my feet to the spinning pedals and the hand brakes weren't even slowing me down…Foot onto pedal and the pedal lifted me right up and off of the bike. I landed on the grass and the bike landed in the stream!

I was pleased to have not broken anything. However, I did face the problem of retrieving the bicycle from the stream. Maybe I should have just left it there.

Since I guessed it was about seven miles back to the Flak Farm, I decided it would be better to ride the bike than to walk.

So, being alone at the edge of the woods, I took off my pants and was pulling my turtleneck over my head to strip down before swimming for the bike, when I was alerted to the fact that I was being watched.

Just a bit into the woods was the silhouette of a horse, standing very still, with a rider on its back. It made me angry to think that I was being spied on instead of the rider coming forward to assist me.

"Hey, YOU!" I shouted. "Get your ass over here and identify yourself."

Slowly the horse and rider came from the woods toward me. It looked to be a woman.

Christ! I'm standing in my undershorts and a woman is coming toward me – at my request.

"Don't come just yet," I said, holding up my hand and trying to do a one-legged dance back into my pants.

The rider obliged my request until I had made myself presentable and walked over to her.

"Can I be of assistance?" she asked politely in what might be called upper class English.

"I just wish you were riding a Western saddle with a good lariat. That way we could throw a loop over my bike and fish it out of the water."

"Sorry to disappoint you," She smiled.

I found my cigarettes and offered her one, but she declined. I lit one for myself and we silently appraised each other.

Not too bad, I thought…She was certainly not any kind of a raving beauty, but she did possess a unique charm, and she did sit well atop a hell of a good looking thoroughbred.

"Beautiful horse," I said, petting its shoulder near the inside of the rider's knee, held high by the short stirrup of the little English saddle.

She watched me judiciously, as if to warn me not to slip beyond the bounds of propriety. Any petting had better be confined to the horse and not to her person. So I slid my hand slowly down the well formed foreleg of her horse, feeling the muscles quiver under the light touch of my hand.

I did have some knowledge of horses, having started riding as a mounted waterboy for my uncle's threshing crew when I was only eight years old, back before harvesting was done with combines.

Later I rode some roundups with friends whose families had ranches. And while most of my experience had been with quarterhorse cowponies, I knew that line-breeding for a pure strain, such as thoroughbreds, could make horses high strung and goosey.

The quiver I'd felt in stroking the horse's leg indicated to me that this lady's horse tended to be excitable. I checked the gender and asked, "Will she ride double?"

That was a question the lady chose to ponder. What was I really asking?

Lady???

That was something that I had to think about, because the girl, while ladylike, could not be much over eighteen. Hmmm?

"They call me Smitty," I said and extended my hand.

She didn't shake my hand, showing her hands to be filled with double-reins.

"What do they call you?" I asked.

It sounded like "Lilly-bet." However, I didn't ask her to repeat, because she obviously didn't want me to know too much. Yet, she seemed uncomfortable about lying to me with a made-up name.

"Okay, Lil," I said. "It's going to get dark in a bit and I've decided not to go into the water after my bike, even though I've got at least a seven mile hike ahead of me. So why don't you just hump yourself forward on that little pancake saddle of yours and you can give me a ride in the rumble seat?"

Slowly I pulled her left foot from the stirrup, alert to any resistance she might offer, but there was none.

Boy, that stirrup sure was high off the ground, plus the fact that the squirrelly horse wouldn't hold still, despite Lil's tugging on the reigns to control it.

"Don't rein her in too tight," I coached. "She'll start bucking."

To avoid the too-high stirrup problem and the jumping around, I grabbed as much of the saddle's pommel near Lil's crotch with my left hand, caught the cantle under Lil's butt at the rear of the saddle with my right hand and heaved myself up into place behind her.

My left leg caught the mare in the left flank and she started to buck!

"Hold on Lil!" I yelled. "It's rodeo time!"

To keep from falling, I tried to re-set my grip on the pommel. Well, the damned English saddle didn't have any kind of a saddle horn, so I missed and grabbed Lil right in her crotch.

Under the circumstances of both of us about to be thrown off, my missed grope was of no consequence and I had to admire Lil's management of the beast. Shortly she had him prancing in place and I was able to release my grips and steady myself by holding onto Lil's waist.

"I'm sorry about that," I said.

Lil excused me by saying that it wasn't my fault and made no mention of my having invaded her privacy.

I pointed in the direction from where I had come and we rode through the woods on a shortcut for the Flak Farm.

We didn't speak; just rocked along, Lil slipping to and fro on the saddle and me squirming around to try and keep from pinching my private parts between the saddle and horse, since my most private part had a mind of its own and kept wanting to go public – until – PINCH!! Ohhh, that hurt.

Lil's blouse was silky slick and my hands wouldn't stay in place on her waist. It was because the bucking around had caused her shirttail to come out and cover her hips. So I took the opportunity to reach up under her shirttail where I found some flesh below her lower ribs to which my hands, the palms of which were damp, adhered better to her skin than to the silk.

I couldn't see her face for a clue as to whether she thought I had gone too far. All she did was to make a quiet little sound. To me, this did not come across as an objection.

As we rocked along on the back of the horse my fingers tested her skin – without objection.

Lil was not fat; not even chunky. I tried, but I couldn't even squeeze up a little half-inch roll in the area of her "love handles."

It made me curious when Lil made another one of those funny little "ahum" sounds, so I whispered into her ear. After all, I didn't want to be too loud, since we were so close.

"Did you say something?" I asked.

The only reply was another one of those little "ahums," as she relaxed a bit and leaned back against me.

Well, my hands naturally went forward that little bit and came to rest on her bare tummy.

It was a pleasant sensation for me, feeling one hell of a lot better than the rigid controls of a Flying Fortress.

As we rolled along rhythmically atop the mare in the forest I became a bit concerned, because the more we rocked the more limp Lil became and the more she moaned – almost whimpered.

The mare slowed and stopped. Lil made no effort to coax her on, but just sat loosely in the saddle. It was as if she had passed out.

I slid off the horse and onto the ground as she folded down out of the saddle and onto me. I had to hold her firmly and lowered her to the ground as gently as I could.

It was getting dark. Not that I was afraid of the dark, but I was apprehensive about Lil's condition. And truly, without her I didn't have a clue as to where we were or where to go for help.

It was a first for me. I didn't know if she was epileptic or maybe she was a diabetic and had gone into shock; nor did I know what to do if she had. All I could do was to examine the situation and knelt down over her closely to see if I could rouse her some way.

Since it was getting dark and I could not see too well, I had to rely on my other senses.

There was a strong scent of – . Whatever it was, it appealed to some basic instinct deep inside of me; a need, a craving, a hunger.

Strange, I thought, why the aroma smelled so much like – bacon and eggs.

Bacon and eggs?

"Are you okay, Smitty?" Moon asked.

Before I opened my eyes I just sat still smelling the eggs and bacon and listening to everyone going into the dining room.

I heard Moon repeat, "Are you okay, Smitty?"

I knew I was sitting, because my butt affirmed that I must have been sitting all night. I had gone to sleep sitting in a large wing-backed chair in the library and I had had a dream.

Therefore, there was no Lil, because she was part of the dream.

"Smitty?"

I opened my eyes and Moon was holding a cigarette he'd lit for me…Unusual, because he normally expected me to light his cigarettes. He was actually showing some concern for me.

"Are you okay?" he asked.

"Maybe," I answered, then asked, "Are you okay?"

"Sure," he said. "Why shouldn't I be?"

Well, they'd been trying to kill us both for three months – and almost succeeded many times – and we were in a Flak House to hopefully mend the unknown scars of our minds; and we were going to have to go back into the insanity of combat; and we are asking each other if we were "Okay?"

Agonizingly, I pushed myself out of the chair and onto the floor face down to let my blood recirculate into my numb butt and to stretch my muscles back to life.

"Ohhhh, me." I groaned. "I feel like I've played all four quarters of a football game, going both ways."

"Come on," Moon said. "Let's get some breakfast. Maybe afterwards we can go for a bicycle ride. That ought to make you feel better."

I groaned again and struggled to my feet with Moon helping to stabilize my wobbly legs. My mind felt as shaky as my body.

Not that my mind was failing me, because I knew with certainty that we still had a job to do – and what a terrible job it was.

The good breakfast and companionship of the other guests was enjoyable until we were reminded of the demons that each of us were doing battle with.

John Shea, one of the skeet shooters, was not at breakfast. He'd gone AWOL.

"How could he be Absent Without Leave?" I asked. "Aren't we all on Flak-Leave?"

Well, there was a technicality: On orders we had to sign in, which meant we also had to sign out when we left. Shea had not signed out and was not even due to depart for another week.

So why had he left?

The rumor was that he'd been found at about seven in the morning; eyes open, standing in his bed, relieving himself.

"Into his potty?" I asked.

"No." Milford replied in disgust. "Into his bed!"

The consensus was, therefore, that Shea had left out of embarrassment.

"In any case," Milford said, "He didn't sign out and he's AWOL!"

I left the table, went to the roster at the main entrance, then returned to announce that John Shea's signature was on the Sign Out roster, just above my name.

Milford said, "If you forged his signature, Smitty, you're in big trouble."

"So ground me, Colonel," I responded sarcastically.

Moon asked, since I'd signed out, where I planned on going. I told him that I had some unfinished business in London.

"LONDON, for Christ's sake!" Moon, exclaimed. "That's the target for all of those goddamned buzz bombs! You've gotta be crazy to go to London now."

I finished my breakfast while the others discussed buzz bombs. Their conclusion was that if D-Day had been delayed for a week, there could not have been an invasion, because the buzz bomb blitz, if focused on the points of debarkation, would have destroyed the invasion force...That was how lucky the Allies had been...And that wasn't all...Before the war would end, the Germans would certainly have some other surprises.

I found Shea at the train station as we both departed for London. At first reluctant to talk with me, he did share in his plans to visit London. He'd not been there, except to pass quickly through on his way from his base to the Flak Farm.

Great. If he didn't mind my company too much, I could likely show him around a bit. Maybe we could even get a room at the prestigious Savoy Hotel. I'd never stayed there, but if we could manage it, it would be an improvement over the Flak House.

Having experienced all kinds of difficulty in trying to get accommodations in London on previous visits, I was surprised at the ease of checking into the Savoy.

I asked for a room as close to the ground level as possible, since I had a "phobia of heights." The desk clerk looked at the wings and ribbons on my tunic. He paused, no doubt wondering if I was "having him on," as they say, and assigned us a room on the second floor.

I was surprised at the availability of choice due to the normal shortage of rooms. However, the explanation came in answer to my question to the bellhop, who was showing the way to our room.

"Which way do they come from?" I asked him as we climbed the stairs to the second flight; which the British considered to be the "First Story," since it is the first story above the ground floor.

He knew without clarification that I was asking about the buzz bombs and replied, "You can see 'em coming."

"We don't *want* to see 'em coming!" I responded.

But that was it. That was why it was so easy for us to have gotten a room. We were on the side of the hotel facing the attack of the flying bombs. That entire side of the hotel was probably vacant, except for expendable Yankee airmen.

What a treat it was. The room was extremely large with unbelievable luxury and grandeur. MIRRORS! The walls, and even the high ceiling, were totally covered with mirrors. In scale and detail, everything was dramatized artistically from the crystal chandelier to the golden handles of the doors. One side of the room was entirely covered with a heavy drapery that was more like a magnificent tapestry.

I didn't open it to check the view, which according to the bellboy, overlooked the Thames. However, I did tug on the drapery and guessed that it must weigh several hundred pounds – at a cost of thousands of Pounds Sterling.

Shea produced a bottle of scotch from his travel kit and wanted to celebrate on the spot. I suggested we go out for the best dinner we could find, and if we got lucky, maybe we could go to a stageplay.

Well, it didn't quite work out that way. Maybe it was better?

We couldn't get tickets to the theatre and the best dinner fare seemed to be mutton or fish. I detested both. This was probably because I'd been raised on beef and potatoes back in Oklahoma.

Some of (but not the sum of) the Windmill Girls.

However, Shea and I did find some worthwhile entertainment at the Windmill Theatre. It was vaudeville that did not lack quantity nor quality of near-nude beauty queens.

While it was a variety show of comics and many acts, it was the backgrounds that were so gratifying to behold. Nudity was not forbidden as long as the models did not move. So they were just there posing in the nude. This, of course, beat the hell out of any pinup picture I'd ever seen.

There wasn't a bad body in the bunch. What made them more provocative was their ecstatic poses and their SILENCE – certainly more restful and recuperative than anything offered at the Flak House. I even forgot to remind myself about the war.

I felt really good and relaxed.

Back in our room I was asleep almost before Shea could pour himself a drink.

Ohhh, me. What a wonderful sleep it was, like being lowered into a deep dark well, and I felt so comfortably calm and dreamy.

The dream was that I was going to sleep and, into that second sleep, I started to dream a dream within the first dream...Weird?

I was in a state of knowing whatever there was to know. There were no secrets.

That dream about Lil??? There was no mystery to it. While appearing to have something to do with sex; it was really not about sex, nor had it been a dream about Lil as a person.

The newspaper article about the 18th birthday of Princess Elizabeth that I had read just before falling asleep back at the Flak House had set the scene for that dream. It had mentioned that the Princess had called herself "Lil-bet" when she was a child, because she could not say "Elizabeth."

Even so, the dream was not even about the Princess and me having a relationship. Rather, the dream was a comment on my involvement with being in England and in the war and – my inability to complete my performance.

So within the second dream of a dream, everything was now so clear, because this was where all of the answers were.

However, the problem was not only in knowing just how to reach this degree of understanding, but how to recall it when I awoke. So how was I now able to call such wisdom to consciousness when I was in deep sleep and the recall of dreams came to me only when I was waking up??? Yet – I was *AWAKE!*

Nobody could have slept through it…The sound of the blast was deafening!! I was in the midst of *DANTE'S INFERNO!!!*

At first I could only see BRILLIANT RED!! My body and bed were jolted as if I were in a colossal earthquake. The sound blast almost knocked the breath out of me!

RED! RED!! RED!!!

The color amplified and multiplied from one mirror to the others, crashing into itself!

The heavy tapestry-drapery extended horizontally into the room; held there by the force and persistence of the blast. And when it dropped back in place, there was total darkness.

Wowww, I thought, THAT was a CLOSE ONE!!!

Unlike Moon's experience of the window being blown out, there was no flying glass, because any glass the window had already had been blown out previously.

That's why the Savoy had vacancies on this side of the hotel.

I thought about it for awhile as I listened to the approach and explosions of other buzz bombs echoing up and down the canyon of buildings along the Thames. There were so many bombs coming in that I imagined them flying in formation.

However, I determined that as close as the last bomb had struck, the odds were that any others had to hit farther away. So dismissing it, I hurried to get back into the comfort of deep sleep.

Except, the sound of tinkling glass in the darkness disturbed me.

It was a bottle clinking on a glass and something being poured from it.

"Are you awake, Shea?" I asked.

"Hell yes!!!" he replied and asked, "You want a drink?"

I declined and listened to Shea express his fear of a bomb falling on us: "This is crazy to be here letting this happen to us…I'm going back to the base and get my plane and get up there where I can *see* what's going on!"

So with only a short delay, to make sure he left enough money to pay for his share of four nights lodging, he dressed and left in the middle of the night.

"Here," he said, handing me his bottle of scotch on his way out. "If you stay here, you're going to need this more than I will."

I got up, took a pee and went back to bed, falling into restful sleep immediately.

With the drapery drawn and the darkness in the room, I slept until almost noon, awoke with a great hunger and called room service for breakfast.

This was living.

All I had to do was to look in any direction – even overhead – and watch myself in a mirror enjoying the luxury.

My only regret was that I was alone and didn't have anyone with which to share such good fortune. And while I had been playing the role of a loner to keep from getting hurt from the loss of a friend, it was getting to me. I was *lonesome!*

Wouldn't it be great to have just one of those beautiful girls from the Windmill with me right now. Hmmmm? I wouldn't even have to know her name. In fact it would be better to not know each other. That way nobody would be hurt when I did get shot down or blown up.

So if I had just one of those beauties – *one?* Why just *one???*

Didn't the Air Force have a reputation to uphold?

"Yeah! You fly-boys have it real tough; plenty of money, running around London with a girlie on each arm."

Well, why should I disappoint them, or myself?

I decided that the time had finally come to enjoy myself.

By four in the afternoon, from the audience in the Windmill Theatre, I was shopping the stage for *two* companions.

The menu – no – the *program* identified all of the performers on the stage by name and photograph.

Within an hour I had made my selections and was at the stage door with a note and a generous tip for the doorman.

Would Ruby and Peggy do me the honor of joining me for dining and dancing at the Savoy?

Who could refuse such an offer?

As I paced back and forth on the sidewalk outside of the stage door, I wondered why it took so long for a response. It made me feel uncomfortable. Maybe I was being auditioned and I was sure that they must have consulted the doorman for his opinion of me, this kid from a small town in Oklahoma.

Maybe it was a mistake. Lacking experience, I wasn't qualified to fulfill any expectations of just one girl, let alone two. My self confidence dropped to zero and I regretted having committed trying to bite off more than I could chew.

Another thing that made me uncomfortable and self conscious was the damned hotel key I had in my pocket. It wasn't really the key, but the ball; a bit smaller than a baseball, chained to the key. This was obviously done to encourage leaving the key at the desk of the hotel instead of taking it with you.

Well, I had taken it with me, thinking to save myself the embarrassment of asking the desk clerk for my key in the single company of two girls. Now I was stuck with it – a huge bulge in my pants.

So, shuffling back and forth outside of the stage door, it occurred to me that I was wearing my battle blouse, which did not have a skirt on it to cover me below the waist. There was no way to disguise that fact that I did have a large bulge in my pants.

Here I was, one of those horny American pilots parading outside of the Windmill Theatre with a lump in my pants.

It took quite an effort to grapple for the key-ball-chain in my pocket. It had dropped in easy enough. But with my hand around the ball to retrieve it, the fit was too tight to get both the ball and my hand out of my pocket.

I almost panicked until I was able to get just the key out and then pull the ball out by the chain. And just in time.

The stage door opened and a rather short female wearing a bulky sweater, sunglasses, no makeup and a scarf about her head emerged into the afternoon sunlight.

She was not very attractive and my opinion must have reflected on my face. For as I walked over to her she said, "I'm not what you expected, am I?"

"Wellll?" was all I could say, because she certainly did not look anything like I had seen on the stage.

"I am Peggy."

She was short – shorter off the stage – and in spite of the scarf, I could tell she was a brunette. Peggy was the brunette and Ruby was the tall blond.

"Ruby and I will meet you upstairs in that pub over there across the street within thirty minutes," she said, leaving me juggling my key-chain-ball.

ALL'S BAD THAT STARTS BADLY.

I had a dream…It was a fantasy that was coming to life…A handsome young Air Force officer leaving a pub with a beautiful babe on each arm. It was the stuff that myths are made of. But in reality, what in hell can you do with *two* girls?

There was no doubt that I was in over my head and I felt as awkward and unnecessary as a second nose on my forehead.

Arm in arm – in arm – in arm we strolled toward the Savoy hotel, each girl with a little bag with a change of clothes for an evening out. We had formalized the date in the pub. They would have to change into something more suitable. I offered them my room at the Savoy, so they had stopped at the theatre for whatever they thought was necessary.

I was trying to think of a subject we might discuss to get better acquainted and to brighten our new relationship when Peggy asked, "Are we going to spend the night together?"

Such straightforward honesty caught me totally by surprise. I had no idea what was going to happen. I had never spent a whole night with even one girl. I had never even kissed a girl on the first date.

"Well-l-l, ahhh, maybe not tonight," I mumbled, "Maybe some other night."

"I'm a virgin, you know." Peggy said.

"No, I ah-h-h – didn't know that," I responded.

What else could I say? Why was she telling me this anyway? The fact that Ruby made no comment gave me even more to think about.

I was glad that Shea had left me his bottle of scotch. It gave me something to do while Ruby and Peggy enjoyed refreshing themselves in the regal atmosphere of my *mirrored cube* quarters.

However, I was not a scotch drinker. In fact I was not a drinker. Bourbon and Coke was about the limit of my experience. I had not even acquired a taste for beer. This was okay with me, because bottles and throttles didn't mix, be it in airplanes or automobiles. Alcohol had killed more people in one way or another than all the wars.

Even so, having a drink appeared to be the thing to do while trying to entertain not one, but two young ladies. The part I was trying to play, as a suave, dashing, rakish American combat pilot, demanded a devil-may-care personality. So I gagged myself on the scotch and tried to appear casual, as if I were in my element.

I'd offered the girls a drink when we first entered the room and they had accepted. I apologized that I didn't have any soda or ice; just scotch. However, it made no difference to them. Scotch was fine. They didn't even want any water with it. Just Scotch. How much?

"A half-a-glass would be fine."

My God! A full bottle looked to hold only maybe four full glasses and Shea had used up a fourth of it. At a half-a-glass for each of us, there might be enough for only two drinks each. But then, I knew I wouldn't drink a half-a-glass. Maybe the girls wouldn't either and the bottle could last all night.

Well, that's what I thought until I saw the girls put it down as if it were water and they were dehydrated.

Americans, for the most part, drink to get drunk. From what I'd seen of the British, they just seemed to drink as if it were nourishment. I concluded, therefore, that the bottle would not last the night; and wondered if *I* could last the night.

We socialized with small talk about the big and elegant room. Was it Baroque or Georgian? I didn't know and I didn't care. I could only wonder how I was to perform. What was the game we were playing, anyway?

To be honest, it had to do with sex. I had been attracted to it, but my experience was definitely limited in the sport.

The ultimate purpose of sex was to make babies. This did not interest me in the least. Just the thought of it brought me to my feet and I walked toward the door realizing I was somehow in a trap.

If I didn't mind, the girls would like to bathe before they dressed for dinner.

It was fine with me. Ruby stretched out across the bed with an almost empty glass while Peggy paraded between the bath and her overnight bag disrobing and organizing her affairs as if I weren't present. I returned to my chair and took a sip of scotch.

Ruby curled up on the bed and pulled off her shoes, commenting that she would be next for the bath and wanted to be ready. So as we talked, she casually removed her clothing in stages. What it amounted to was an informal striptease.

How could she do that? I was shy about getting undressed in a barracks with other guys. Group showers made me feel uneasy. Yet these girls were no more self conscious about disrobing than I was in doing a pre-flight inspection.

Well, I could see that this was going to lead to an embarrassing problem, because I was not about to expose myself to one, let alone two females, especially in a *Hall of Mirrors*. While I had fantasized about being with several nude beauties, that was dream stuff. This was real and I knew I couldn't handle it.

I couldn't sleep very well with all of the shooting going on up on the screen of the all-night newsreel cinema where I'd hoped to rest a bit before getting on the train to go back to the base. It was the only thing to do, since I was out of money.

I had taken the two girls to dinner in the Savoy. Besides dinner there had been dancing. But unable to dance with both of them at the same time, I realized that I had exceeded my level of competency. So after dinner I told them to go up to the room and that I would be up later.

However, I never made it up to the room. Instead, I paid for everything, including the night's lodging and I asked the clerk to make sure to not disturb until noon. He responded with a smile and a tick of his eyebrows, assuring me that I would not be interrupted.

It might have baffled him to watch me leave the hotel. I didn't really know, because I didn't look back. I didn't even bother to pick up my toiletry kit. It could be replaced.

The myth about "You Air Force guys with a gal on each arm and plenty of money" wasn't as great as it sounded. I was broke, if not broken, and it was time to go back to work.

MISSION # 29
Sautrescourt, France, 6 July 1944
Thursday: 13 ships up   (4:30 Flying Time)
Target: Airdrome

Dyer did not fly the left waist gun position for us, because he was dead.

While the crew had gone on flak-leave, Dyer had volunteered for some extra missions, because he had fallen behind the rest of us when he had broken his arm riding a bicycle. By flying the extra missions, he could catch up with the rest of us in order for everyone to complete his tour of combat at the same time.

We were told that he had died of anoxia. It had been during a fighter attack when the right waist gunner saw Dyer fall to the floor without his oxygen mask on his face. So the right waist gunner quickly placed Dyer's mask onto his face and helped him get back up to his feet and onto his gun.

Just a bit later the right waist gunner again noticed that Dyer was back on the deck without his mask. Due to the intensity of the battle, he didn't know how long Dyer had been unconscious. But then, it made no difference, because Dyer was dead.

It was Thursday the sixth of July, thirty days after D-Day , when we went to Sautrescourt, France.

Almost a million Allied troops and 177,000 vehicles had been landed on the Continent by then. Our mission as bombers was to support the the ground forces by overflying the line of battle and destroying the German's overwhelming advantages, such as supplies, airfields and aircraft.

It was a good feeling to be sustaining the troops on the ground after fighting the war by ourselves so far behind the enemy lines without any obvious results. It finally felt like we were accomplishing something.

Even so, the Germans were still very much in business.

Sometimes there were smiles AFTER a mission.

NOT YET
CHAPTER 14

Dyer's loss was a stern reminder that calamity awaited each of us and that life was only as long as the *PRESENT MOMENT*.

Just where were we at this moment?

We were down to the last half of the final quarter of the most critical contest of our lives. I personally had only six more missions to complete – unless they moved the goal again. If not, I had only six missions left on a 35 mission tour.

So, what was the score?

Since it was like apples to oranges, it was difficult to assess. Collectively, the crew had credit for shooting down seven fighters, three Purple Hearts, and over a hundred other awards and decorations for our efforts in destruction.

The damage against us was also hard to determine, but there was the obvious: Dyer and Rudolfsky were no longer flying with us; Eutrecht sometimes flew, but his personal fitness was being evaluated. Maybe the rest of us should also be assessed, because we all seemed to be losing some of our starch.

Ears was the riddle. Was it booze or bravery that gave him such indifference? While I'd never known him to pass up a drink, he had always been dispassionate about any crisis, even in times of sobriety. It was his character to be nonchalant and blase. And while he gave the impression that the only time he was sober was when he was on oxygen and somebody was shooting at us, it could have been an act, because he remained unflappable even in the killing field.

Moon also was a bit of a mystery, because he never revealed any of the terror that had to be within each of us at times. He never panicked nor hinted that he had a breaking point. But then, like the rest of us, he kept his true feelings from surfacing.

Moon reported to Sick Call before the next mission, since he had a head cold and was having trouble with his sinuses. So with him out of action, Burnell and I were assigned to fly with 1st Lt. George M. Jacobsen. Or was it the other way around?

This was one of those missions for the combat-experienced to check out the inexperienced.

However, it was a break with standard operating procedure, because I was made the Instructor Pilot. And, even though I was outranked, I was the Pilot in Command.

While it struck me as odd that I was the Check Pilot when I hadn't yet even been checked out as a First Pilot, my combat experience evidently counted for a great deal. In any case, the outcome should prove interesting.

MISSION # 30
Conchise, France, 8 July 1944
Saturday   (6:00 Flying Time)
Target: Airdrome

We did bomb the airdrome at Conchise, but only because all other targets under consideration were destroyed before we got to them. This accounted for a six hour mission that could have taken less time had we known to go straight to it.

Thus, for the time being, the focus was more on the tactical destruction of targets that could be used against the Allied invasion rather than in our designed role of strategic bombing.

In other words, we were helping out the ground forces, because it had been a month since D-Day and the invasion of Europe was not moving as well as hoped for.

While the American forces had taken all of the Cherbourg peninsula, Field Marshal Montgomery was unable to move his troops more than 20 miles.

Over a month after the invasion Monty was still hung up around Caen, despite the help of the French Resistance, the saturation bombing of the RAF, and even our help in shutting down the Luftwaffe.

It appeared that the boastful Field Marshal Montgomery, who wanted to be the first in victories, was not up to his bragging. And despite his route being the shortest to Paris, Monty was not able to pull it off despite his smug optimism.

But then, our mission for the day was also taking too long.

On the way to the target I noticed that, for some unknown reason, the flow-rate of Jacobsen's oxygen was not normal. He was using it up too fast. I warned him to keep an eye on it. I even warned him a second time. So it should not have been a surprise when, after leaving the target and while I was flying, that Jacobsen passed out from a lack of oxygen.

As soon as he folded over and hung down between us, I called for Burnell in the top turret to, "Get this guy some oxygen!"

I couldn't take my attention away from flying formation. That was my job: FLY THE AIRPLANE *FIRST*. Besides, I already knew Jacobsen's problem and its solution: oxygen. I'd seen it coming – and I'd warned him – twice!

So while Burnell got him hooked up to a spare oxygen hose, I did the flying and swore at Jacobsen. Not that he could hear me, even if he was conscious, since the atmosphere was too thin to carry the sound of voice. I could have pushed my mike button and reprimanded him over the intercom, but it would have shaken up the crew. So I simply shouted into my oxygen mask.

"YOU DUMB SON OF A BITCH!!! YOU ASS HOLE!! You're supposed to be the commander of this crew and you can't even take care of YOURSELF! You've got SHIT FOR BRAINS! You haven't even STARTED to fly combat, and you pull a dumb stunt like that? You ain't gonna make it buddy when it comes to the REAL nut-cuttin' unless you get with the program! What do you think this is? Some kind of pleasure cruise? PEOPLE DIE UP HERE!!! There's a goddamned WAR going on! Get your head out of your ass and pay attention, or you're gonna get somebody HURT!"

I was mad as hell!

Too bad he didn't hear me.

At least I'd released some tension for myself.

Dumb bastard – I'd warned him twice.

As soon as the oxygen started to bring him back to consciousness I forced him back onto the "horse" that had just thrown him.

"You've got it!" I said, giving him the controls to make him fly. I knew he was confused and worried – if not scared.

Good! Hopefully it was a lesson he wouldn't forget. I'd go over it again with him when we got back on the ground – if we made it.

He didn't screw up again until we got back over England.

Clouds awaited our return. So in group formation we let down, following on each other's wing in formation: into the clouds, into the clear, into the clouds, and so on. Finally Jacobsen lost it! That is, he lost contact with the ship on which we were flying!

Anticipating that this would happen, I grabbed the controls and pushed forward into a 1,000 feet a minute descent. Our Group was letting down at 500 feet a minute. Either we had to let down at a faster or slower rate, because it was too dangerous to try and stay amidst thirty-two other unseen B-17's inside of the same cloud.

"*TAKE IT UP! TAKE IT UP! TAKE IT UP!*" someone yelled on the intercom!

Immediately I pulled back and banked to the left – as a guess as to where the Group would *not* be – added power, and started a climb.

It was the navigator who had taken my advice to the crew that it was more important to communicate information than to make identification. I had also told them to learn to recognize each other's voice to eliminate the delay in identification.

Even so, having first acted on the warning, I then requested clarification and learned that it was the navigator who had called. He reported that the bombardier had started screaming with pain when we had descended, because his sinuses and ears would not clear.

Fortunately we broke out and I was able to circle around and around in the clear while the bombardier worked on trying to get his ears pressurized.

He was a human altimeter. When I very slowly descended he would start yelling at 12,000 feet and I would pull back up. No matter how slowly we lowered, he could not take the pain below 12,000 feet and I personally knew how excruciating that could be.

As difficult as it can be in life to push yourself to succeed, there are many times when it is better (even though it can be even more difficult) to stop pushing and to just *slow down*, or even *stop*, if that is possible.

Well, we could hardly stop and park on a cloud, but we could take a pause before descending to the base. At least for awhile we could do that within the limitation of our fuel. And even though we were supposed to be on oxygen above 10,000 feet, we weren't in any real danger without it at 12,000 feet. So we took a time out. Being late would even keep us out of the traffic congestion back home. Even so, patience is not easy.

However, after orbiting for forty-five minutes and just waiting, without success, for the ears of the bombardier to improve, reduced fuel and worsening weather finally pushed me to resolve the problem. There were no options; we had to go down!

I relayed my decision to the crew and advised the navigator to help the bombardier hold his head on, because we were going to "DO IT"!

There was a chance that both of the bombardier's ears could cave in and rupture, so I would not prolong the agony. Maybe a swift change in airpressure would even help; for going at it slowly had certainly not worked.

At 2,000 feet a minute – and not exceeding the red-line – the dive lasted four minutes. And fortunately I was right. It didn't burst his ear drums.

"He's doing just fine," the navigator reported.

"Good." I replied. "Give me a QDM (heading) to base."

"I'll work one up," he replied.

"Work one up?" I questioned. Ears would not have said that he would "work one up." He would already have a heading for home and would have responded immediately…Of course he would probably be making corrections all along the way, but Ears would have us going in the general direction of home and not wasting time to "work one up."

I knew the navigator had been distracted by the bombardier's problem, but I admonished him, reminding him that it was his job to know where he was at all times and that it was his duty and not a Constitutional RIGHT for him to know!

"I don't want any excuses or conversation," I told him. "You'd better give me a QDM to base! RIGHT NOW!"

"Yes, Sir!" he snapped. "Steer one-two-zero."

"GUESS AGAIN YOU DUMMY!" I boomed back at him.

I could see Ipswitch just north of us. Our base was to the north and west of Ipswitch and not 120 degrees to the southeast in the exact opposite direction. So I knew what mistake the navigator had made.

He had figured out where we were alright, and he had even plotted the course back to base correctly; but under the strain of his first combat mission he had given me the reverse heading, which would have taken us right back over the Continent.

So in order for him not to repeat such a grave error, I leaned on him.

"You gave me a RECIPROCAL!" I scolded. "Do you know where that would have taken us?"

I could imagine his surprise, confusion and embarrassment – if not also his feeling of incompetence and fear for having made such a fundamental error and the realization of its disastrous outcome had I followed his direction.

"You don't really want us to go back to the Continent this evening, do you?" I asked sarcastically, knowing that he was probably seeing that the reverse heading would have put us over Calais, France.

"No, Sir," he replied.

I left him alone to figure it out.

I didn't need a navigator to find my way home from Ipswitch. That wasn't the problem. The main concern was avoiding the barrage balloons around Ipswitch.

With the coming of the buzz-bombs there were more barrage balloons. These ominous "creatures," like giant prehistoric behemoths, were tethered by cables to the earth; and on the cables were explosive charges, which could not tell the difference between a Flying Bomb or a Flying Fortress. And to make it more difficult, the balloons were flown in the clouds. That way you could not see them, nor could you see the cable with explosives, until it was too late to avoid them.

For the benefit of Jacobsen and his navigator, I told them to avoid Ipswitch and its barrage balloons. Such information was not always covered in briefings and depended on experience and word-of-mouth.

The reason I didn't need a navigator to get home was that once I got north of Ipswitch, all I had to do was to follow the "iron compass." The railroad tracks running north out of Ipswitch marked the course. By taking the spur to the west, it led directly to our home station of Great Ashfield.

On Tuesday evening, the 11th of May, there was a dance at the Officers Club, for no apparent reason other than they must have been able to recruit some females to dance with. And as usual, there were more guys than gals, which resulted in more drinking than dancing.

I arrived late. Which is to say, most everyone was ahead of me and well into their cups. This always added to my enjoyment, since drunken behavior can be entertaining if it doesn't go too far.

Well, Ears and McDonald from our billet – while they were already pretty far gone – weren't really getting anywhere. None of the girls wanted to dance with them. In fact, a girl that McDonald had his sights on tried everything to stay away from him. It amounted to a very funny game of hide-and-seek.

Finally, out of desperation, and almost caught by McDonald, the girl avoided the encounter by side-stepping into the ladies room.

McDonald relaxed against the door frame and waited.

He waited and waited, and I waited and waited to see what would happen when she reappeared. But, she didn't. She must have been in there almost a half an hour. It became apparent that she was not going to come out of the ladies room until McDonald left.

The idea must have also occurred to McDonald, because his shoulder eventually slipped off of the door frame and his body and feet followed his shoulder straight away into the Ladies Room.

Screams announced his presence!

Screams also brought the Provost Marshal, who dispatched two Military Police from the entrance of the club into the ladies room to retrieve McDonald.

Ears confronted the Major and the two MP's who were carrying McDonald out of the club. Ears told the Major that he and the MP's had *no right* to remove McDonald from the club.

Wrong…They also took Ears with them.

Both Ears and McDonald were kept in the Provost Marshal's office for the night to "sleep it off." It was decided that they should not be charged or officially be put into the brig. As such, they didn't have a bed to sleep in and tried to rest for a couple of hours on the floor.

Prior to D-Day almost everyone on the base had been armed, because nobody really knew what the consequences would be. Even in November of 1943, seven months prior, the Germans had landed paratroopers in England. It was thought that they would try it again when we invaded the Continent.

Therefore, from time to time announcements were made over the P.A. , called the Tannoy, that the base was under a "Yellow Alert." A Red alert would signal that the Germans were bringing the war to us.

All of this came to mind when I had left the club and went back to the billet alone to try and get some rest after McDonald and Ears had been taken into custody. After all, they had been the star performers and anything else would be anticlimactic.

I was in my bunk, staring into the dark and trying to recall when I had last heard a Yellow Alert, when the door at the far end of the billet slowly opened. A figure in silhouette appeared and just stood there.

If it was one of us, he would turn on the lights, but he didn't.

I reached over and unholstered my .45 that hung on my chair. It was always loaded and I carried an extra round in the chamber.

Quietly I slipped the safety off and pointed it at the figure that was starting to move slowly toward Baumersbach's bunk. And as it bent down over the bed I said, "You'd better say something, and it had better sound American."

"Whoozzatt?? Smitty?? It's me – Baumersbach."

He was *bombed* and there was vengeance in his sloshed mind, because he had come for his .45 and was going to "find that goddamned Provost Marshal an' shoot the sonovabitch for lockin' up Ears an' Mac."

"Well, don't stay out too late," I told him. "We're probably going to have to go on a mission in a couple of hours."

I worried about it for a little while until I heard what had to have been Baumersbach firing every round of his .45 from what sounded like the middle of the wheat field between the club and our billet. He wasn't going to hurt anybody out there.

After the time it took him to stagger back from the field, the far door of the billet opened again and Baumersbach announced himself.

"Smitty?"

"Yeah."

"The sonovabitch got away from me," he said. "I missed him."

"Good night." I said.

"Good night, Smitty."

MISSION # 31
Munich, Germany, 12 July 1944
Wednesday: 42 ships up, two down. (9:30 Flying Time)

A tailwind got us down to Bavaria early. The bad part of it was that we would have to eat up the time gained, because each group had to be over the target and drop at a specific time. If not, they would be dropping onto and through each other.

Our course was to pass north of Munich from west to east. Then, northeast of Munich we were to fly south until we were east of Munich, where we would turn onto the I.P. and make our bomb run from Initial Point from east to west.

In order to get back on schedule we flew a zig-zag time-turn while north of Munich. This "dog-leg" along the way would kill some time. This it did – and more.

Captain White's ship was above McDonald's in the turn. They should not have gotten into such a relationship. Maybe McDonald, short of sleep, might have been late in reacting to the turn. But in any case, it was a no-no situation.

It was not clear whether McDonald pulled up into White or whether White had dropped down onto McDonald. All we saw was that they collided and locked into each other for a moment. Then

Formation flying.

McDonald's ship broke half in two and the two ships and their separate parts spun and twisted downward.

Out of the twenty men in both ships, I saw no chutes.

On our return, Captain Stern, our Squadron Executive Officer, asked us to go through the belongings of our billet mates: Pilot McDonald; Copilot Ryan; Navigator Henry and Bombardier Chrisman, to make sure there was nothing in their personal effects that would cause embarrassment to their families. The government would retrieve all G.I. property for salvage and anything else would be destroyed.

It was an unwelcome task, so we spent some time just sitting and thinking and remembering our mates.

Finally, Moon stood up and said, "I'm out of cigarettes."

He walked over to McDonald's bunk and said, "Well, they won't need these anymore," tossed me a carton and kept a carton.

Ears and Eut joined us as we collected their stuff.

McDonald had left his A-2 flight jacket and it was in better shape than mine, so I asked Moon what he thought.

"It'll go to salvage," he said. "Keep it if you want it."

Without much rest, we were briefed for a return to Munich the very next morning. It would be the third day in a row to the same target and well rehearsed – for the German flak gunners.

MISSION # XX
Munich, Germany, 13 July 1944
Thursday: 32 ships up, one down. (4:00 Flying Time)
Turner and crew missing in action.

What was to have been MISSION #32 to Munich did not work out for us. Which is not to say that it didn't provide some excitement, because the weather was definitely not good for flying.

While most of our takeoffs were in the dark, today was different. All times had been pushed back to allow the bad weather to move out, but it didn't.

With clouds hanging very low and the heavy humidity, which was close to putting everything inside of a cloud, the decision was made to go for it. After all, Munich was far away and in eight or nine hours when we returned the field "should" be open.

WOOOMM-WOOOMM-WOOOM-WOOOM – Our four 1200 horsepower Wright Cyclone engines slowly developed their full potential as we opened the throttles, the sound of them beating against each other in search of synchrony.

In the strange light of morning the four huge propellers cut circles of water vapor from the saturated air…It was an exciting sight to behold. The normal invisible air was transformed into white discs of moisture, auguring themselves farther apart as we accelerated down the runway.

Every thirty seconds this drama was repeated as thirty-two B-17's followed each other into the air from Great Ashfield. Then thousands more duplicated the performance across East Anglia. Being a part of such a force was a very emotional experience. It cast a spell and was an experience not to be forgotten.

I felt that this was a special time in our world's history and was pleased to be a part of it. What a phenomenon it was! But as awesome and thrilling as it was, I hoped there would never be a need for it to happen again…

But what about that spray of gasoline coming from the top of our right wing? The fuel cap had not been secured!

I recalled a pilot telling how it had happened to him in the States. That the fuel had somehow become ignited and he had run a hell of race with a ball of fire chasing him at 160 mph for hours!

I naturally called the fuel leak to Moon's attention.

We were into the clouds in trail at 30 second intervals with 32 others on our way to the radio Buncher beacon. It was hardly possible to turn back against the stream of traffic.

Yet, there was no point in going with the Group, because our fuel was siphoning out and we wouldn't have enough to make the trip.

What to do?

When we eventually broke out of the top of the clouds into the bright morning sunlight, we notified Hotshot Yellow that we had to abort because our fuel was siphoning out.

That done, we turned east to get over the North Sea and away from all of the traffic over England.

Our plan was to burn up enough fuel so that any fuel left in that tank could be transferred to the other fuel cells. After which, we would then try to figure out how we were going to get back down through the weather and land.

It was back to that old game of *Patience*.

No problem, we had four good engines, nobody shooting at us, and we could spend the day flying around until the weather cleared.

Okay…I called our radio operator and asked if he could get us a good radio program to help us while away the time and noticed that – *THERE WAS NO OIL PRESSURE ON # 2 ENGINE!!!*

Son of a bitch. I alerted Moon as I automatically hit the #2 feather button.

Too late! Whenever the oil level dropped below the standpipe in the engine, the propeller would not feather…And it didn't!

The sooner we got down the better, because one of two things would definitely happen: without oil the dry engine, still being driven by a "windmilling" propeller (metal against metal) would start to melt. This would cause the engine to seize and lock up. The other liability was that the prop would break loose and possibly fly into the ship, or even *cut through the cockpit*.

I called "Hardlife" to declare an emergency and requested "Landing Advisory."

"Sorry to advise, Alfrek 'C' Charley, the field is now closed."

Now, that's not exactly what I wanted to hear.

Here we were with a broken airplane that weighed more than a furnished two story house and we had to set it down someplace – the sooner the better.

I demanded that Hardlife give me some advice!

"'C' Charley, you might contact 'Chair-Leg.'"

Who in Hell was 'Chair-Leg'?

"Hardlife, this is 'C' Charley. Give me a frequency for 'Chair-Leg,' please."

I got it and called 'Chair-Leg,' but they were also below minimum landing conditions. In fact, they advised that all of England was socked in!

Did they have any suggestions?

No.

The #2 engine reminded us that it would soon come apart or weld itself together, because it started jerking violently on its mounts. Best we stay in clear air over the sea and keep close to the shoreline, because we didn't know if, or how long, we would have an airplane to fly.

"Get ready, Smitty," Moon said, "If that prop comes off, I'm gonna say, 'Smitty, you've got it!'"

I replied, "If you say, 'Smitty' you'll be talkin' to *yourself*, cause, I ain't gonna be here!"

It was obvious that something was about to happen, because the vibration of the engine had compounded itself into a savage buffeting.

Moon had difficulty holding the controls and my assistance made no difference. The plane was flying us. The instrument panel was jumping so vigorously that the instruments could not be read. Then – ?

Instantly, there was no more vibration. The fight was over.

The prop did not windmill. The metal in the engine was welded tightly and the prop had not been thrown off and into our laps.

Thank God!

We were low enough to not be wearing oxygen masks. My nose was running and when I wiped it on my sleeve, Moon chuckled and said,"That sure was a snot-shaker, wasn't it?"

I smiled back at him and asked, "Okay, what's next?"

He lost his smile, looked out at the clouds over England, looked back at me and gave a thumb-down.

With a heavy load of bombs, an engine out, not feathered and creating a lot of drag, we dropped down to sea level, then pumped ourselves back up a couple of notches to 200 feet and headed inland.

Ears gave us a QDM to base. Our penetration was into cloud scuds, so Moon had to drop us a little lower to maintain visual contact with the ground. We would be "scud-running" at less than 150 feet altitude between cloud scuds.

I checked with Moon and ordered everyone into the radio room to *"PREPARE FOR CRASH LANDING"*!

As often as we had practiced this low level "shit" and were as good at it as we were, it was dangerous! Any chance of success depended on both skill and a hell of a lot of luck.

While we had received no formal training in "hedgehopping," if there had even been such a course for B-17's, Moon and I had developed our own routine: Moon would fly instruments, the same as if he were flying at thousands of feet higher, while I would fly visual contact with the ground.

This was a critical and a very risky game of I'll-Pull-You-Push – and visa versa. It was two human nervous systems interlocked as one in total harmony. Any conflict of action or reaction – within a fraction of a second – could result in disaster.

The truth was, neither one of us were in full-time total control; yet taking full control, and giving it up, depended on everchanging circumstances. It took guts, sensitivity, strength and complete confidence in each other. No bond could have been stronger.

On instruments, Moon flew the heading toward the base, given to him by Ears.

The sails of a classic Dutch-like windmill reached for us out of the scuds!

I heaved back on the controls and lifted up our right wing!

We missed it. I turned loose and Moon had us back on course and in level flight.

CHRIST!!! A church steeple!

I missed it also.

My faith told me that, if Jesus had a say in the matter, they wouldn't have built that goddamned steeple where somebody might fly into it.

And so it went: steeples, buildings, barns and even tilting at windmills. We were crazy, but alive – so far. But, where was our base?

It was said that you could fly three minutes in any direction in East Anglia and find an airbase…Not so. We'd been beating the weeds and bushes for almost an hour and not a single airport. But then, we couldn't see more than a mile away.

"AIRFIELD!" I yelled and Moon banked left in a standard rate turn. Within 120 seconds we would be back over the same spot, without any wind. There was no wind to worry about, since the air was stagnant.

Moon called for: "High RPM. One-Third Flaps. Give Me WHEELS!"

He was going to try for it, even with the weather well below minimum standards.

However for us, there were no standards, because we were already less than 200 feet. The standard traffic pattern was four times higher and we couldn't even maintain visual contact where we were. It was getting worse and raining, but –"THERE!" I said, pointing to our left.

Moon finally left the instruments, looked left and tightened the bank to make it fit. Many pilots in other aircraft had crashed from a high speed stall under such circumstances, but few pilots were strong enough to force a Seventeen into such a stall.

I helped him roll it out level so we wouldn't catch a wing and "KISS-KISS" – the wheels contacted the runway.

It wasn't our base, but we didn't care. We were safely on the ground. Transportation was arranged. We left the ship there and a truck took us all back home in time for lunch.

The rest of the crew talked excitedly all the way back to base. Theirs had been a different experience.

Prepared for a crash landing, their positions were in the radio room where they sat between each other's legs in a line facing toward the rear of the ship.

Hill, being the tail-gunner was the last one in the row. Sitting there he faced the heavy emergency cranks snapped to the bulkhead; which he removed, because he didn't want them to come loose and hit him in the head if we impacted in a crash.

Ears had been frustrated, because he was unable to do his job of navigating. "After all," he claimed, as he always did, "I'm the navigator and I have a right to know where we are at all times."

It was a joke, because none of us had known where we were.

The humor faded and Eutrecht spoke heartfelt for the crew about how they had always owed their lives to "Moon and Smitty" since we had become a crew. It was not a prepared speech – more emotional than polished and a bit embarrassing. He ended by saying, "I would go to Hell and back any time with Moon and Smitty!"

Everyone echoed with "HERE! HERE!" and Moon responded that we felt the same way about our crew.

That's what made even the *WRONG STUFF* work. I would call it "Crew Glue." Other crews felt the same about their own. And with the ground troops, they too must have had the same bond within a squad.

I had heard that even kidnappers and their hostages bonded when they shared a life-threatening experience…So strange that people could bond, regardless of religion, race culture or nationality, out of sharing in a struggle for their lives.

Word was that a Luftwaffe pilot had bailed out over England and remained hidden for three days until he could turn himself in to an American airbase. That while waiting to be picked up and interned by the authorities, the pilots on the base had taken him to the club, where they all got drunk. When he was taken away, there were tears in the eyes of some of the Americans.

Likewise, we had all heard how the Luftwaffe had rescued American flyers from hostile German civilians, as well as the Nazi SS.

There was not only togetherness among crew members, but among crews, billets, squadrons, groups, and – God Bless it – the United States of America.

Sure, there was patriotism, but what it really came down to was fighting for survival of Self and your buddies – sometimes in reverse order.

I had gone to sleep on my bunk after lunch and awoke to hear Captain Stern talking with Moon, Ears and Eut. He was asking us to go through personal effects of those shot down.

We'd already done that yesterday.

"No," Moon said when Stern left. "Turner and his crew didn't make it back today."

That meant eight billet-mates had gone down since yesterday morning: one-third of us wiped out in two days.

Oh, well, it was only a matter of time. I knew that, didn't I. The only thing I could recall from the address at the graduation of our pilot class was that only three percent of us were expected to survive the war. That would be 291 of us killed out of the class of 300. But then, those were just words spoken eight months before – so long, long ago.

"We looked to the south and saw hundreds of earthen fountains playing skywards."
This picture of American bombs bursting on German lines in the big push near St. Lo
was the last one taken by G. Bede Irvin, an American war photographer for the Associated
Press, before he was killed instantly by a bomb fragment.
(Reprinted from YANK, the Army Weekly).

BREAKDOWNS
CHAPTER 15

McDonald's crew went down on Wednesday, the 12th of July. Turner's crew went down on Thursday. It was Friday at 2 a.m. when Sgt. Gatt woke us all and Lt. Borns, a relative newcomer who bunked at the far end of our billet with his crew, and called to us, "Good morning *other* crew."

By 3:30 a.m. we were filing in for our briefing and the Squadron Commanders were identifying each of us personally again. Would it mean another trip back to Southern France?

Major Tesla identified me as one of his and said, "Smith, you're out of uniform. You're not even wearing any rank! Just what the hell are you, anyway?

"Second Lieutenant, Sir. ," I answered, turning up the neck of my unofficial Red Cross turtleneck sweater to reveal my rank and Air Force insignia pinned on the underside of the collar.

"They'll shoot you as a spy," he said.

"Not if I see them first."

I was ready and determined to survive.

My cap looked to have a hundred missions on it – oil stains, crumpled, and soft from use and abuse. It looked more like it belonged to a Nazi "U" Boat commander. I could throw it away if necessary and temporarily pass as a civilian, because beneath the sweater I also wore a civilian shirt that I had kept after getting the "civilian" bailout pictures taken, which we carried to avoid capture.

It was summertime and I could get by wearing my short A-2 leather jacket unless it was to be a real high-altitude flight. I would decide after the briefing what best to wear.

I still carried two pistols: a .45 Colt automatic on my hip in a custom-made holster I had fashioned myself, and a smaller caliber pistol under my armpit, which would leave me armed even after I might have to surrender my standard weapon. I figured that, if necessary, I could always throw my weapons away. But if I didn't have them to start with, there was no way to get them from out of thin air.

I kept my old civilian hunting knife very sharp in case I had to cut the shroud lines of my parachute in a hurry, should I land in water, or other emergencies. In my pocket I carried a light switchblade that had a six inch blade. It was long enough, according to an undertaker friend of mine back home who had instructed me on its effective use.

Concealed on the back of my hip holster was a stiletto, which was more like an ice pick.

I also had one more weapon. It was my throwing knife.

Moon was somehow amused that Herby Hill and I spent endless hours practicing with throwing-knives. It was a hobby that I had acquired as a kid; along with bullwhip cracking and trick roping. My dad had even paid for my roping lessons from the Shultz kids, who were rodeo and show performers.

Well, Herby and I had developed our own performance of knife throwing. While I could even throw and hit a target with a machete, our real speciality was taking turns throwing the smaller knives at each other – outlining our bodies – since we could accurately hit where we aimed.

"You guys are crazy," Moon would say, but I silently disagreed. If dropping bombs and having flak thrown back was considered normal behavior, why should throwing knives be crazy?

MISSION #32
"Cadillac," France, 14 July 1944
Friday: 36 ships up.   (10:35 Flying Time)
Target: Arms-drop to Maquis in Southern France.

Among the risks to life were: flak, fighters, the Nazi SS, enraged civilians, sub-zero temperatures, anoxia, loss of self control, fatigue, mid-air collisions, mechanical malfunctions, lack of fuel, and – the Alps!

The target made it a long mission behind enemy lines, south of Grenoble, France, and into the foot-mountains of the Alps, in a valley that was above 10,000 feet!

Now, I had seen some astounding feats of airmanship at airshows that demonstrated exceptional skill and daring do, but we were undertaking a bold venture ourselves that had never before been attempted and it was in no way less challenging.

The task was more like attempting to pass a camel through the eye of a needle by flying thirty-six Flying Fortresses up what was a dead-end canyon, depending on the altitude flown.

The canyon consisted of mountains high above us on either side. At the far end of the canyon was a solid wall on the top of which was a level field, or "table top," at 11,500 feet. This was the drop zone.

Once into the canyon, each ship in the group was committed because there was not enough room to make a turn back toward the entrance and escape. The only way out was straight ahead and over the drop zone, and hopefully not into the immovable wall.

The scary part was that, from where I sat, it did not appear that we were high enough to clear the wall!

We had been briefed that qualified personnel were on the ground and that they would transmit the correct barometric pressure that would give us an accurate altimeter setting.

So, what it amounted to was that we were staking 360 lives on the word of someone who someone else had said was qualified to bring us effectively and safely over the drop zone.

Except, my perception was that we were flying straight toward a stone wall in the midst of thirty-six four engine bombers and it did not appear to me that we were high enough to clear the wall!

It was different. No flak or fighters. Yet, it was still fearful. Some misjudgment in establishing the proper altitude, the propwash, midair collisions, or a loss of power from any of 144 engines would get somebody hurt in a big way – in a remote place where there was no help.

Therefore, it was a great relief when we all skimmed over the lip of the mesa between the towering peaks and dropped our cargo to the Free French Forces of the Interior.

Our success was worthy of celebration when we returned and there was much festivity at the club after dinner. Wouldn't it be great if all the remaining missions would be that rewarding? After all, I had only three more missions left to finish my tour.

I finally got to my billet at around nine-thirty and met the replacement crew for McDonald's crew. They were tired from their travels and were already going to bed in the bunks that were still "warm." I, too, was tired and went to bed, dropping off to sleep without a problem.

Moon woke me briefly when he came in and turned on the light. He was sloshed and wearing the cap of the RAF Wing Commander who had briefed us in the morning and had remained on base to join in the festivities.

How Moon had come by the cap I didn't ask, but tried to get back to sleep despite the fact that he wouldn't turn out the light. He was in a good mood, singing, and disrobing like a strip-tease dancer, peeling off everything except his socks, long underwear, and the Wing Commander's cap.

Dammit, Moon flopped face down on his bunk and passed out, leaving the light on and me wide awake.

Some of the replacements rustled around a bit and started snoring. So while I lay there thinking that it might help me to go back to sleep if I made the effort to get up and turn the light out, Colonel Vandevanter entered the billet with the bare-headed Wing Commander in search of his cap.

They found it on the floor where it had fallen when Moon had slammed into bed. They retrieved it and left without any endeavor to reprimand Moon and without turning off the light.

I was damned if I was going to turn it out either.

I don't recall going to sleep, but my waking up was shocking.

"BAIL OUT!! BAIL OUT!! WE'RE ON FIRE!! BAIL OUT !!"

It was Moon, standing in bed, eyes wide open, holding his pillow to his chest and yelling at the top of his voice. He had finally come unglued. Or maybe it was just a nightmare. I was no expert.

"Moon! It's me, Smitty! Wake up!"

"Smitty, save the crew! WE'RE ON FIRE!! BAIL OUT!! QUICK!!"

Before I could reach him he bailed out of bed head first, clutching the pillow to his chest like a parachute! His forehead hit the concrete floor, splitting the skin in an ugly gash and knocking him out!

Dammit all to hell anyway!

I was over him and called for the replacements to come and help me, but they didn't come. I knew they weren't sleeping, because their snoring had stopped. Yet, they refused to help. They were probably scared motionless and were wondering what they were getting into.

The only compress I could find to stop the bleeding was one of my handkerchiefs. And as dirty as it was, it did help. However, my big job was to get Moon to the hospital – without any help from the replacements. They wouldn't even leave their bunks!

Surprisingly, Moon regained consciousness rather quickly. I got him to his feet and wrestled him out of the billet to take him to the Orderly Room where the Charge of Quarters could call an ambulance. However, Moon had a different idea and tried to go a separate direction, which took us off the walkway and into the cold mud.

It was cold, because it had been, and still was, raining and we didn't have any shoes on. We were in stocking feet and standing in a mud puddle.

We were as one, because I was holding Moon up with his arm around my neck, as well as struggling to keep the bloody compress on his forehead, but evidently not very well. His eyes were filled with blood and he couldn't see. His blood was all over the both of us.

It was a Halloween scene. Two guys dressed in white long underwear, covered in blood, hanging onto each other and standing in a puddle of mud.

Moon wanted to go "over there," but I wanted to go "this way."

"No," Moon said. "I want to go see the Doc."

"Okay," I said. "You'll see the Doc at the hospital."

"No," Moon insisted. "I know where he lives. Over there. Let's go!"

Well, as we walked in place in the puddle of mud, arguing where we were going, my socks started to come off. So when Moon tried to pull away from me and go for a walk in the blackout, I tripped over the toes of my socks and pulled Moon down with me into the puddle of mud.

It was Trick or Treat when I snapped on the light in the Doc's quarters.

He awoke with a start, seeing two bloody-muddy figures holding onto each other in his doorway.

The Doc pulled his bed covers up under his chin and yelled, "*GET AWAY!! GET OUT OF HERE!!*"

Moon staggered toward him, pulling me along holding the compress to his head, and started to speak, "Doc – ."

"*HALT!!*" exclaimed the Doc. "Don't you take one more step! You're bleeding all over my floor!"

"Yeah, Moon," I said, "We're kinda all muddy too. Let's get outa here."

Moon, still intoxicated and knocked silly from the blow to his head, would not disobey the order to not take "one more step," so he dropped to the floor, taking me with him, and started crawling across the floor toward the Doc, who recoiled on the head of his bed and yelled at me, "*GET HIM OUT OF HERE!! GET HIM TO THE HOSPITAL!!*"

Well, it wasn't exactly easy, since we and the floor were pretty slippery, but I did my best while Moon pleaded.

"Doc, you can ground me, but don't let my crew fly without me. We're all together. We're going to finish together…Even if we don't finish, we'll be together. Keep us together, Doc!"

Eventually I got Moon into the ambulance and I stood in the road as it drove away with Moon's voice fading in the distance.

"SMITTY…Smitty…smitty…"

Moon's voice and the ambulance faded into the dark night.

"Would you like a cup of coffee, Sir?" asked the Corporal who was on duty as the C.Q. , Charge of Quarters, who had called the ambulance for me.

"No thanks," I said. "It might keep me awake."

The whole crew went to see Moon in the hospital the next morning, but he couldn't see us. His eyes were swollen shut and his eyelids were shiny purple-black.

By that afternoon, Captain Vance had me on the flight line to check out as First Pilot, along with a couple of other contenders.

The check-out was simple, but certainly not easy.

"Take it off," Vance said. "Keep it in the pattern."

I did. And when I got to the 800 feet traffic pattern altitude, he feathered and engine and said, "Now land it."

I did.

"Take it off," Vance said

I did. And when we got to pattern altitude, he feathered *two* engines and said, "Now land it."

Well, the ship got rather heavy, but I managed a pretty good landing in spite of it.

"Take it off," Vance said.

Ohhh *SHIT*, I thought, surely he's not going to feather *three* engines on me, but he *did*!

Just as I turned onto the downwind leg in the traffic pattern, Captain Vance feathered three engines and said, "Now, land it."

What in hell did he think I was going to do? Even an empty B-17 will not fly very long with just one engine, and we were only up 800 feet to start with. No question, we would land.

The question was, would there be a runway under us when we met the ground?

What it turned out to be was a race. Could I get it safely back onto the runway before I ran out of altitude and airspeed? Could I even hold it on course? Only the #1 engine, way out on the left wing, was pulling. Everything else – three dead engines and the entire plane – was *drag*.

It was a physical battle, but – to my surprise – *I did it!*

"Congratulations," Vance said. "Your next mission will be as Pilot in Command."

WOW! I'd finally made it. I'd turned twenty years old in January and now, the middle of July, I was the Command Pilot of a B-17 Flying Fortress. I'd come a long way from Piper Cubs just two years ago, thanks to Moon and the war.

The WAR?

Yes, the war had made it possible. But maybe, just maybe, that might not be such a good deal after all.

There was only one possible catch. I had to have a check-ride to update my instrument rating.

My check pilot was 1st Lt. Jacobsen.

That's right, the guy I had checked out on his first combat mission, who in my opinion, had screwed up pretty badly. This was the guy who had passed out on me on the Conches raid and lost the formation in the clouds on our return. Now he was going to check me out on instruments.

Before we started he said, "It seems like you should be checking *me* out."

Although I agreed with him, I didn't say anything, except to myself, which was, "You'd better watch this guy. He can get you into a lot of trouble."

Jacobsen had me lower my seat so I couldn't see out of the cockpit to simulate blind flying. He then tuned the ADF, Automatic Direction Finder, to our Buncher beacon frequency and asked me to show him an instrument takeoff. I did and we climbed toward where the ADF indicated the Buncher to be.

I naturally checked the time we started for the Buncher.

However, the ADF did not signal our passing over the Buncher within the normal time it took to reach it.

I continued a bit longer to allow for a delay by a headwind, but the needle on the ADF still did not signal reaching the Buncher. Something was wrong and I knew what it was.

"Do you know where we are and where we're going to end up?" I asked Jacobsen.

"The Buncher?" he replied with more of a question than a statement, because – . Well, why else would I ask such an obvious question?"

"I'll bet you money, marbles or chalk that we are over the North Sea," I said. "And when the flak starts, it'll be coming up from Dunkirk."

"FLAK?" came his surprised reaction.

I raised my seat, looked down and then pointed for him to look at the ocean between the broken clouds below us. I then banked to the right for him to get a better look and headed us back to England.

Jacobsen was totally confused, and justifiably so. So along the way I explained the puzzle:

(1) He had tuned the Buncher frequency by the numbers.

(2) When the strength meter indicated a signal, he assumed it was the signal from the Buncher.

(3) He had not listened to the signal and identified it as the Buncher.

(4) He did not know that the Germans had bracketed both sides of our Buncher frequency with a stronger signal. Should the tuning be off just a bit, the ADF would point to the stronger German signal.

"Then what happens?" Jacobsen asked.

"Well," I said. "They track with radar and if the 'Spider' catches you in his web, he shoots you down and eats you."

Was there anything else he wanted to know?

By the 21st of July 1944, First Lieutenant George M. Jacobsen and Captain William T. Vance both certified me qualified to fly as Pilot in Command.

The 17th of July 1944 was the start of a lively week –

MONDAY, 17th:
FIELD MARSHAL ROMMEL badly wounded by air attack.
FIRST USE OF NAPALM by USAAF P-38s on Normandy depot.
8th ARMY, crossed the Arno River in Italy.

TUESDAY, 18th:
AMERICANS capture St Lo, France.
BRITISH still fighting around Caen, France.
JAPANESE WAR LORD TOJO, resigns.

WEDNESDAY, 19th:
AMERICANS capture Leghorn, Italy.

THURSDAY, 20th:
HITLER NARROWLY ESCAPES ASSASSINATION.
PRESIDENT ROOSEVELT renominated to run for fourth term.

FRIDAY, 21st:
AMERICANS land on island of Guam in South Pacific.
LT. TRUMAN SMITH (age 20) certified as Pilot in Command.

Moon, still grounded, was able to see after a few days and congratulated me. However the rest of the crew tried to give me a rough time. For with Moon out of commission, I had been given the responsibility as the Aircraft Commander and the crew – according to them in their joviality – had been given the unwanted embarrassment of having an "Old Man" who was not even old enough to vote. In fact I was the youngest guy on the crew.

"Maybe you'd look old enough to be a pilot if you grew a mustache."

I agreed with them, but had to confess that I had tried, but nobody had even noticed it.

"Yeh, Yeh, I see a little hair there," Carmen said.

"Use a pencil," Corky added.

"Right," Burnell made fun. "Like the gals who draw those lines on the back of their legs to make it look like they're wearing stockings that they don't have and can't get."

Well, I didn't have an eyebrow pencil, but when nobody was around, I did try to emphasis the few hairs I had on my upper lip with a regular lead pencil. Puberty was hard to come by.

My first mission as First Pilot came on Monday the 24th of July. I was fortunate to have old *BARBARA "B"* to fly and the old crew to fly with me, except for Eutrecht who had been given some extra time off to recuperate. Evidently he had been evaluated as needing more time to bounce back into "good form," as the British might put it.

Therefore I was given a new "old" bombardier, who might have been just as used-up as Eut. I didn't know. It was not my choice. Nor did I have the choice of a copilot.

Unfortunately, the copilot assigned to me was one of the other two copilots who were trying to qualify when I did. The one who failed the test was the copilot that I got. I was, therefore, as skeptical of his abilities as he was resentful of mine. This, of course, would have to result in a show-down.

OHH OHH...

On the way out of the briefing I saw Major Tesla standing at the back door. I hoped he wouldn't notice me in the crowd. But why not? I was the only one out of uniform, because I was still wearing my comfortable Red Cross hand-knitted turtle-neck sweater, to which he had objected. It was khaki colored, so maybe I would blend in and he wouldn't see me.

A fist knotted the sweater on my chest and it stretched me right over eyeball to eyeball with a scowling Major Tesla.

"Smith!" he said very firmly and paused. It was obvious that he was not happy.

Well, I deserved the hell he was going to give me for ignoring his suggestion to dress like an Air Force officer and not look like a German submarine commander. After all, he was my Squadron Commander and the Officer's Manual said, "The wish or suggestion of a Commander is to be taken as an order."

"Yes, Sir!" I responded as official as I could make it.

"Smith," he said sternly, "You bring that goddamned airplane back today! Do you understand me? That's an ORDER!"

"Yes, Sir," I said and smiled at him.

The hardness and strain in his face softened. He loosened his grip on my sweater, smiled and – making no comment about me being out of uniform – said, "Go break your neck."

The meaning was not lost on me.

Telling me to break my neck was a *blessing* to deceive the God of War. It had come out of superstition and mythology. Theatre people wished each other good luck by saying, "Break a leg." I'd read that Luftwaffe pilots said, "Hals und Bein bruch" (Neck and leg break).

The logic of such deception was to prevent the gods of war or theatre – or whatever – from thinking that mortals had the power to bless each other. Such power belonged only to the gods. If a mortal blessed someone with good fortune, it was an attack against the powers of the god. Therefore, the god would punish the mortal by reversing the blessing...Well, mortals weren't stupid. All you had to do was wish someone "Bad luck" and the gods would reverse it to "Good Luck."

MISSION # 33
St. Lo, France, 24 July 1944
Monday: 42 ships up.　(5:00 Flying Time)
Target: German Infantry South of the St. Lo Road.
Bomb Load: 6,000#'s of 36# AP's (Anti Personnel)

Based on what I had seen of my copilot's abilities, I was reluctant, make that "scared," to let him fly. Even so, after we were formed up into group formation and on our way, and since I was tired from doing all of the flying, I handed the controls over to him.

Now, we were flying off of the right wing of our guide ship, which meant the copilot would be flying cross-cockpit and seeing through my window. This made the job more difficult and somewhat less accurate than for him to look through his own window and fly on a ship to our right. Except, circumstances demanded he look through my window to guide on the ship to our left.

Jesus Christ! He damned near rammed our guide ship and almost stuck our left wing into their right waist window!

I started to grab the controls, but found he'd done it on purpose to scare me in having a go at trying to prove that he was a better pilot than I – when he said, "How do you like *that?*"

I thought, you dumb son-of-a-bitch! If you want to play games with our lives to make a point, you're, by-god, going to have to earn that right.

"*That* is *exactly* the way I like it," I said, "Now, you hold it right in there good and tight-like for the next five hours and I'll be able to get a little rest."

Well, damn it! He wasn't as good or as gutsy as he thought he was...He worked his ass off trying to maintain the level of standard he'd set for himself...That is, I worked his ass off, because every time he tried to relax for a moment I'd remind him to, "Tighten it up! Tighten it up!" – forcing him to try and prove himself.

I knew exactly how difficult his job was and what his mind and muscles were going through. Within five minutes he would be in agony, full of regrets and blaming me for it. Even so, he didn't dare chicken out. Yet, he had an important lesson to learn about eating crow and shrinking his ego. He was lucky to have me as his instructor, because I was really good.

After fifteen minutes by the clock and with four hours and forty-five minutes to go, I told him, "Now, if you happen to get tired, or you figure you can't do it anymore, and want to give up; I'll be glad to take it for you." Then I reminded him, "Go on, and get it back in there." Then I would encourage him that I knew he could do better, because, "You started off real great. Get it back in there! Show me how good you are."

After thirty minutes he was all over the place and no more effective at holding formation than sticking a limp noodle up a wildcat's ass. His depth perception, reflexes and judgment had left him to the degree that he could have caused us a calamity. So I took over.

"You know," I said, knowing he really didn't have too much experience flying formation, "I really did like to fly tight formation for my first thirty missions, or so, but now, well I just enjoy taking it easy."

While the Americans had taken the Cherbourg peninsula and moved as far south as St. Lo, their six weeks advance had been made most difficult by the disadvantage of the terrain, namely the hedgerows that favored the defensive forces of the Germans.

The hedgerows were more than rows of hedges. After centuries of existence, their tangled roots bound each row into solid walls of actual fortifications. And since they were practically impenetrable, it was considered more feasible to go over them than through them.

Therefore, over 3,000 heavy bombers of the Eighth and Ninth Air Forces were armed with 9,000 TONS of small 36 pound Anti Personnel bombs carried in clusters, designed to scatter like the broadcasting of seeds.

The Drop Zone was everything south of the east-west road, west of St. Lo. So we took off, got to the target and were prevented from dropping due to the visual obstruction of clouds.

This meant that we had to bring our bombs back to base and land with them. In so doing, it was understood that everyone would try to make their best landing.

MISSION # 34
St. Lo, France, 25 July 1944
Tuesday: 42 ships up.   (5:45 Flying Time)
Target: German Infantry South of St. Lo Road.
Bomb Load: 6,000#'s of 36# AP's (Anti Personnel) clusters.

War correspondent Ernie Pyle wrote, "…July 25 of the year 1945 will be one of the great historic pinnacles of this war."

He was referring to the "BREAKTHROUGH" of American forces at St. Lo where he observed the action from the ground.

"The first planes of the mass onslaught came over a little before 10 A.M.. They were the fighters and dive bombers. The main road, running crosswise in front of us, was their bomb line. They were to bomb only on the far side of that road. Our kickoff infantry had pulled back a few hundred yards from the near side of the road. Everyone in the area had been given the strictest orders to be in foxholes, for high-level bombers can, and do quite excusably make mistakes...

"Our front lines were marked by long strips of colored cloth laid on the ground, and with colored smoke to guide our airmen during the mass bombing. Dive bombers hit it just right. We stood and watched them barrel nearly straight down out of the sky. They were bombing about a half mile ahead of where we stood. They came in groups, diving from every direction, perfectly timed, one right after another...

"The air was full of sharp and distinct sounds of cracking bombs and the heavy rips of the plane's machine guns and the splitting screams of diving wings. It was all fast and furious, yet distinct.

"And then a new sound droned into our ears, a sound deep and all-encompassing with no notes in it – just a gigantic faraway surge of doomlike sound. It was the heavies. They came from directly behind us. At first they were the merest dots in the sky. We could see clots of them against the far heavens, too tiny to count individually. They came on with a terrible slowness. They came in flights of twelve, three flights to a group and in groups stretched out across the sky. They came in "families" of about seventy planes each. Maybe those gigantic waves were two miles apart, maybe they were ten miles. I don't know. But I do know they came in a constant procession and I thought it would never end. What the Germans must have thought is beyond comprehension.

"The flight across the sky was slow and studied. I've never known a storm, or a machine, or any resolve of man that had about it the aura of such ghastly relentlessness. I had the feeling that even if God had appeared to beseech before them in the sky, with palms outstretched to persuade them back, they would not have had within them the power to turn from their irresistible course...

"The Germans began to shoot heavy, high ack-ack. Great black puffs of it by the score speckled the sky until it was hard to distinguish smoke puffs from planes. And then someone shouted that one of the planes was smoking. Yes, we could all see it. A long faint line of black smoke stretched straight for a mile behind one of them. And as we watched there was a gigantic sweep of flame over the plane. From nose to tail it disappeared in flame, and it slanted slowly down and banked around the sky in great wide curves, this way and that way, as rhythmically and as gracefully as in a slow motion waltz. Then suddenly it seemed to change its mind and it swept upward, steeper and steeper and ever slower until finally it seemed poised motionless on its own black pillar of smoke. And then just as slowly it turned over and dived for the earth – a golden spearhead on the straight black shaft of its own creation – and disappeared behind the treetops. "There's another one smoking – and there's a third one now." Chutes came out of some of the planes. Out of some came no chutes at all. One of white silk caught on the tail of a plane. Men with binoculars could see him fight to get loose until flames swept over him, and then a tiny black dot fell through space, alone.

"And all that time the great flat ceiling of the sky was roofed by all the other planes that didn't go down, plowing their way forward as if there were no turmoil in the world. Nothing deviated them by the slightest. They stalked on, slowly and with a dreadful pall of sound, as though they were seeing only something at a great distance and nothing existed between. God, how we admired those men up there and sickened for the ones who fell…

"Then fate stepped in and all Hell broke loose onto the ones on the ground, because a gentle breeze blew the smoke back over the St. Lo road that marked the beginning of the drop zone – and the American bombs began to fall on American troops. It's called

"Friendly Fire" but it is a friend only to death. Several hundred American troops were killed."

I didn't know this at the time, because I had my own problems. First off, I had told my copilot that I would do all of the flying as long as I was able and his only job was to watch the oil pressure gauges. That if we took a hit, or for any other reason that the oil pressure should start to drop on any of the engines, to hurry and hit the feathering button, at the same time telling me what he was doing. There could be no loss of time, otherwise the loss off pressure could lose us the chance to feather the engine.

"MY GOD, LOOK AT THOSE GERMANS RUN!!!"

He was not watching the gauges as I had told him to do, but was viewing the spectacle beneath us. I regretted not seeing it myself. But for our own safety, I had to keep my attention on the ship on which we were flying formation, which was above and to the right of us. Even so,

I took a swing in his direction with a heavy backhand and caught his left shoulder with quite a force, as my adrenalin was pumped up pretty high.

"*WATCH THE GODDAMNED GAUGES!*" I ordered.

We were the bottom ship in the bottom of a three-ship Element, of the bottom Flight, of the bottom Squadron, of the bottom Group. The entire Air Force was above us and had cut loose their bomb loads, which were tumbling down toward us. Tumbling, because the clusters of the smaller bombs spewed out in all directions in their fall.

When the Lead ship of our Squadron made an adjustment to escape the falling bombs, his wingman banked sharply to avoid a collision and scattered his bombs right above us!

My only choice to avoid the falling bombs was a sharp bank. I peeled off to the left in a dive. And while we didn't get hit by a single bomb, we ended up less than a thousand feet above the ground and, naturally, as far away from our Group as I could get.

What if we got separated in all of the chaos? Did Ears have a good fix on our position to get us out of the bedlam?

"Ears?" I called on the intercom, but he didn't respond.

What had happened to Ears? The worthless copilot had also not been running Crew Checks, assuming everyone was okay since we weren't on oxygen. So I called for Ears again and again did not get a response from him.

I switched my communication selector box to CALL, which was an over-ride to all channels of communications and called for Ears… He did not speak back to me, but I could hear Dinah Shore singing.

…Why did I hear Dinah Shore singing?

Into the inverted "fish bowl" astro dome, about six feet in front of me, appeared the helmeted head of Ears with a big smile, mouthing the words to Dinah's song. He was also dancing.

"What's up?" he asked over the intercom.

Whatever it was that I wanted to ask him had left me and I told him, "Never mind."

On the way back to base I thought how much I missed having Moon along to share in the concerns of such insanity.

However, it didn't end with the St. Lo mission. We were scheduled for another mission in the afternoon. True, I only had one more mission to complete my tour of 35 combat missions, but to fly two-a-day was a bit too much.

So despite the agony of suspense, I would really have preferred to wait until tomorrow to finish up. However, the choice was not mine.

A LITTLE MISTAKE
CHAPTER 16

After lunch and another briefing, planes were rearmed and fueled. And for what ever ill-conceived reason, we were the first to take off in what was becoming marginal weather.

The plan was to climb out on instruments toward the radio Buncher beacon. Except, we didn't climb *out*. When we reached the Buncher we were still *in* the "soup."

Okay, we circled the Buncher in a climbing turn, winding our way up to 10,000 feet where we would surely be in the clear and ready to assemble before going on oxygen.

It didn't happen, because it was one of those phenomena when it looks like you're almost about to break out on top, but it just doesn't happen, because the clouds build up as fast as you climb.

I reported this to "Hardlife," our control back at Great Ashfield. They replied, "Keep climbing."

So at 10,000 feet we went on oxygen, turned booster pumps on to insure fuel pressure and kept climbing up to 15,000 feet, where we were still on instruments.

It was not a good situation for anyone, especially me, since this was my last mission and I didn't want to end it by running into anyone in the clouds. My only advantage was that we were in the lead and at the top of the stack. However, right behind us at 30 second intervals were 30 other bombers climbing up the same radio marker as if it were a "pole."

I reported to Hardlife that we had not yet broken out of the clouds at 15,000 feet.

"Keep climbing," was the reply.

Okay. We kept climbing up to 20,000 feet where I reported to Hardlife that we were still on instruments.

The reply came back, "Keep climbing."

It occurred to me that even if we should break out at 25,000 feet, we had never assembled that high. So what was the deal?

Since the weather forecast had been so far off, my guess was that we were trapped in a SNAFU (Situation Normal: All *Fouled* UP). It was as if the "planners" were so caught up in the enthusiasm of the invasion of Europe, that caution had been abandoned in the rush to bomb every target on the Continent. In fact, the particular target was insignificant; just bomb anything and everything.

Well, bombing was our business, but give us a break. You've got to assemble all of the bombers together in formation before you can effectively destroy any target. Otherwise, you'll destroy your own bombing force. And in order to assemble, you have to be in the clear for the bombers to see each other. Besides, this was usually done down at 10,000 feet before going on oxygen.

Since this was the first time we were going to assemble at, or above, our mission altitude, I worried about whether any thought had been given as to how 30 bombers were to be unscrambled from around, what I imagined was, a *barber pole*.

Now, except for trying to maneuver in the thin and sloppy air at high altitude, there shouldn't be too great a problem, as long as everyone could see each other. However, what was to happen when everyone reached their altitude limitation and we were still flying blind in the clouds?

I sure as hell didn't know the answer to such a predicament and I wasn't so certain that Hardlife knew how to unscrew us from the *barber pole* either.

"Hardlife, this is Alfrek "C" Charley. I'm at twenty-five Angels and I'm still not on top of it."

"Alfrek 'C' Charley...Keep climbing."

"You sonovabitch," I mumbled and thought. It's easy for you to say, down there 15 feet off the ground, standing still in a concrete control tower, but I'm up here in an aluminum tank with over two-thousand gallons of high octane gasoline and six-thousand pounds of high explosives stacked about six feet behind me and in a little bit I'm gonna' be playing blind man's tag with 30 other idiots!

BARBARA "B" didn't like the idea of it either, as *she* reluctantly no longer climbed at 500 feet a minute.

Finally, at 30,000 feet the top of the clouds was still somewhere above us and there was no end in sight. Hoping that Hardlife had an answer to the problem, I reported the situation and the order came back: "Alfreck 'C' Charley. Keep climbing."

Well…there are limitations.

At 33,000 feet there was no more climb left in BARBARA "B." It was there that I entered a new dimension, because I had never had such an experience as just hanging in space: NOT MOVING.

With the superchargers on, the airspeed read 150 mph, but we were not climbing – just hanging still inside of a giant white cloud. I would not have been surprised to hear trumpets playing, the gate of heaven appear and the angel Gabriel reach out his hand and welcome us. It was pure fantasy and I was caught up in the rapture of it.

"Alfreck 'C' Charley. Are you in the clear yet?"

"Nope." I replied. "No, I'm not in the clear yet."

"Are you still climbing, 'C' Charley?"

"Nooo," I answered. "We're just sitting still up here at thirty-three Angels waiting for instructions…It won't climb any more."

I decided to let them worry about it.

"Stand by Alfreck 'C' Charley…"

"Roger, Hardlife. I'm not going any place."

Hanging still at 33 Angles, waiting for Hardlife, it occurred to me that the mission would have to be scrubbed. If so, we would be recalled – and the first up would have to be the last down. That was us. Therefore, it was no time to get in a hurry. It was a time for *patience*, because it would be fatal to dive down through the clouds that were filled with 30 loaded bombers.

No, we would just hang around for awhile.

Hardlife eventually called back to issue the Recall.

Okay Smitty, I thought. Don't get in a hurry. With only one last mission to complete the combat tour, don't screw it up by getting in a rush. Let everyone get out of the way.

A SUCKER HOLE is an opportunity that presents itself as a gift from God to get you out of a predicament. But as most pilots who have survived, have learned that, in most cases, a SUCKER HOLE will usually put you in deeper trouble, thus its name.

I didn't even recognize it as a *Sucker Hole*, but there it was.

PAHWHOOM! I was flying in the clear!

I hadn't gone for it, because I couldn't have seen it in the clouds. But I had been flying in the clouds too long, and then suddenly I was flying in the *clear*…Thank you God.

It was as if we had entered a giant well. The clearing was just a few miles across, but it went 33,000 feet straight down to the earth, which was very dark at the bottom of the *well*.

Well, maybe it was more like an elevator shaft. At least that was what I was going to use it for, to express us from the top floor to the basement the quick and easy way – in the clear and not by flying instruments amidst other bombers that I couldn't see.

It was about time too, because I had been doing all of the flying, not trusting the questionable skill of my copilot, and I was tired. At least now, I thought, I can take a little break, because, even my copilot couldn't screw up a simple let-down under visual flight rules?

However, my copilot proved me wrong.

I established a 500 feet per minute descending turn to the left, trimmed the ship and turned it over to ol' *Shit-For-Brains*.

If he'd done nothing at all, BARBARA "B" would have found her own way back to the barn. But nooo, SFB had to jack around and still try to prove that he was a better pilot than I.

Except, he wasn't! He was older and taller. But a better pilot than I? Captain Vance and I didn't think so.

I watched the rate-of-descent creep down from 500 feet per minute to 1,000 fpm and I looked at him. His eyes were smiling and dancing, obviously for my benefit; flaunting his casualness – and stupidity – to spite my concern, if not the anger that he must have seen in my eyes.

I took my feet away from the rudder pedals and twisted my body in his direction to give him my full attention. After all, he made it clear that he was going to show me something and I wanted him to know that I was going to *watch* him.

Even so, I also made it a point to glance at our descent from time to time as a suggestion that he might wish to do likewise.

Our descent increased from 1,500 fpm to 2,000 fpm.

I was infuriated! With only one mission left on my long and agonizing tour of combat, this dumb sonovabitch was going to kill me. Maybe he had a death wish – and maybe he deserved to die – but I was damned if I was going to let him take me with him!

The rate of descent passed 2,500 fpm to 3,000!

My rage turned to madness. I wanted to smash his face with my fist, but I saw he was in trouble. Sweat washed into his eyes, but he couldn't wipe it away because both of his hands were locked onto and tugging at the control wheel.

His game of *chicken* was about to bite him in the ass. It also meant we were *all* in trouble!

His eyes were jerking all over the instrument panel. He was in a panic, not seeing anything, and he mumbled something.

"Look at the fucking altimeter!" I ordered. It was spinning so fast that it couldn't be read. The rate of descent could be read and it showed that we were dropping at 4,000 feet per minute and the instrument had reached its limit!

Obviously we had exceeded the limitations of *Shit-For-Brains*. But, had we passed *my* limitations? What about the limits of the ship?

"Help me," he mumbled.

"What?" I asked.

"*HELP ME!*" he bellowed.

I had already pulled a bomb load loose from the bomb racks over Zwickau; which the Engineering Officer had said couldn't be done. But besides sheer musclepower, especially with the adrenalin pumping, some consideration had to be given to the "G" Forces from both gravity and momentum. And, yes, we had a full bomb load. That plus the fuel and the aircraft made us extremely HEAVY!

Well, it was a problem that would be resolved one way or the other within minutes. We would either be free, or we would blow one hell of a big hole into the earth, because we were literally going from Heaven to Hell too rapidly.

As the Aircraft Commander, I was the "Old Man" of the crew. However, age did not matter, only ability. There was no flight instructor to advise me, so I instructed myself internally as I took the controls.

"Smith, you are in deep shit!"

"You haven't much time, but don't panic!"

"If you panic, you'll lose it for sure!"

It was getting darker, since we were spiraling deep down into the hole. Exactly what the altimeter read I couldn't see, because it was spinning wildly.

It didn't make any difference, because I didn't know how much altitude or time I needed to recover. All I knew was that we had to hurry before we hit bottom and I would have to work with whatever was given.

"Not so hard! Don't pull back so hard! You'll break it!"

Ohhh, boy! If I didn't pull hard, it would suck us right down into the hole like a beetle in a flushed toilet.

"Goddamned, she's heavy. She's going to take us in."

"Talk to her. Talk to her!" I became vocal, the same as I had as a kid when I was the water boy for a threshing crew, riding old one-eyed Nellie and she ran away with me and headed into the timbers at full speed.

"COME-ON-YOU-SON-OF-A-BITCH! I'LL BREAK YOUR DAMNED NECK!"

I could feel the "G" forces loading up on me. I was already three times heavier than my normal weight, as was the ship and everyone in it. That meant the ship was up to almost *100 TONS!*

Higher "G"s over an extended time would black us out as a result of the blood being pulled down and out of the brain and we would be blind. So either we forced more "G"s for a shorter time or less "G"s over a longer period. But did we have a longer period before running out of altitude? Probably not.

Not jerking, but with a steady pull, I heaved back on the controls with all my strength, tightened my belly muscles to compress my guts back against my main aorta artery to try and keep all of my blood from going into my legs and I shouted, "YEOOOOOOH!" until my breath left me.

Starting to black out, I heard a "THUMP" from somewhere behind me and hoped it wasn't the main wing spar giving way. I eased off on the back pressure, taking the opportunity to judge our progress.

We bottomed out of the clouds below 500 feet and were still heading down. However, our rate of descent had been slowed and I kept nursing her back until we were flying level and parallel to the earth a bit below 200 feet.

Not bad. We made it without exceeding the 250 mph Red Line by much, and had probably not pulled any more than six "G"s at the most; and I was wet with sweat.

I took my hands off of the wheel and raised them above my head like the winner of a prize fight, turned to my copilot and said, "It's all yours, *Junior*. Now see if you can keep it straight and level until we get home."

I knew he didn't like being called *Junior*, because he was at least four years older than I and had an ego problem anyway. However, he took the insult, since he knew he deserved it. And then to rub it in some more, I told him, "Don't *ever* try that again. Not even if I'm along to save your ass. Because if you do, and you survive, I will *kill* you!"

Ears gave me a steer back to base without any comment. However, the bombardier came forward on his way to the nose and said, "That sure was some kind of a ride."

"You were in the bomb-bay?" I asked with surprise.

"Yeah," he replied, "When I heard the Recall, I went back to safety the bombs."

"You mean the bombs were *armed?*" I asked. "You'd already armed the bombs?"

"Well, I had plenty of time, climbing up to altitude."

"You *never* arm the bombs until you're over the Channel!"

I made it a point to finally really look at this guy whom I had taken for granted as my assigned bombardier. He smiled back at me in appreciation of the recognition.

"And you were back there during the descent?" I asked.

"Yeah," he said, but not complaining. "I damn near came out through the bomb doors."

Thinking what he must have gone through and looking him over carefully to check his condition, I noticed that his A-2 flight jacket was full of little tiny holes, as if someone had torn bits out of it with a pair of pliers.

"Are those moth holes?" I jested.

"No," he smiled and chuckled. "They're flak holes from a mission last week…I'm one lucky guy."

He then ducked down and went forward into the nose and I marveled that he was still alive. It was unbelievable.

The fact that we were the first of our Group to land was also considered unbelievable. Captain Vance asked how we had managed to have been the first off and the first back.

A *Sucker Hole*, I said. "We got lucky…But if you don't get me a different copilot, I'm going to kill that sonovabitch before he kills a lot of people…I mean it Captain."

Since Vance had tried to check him out, he knew what I was talking about and said he'd try to work out something.

Well, three days later I was scheduled to fly my last mission and Captain Vance had not been able to get me a different copilot. It only added to my stress that my worst enemy – having impressed me that he was out to destroy me – would be flying as my copilot.

MISSION # 35 – THE LAST MISSION
Merseburg, Germany. 28 July 1944
Friday: 41 ships up.   (9:00 Flying Time)

"NOOO! NOOO! NOOO! WE'RE NOT SUPPOSED TO GO! NOOOOO!!!"

It was Corky. I could see him in the dark as I looked out and down from my cockpit window. He was shouting up at me and swearing that it was not meant for us to go. Carmen and Herby tried to calm him

My last mission – Merseburg, Germany.

and get him back into the ship, but they could not change his premonition that – "WE WON'T MAKE IT!"

As Moon's copilot, I would never have allowed him to taxi our right wheel off of the hardstand and into the mud. But not *my* copilot!

We were stuck hub deep in the mud – thirty tons of us! So I called on the radio for a cleat-tractor and we just sat in the dark with our thoughts on the day's mission over Germany and waited for the "cleat-track" to arrive and pull us free of the mud.

Corky was upset with the delay of our misfortune, taking it as a bad omen, and he protested loudly.

"I hear you, Corky," I yelled down to him and invited him to express himself, which he continued to do. Then I asked him, "Corky, do you want to get this over with *TODAY*, or do you want to stretch it out until tomorrow, or maybe next week?"

He thought about it and scuffed his feet around and talked with Carmen and Herby, then strolled away toward the rear of the plane.

By comparison to thirty-four previous missions, the trip to Merseburg itself was rather anticlimactic, which was a welcome climax to the most terrible period of my life.

There was flak. Of course there was flak. There had to be opposition from the enemy or it could not count as a mission.

It was a long trip, nine hours long, but not the longest. My copilot even eased my burden by cooperating. He didn't even object to pissing on the tent peg for good luck.

As for kissing the props, I'd given that up somewhere along the line, because it really didn't seem to make any difference. For as much as I loved those engines, and they loved me too, it had been proved that kissing them had not kept the flak away.

I'd become rather fatalistic about the flak, since there was nothing I could do about it. Even so, I had tried to work Turner's magic by trying to keep my mind tuned to receive some message or impulse to avoid the flak bursts. However, there was no sign that it worked for me, or that I could control it.

In the search for much needed morale I recalled a prayer my father would give at the family dinner on Sundays. I wasn't good at praying aloud like he was. I couldn't even recite it exactly, but it had to do with: "Heavenly Father, give us the strength to change those things we must and to abide those things we cannot change, and the wisdom to know the difference…"

Well, I certainly couldn't change the flak. Therefore, I would just have to "abide" it. However, I could change the way I flew formation, within limitations. And since I had probably seen more ships go down from collisions and the effects of propwash than from flak and fighters combined, I would – on this last mission – change the way I flew formation.

We started out in the High Squadron; except I flew even higher because there was the Group, and there I was above it, more like I was flying fighter escort…That way, if we got hit by bandits, I could dive down and into the Group for protection.

It was a luxury allowed me and there was no objection from our leader, since nobody in the Group had more missions than I did. In effect, I was the oldest combat pilot in the Group.

However, when we finally approached the target and the flak began in earnest, I dove down and joined in on the Bomb Run so that our bombs would be concentrated on the target.

PUMPH! BUMPH! BANG!

Thank God, this was the *last* time!

"BOMBS AWAY!"

That was *IT*! I'd done it! What a feeling of exhilaration! It was intoxicating. I was without fear. I wanted to celebrate and went my own way...The Group broke to the right for the Rally Point and I flew straight ahead alone, making a wide leisurely turn above the target...I was, for the first time, totally without fear and I felt immune to mortal danger as we sailed in a giant turn all alone above Merseburg, Germany, between the flak bursts that failed to do us any damage..."Goodbye, Germany!"

"JESUS CHRIST, Smitty!" It was Ears on the intercom. "Get back into the goddamned formation! Get us to hell outa here!"

It was the first time ever that Ears had tried to tell me how to fly – and he was right, of course. I must have gone a bit "bonkers." But in spite of the wide swing I made over Merseburg, which Ears considered foolhardy, it was a perfect last mission. There was fighter support all the way to the target and back. And even better, they had not been needed.

My combat experience was in April, May, June and July of 1944. I had flown over 50,000 miles (twice around the Equator) in harm's way and considered it a miracle to have survived. Except, "It ain't over till it's over."

Back over England my copilot – somehow turned appreciative – said, "I've never known anyone to have completed 35 missions. Are you going to buzz the base when we get back?"

No, I was not going to give the base a "buzz job" when we got back. Flying low, buzzing across the field and showing off had cost other crews their lives. I was tired and I knew my judgment had to be off. It was not worth the risk of killing us all for the sake of playing to the grandstand to please the fans.

There were plenty of fans to support us after the missions. It seemed that everyone who could pause in their many duties flocked to the flightline to greet our return. Sometimes they were even moved to applaud.

As much as I would have enjoyed buzzing the field to celebrate the completion of my last mission, I recalled the failed attempts of others. Failed, because of distorted judgment.

Good judgment is critical for survival. After a nine hour mission, judgment was probably way out of alignment. Therefore, a Buzz Job would have to come at some other time.

Thirty B-17's, taking up about the same airspace as ten football stadiums, approached Great Ashfield in formation in preparation for landing on a single runway; the intention of which might be like trying to poke ten pounds of shit into a one pound bag.

Added to the suspense was the time element. It had been a long mission, nine hours flying time, and fuel on board was running low, and the guy I followed in the landing pattern just kept flying past the middle of the runway without peeling off. It was as if he was on a leisurely cross-country flight.

One of the first rules that I had learned when shooting Overhead Dead-Stick Landings as a kid in Ponca City, was to be in a position to land on the runway whenever the power was cut off; because, it just might not come back on again. A friend of mine once pulled the throttle back and it came off in his hand. Fortunately it was a small plane and he was able make a soft crash into the top of a tree.

Well, to hell with following the guy wasting time and fuel by not keeping a tight landing pattern. I peeled off and tried to catch up to the last ship in the pattern.

Somehow, without any explanation, my crew knew what I was doing, because Herby called from the tail, "That guy finally just peeled off and he's going to try and cut us off at the *pass*."

That "guy" had one advantage. Being higher, he could pick up speed in a dive and pass us. Our advantage was being at the exact pattern-altitude and we were just a bit closer to the only slot in the *parade*.

So as the "guy" and I jockeyed to join onto the third B-17 in the traffic pattern, in terms of the analogy, we were narrowing the competition down into a three dimensional arena not much larger than a single football stadium, which was flying along at 150 mph.

"Yea-Yea!" Carmen cheered, "Break Left!! Break Left! He's comin' over the top to our left!"

This meant that he planned to dive down on my left and beat us into the slot behind the "target" ship as it turned 90 degrees to the left and onto the base leg prior to turning on to the final approach.

Even so, unable to actually see him above me, I followed Carmen's instructions and broke to the left sharply, filling the space he intended to capture.

My copilot, with the extra beef-strength needed, backed me up on the controls and I was pleased that he was finally with the program and synchronized with my movements. In fact, his thinking was almost ahead of me.

We locked into the slot, cutting the other guy out of the pattern, because he was still above us and the rule is that the lower ship has the right-of-way. Besides, we were in the *slot* and there was room for only one of us.

However, in grabbing the advantage, we ended up going too fast!

Approaching the last 90 degree turn onto the final approach, I was too busy looking outside to read our airspeed, but I knew we were flying too fast.

"Wheels down and locked!" I called as we both hauled back to force the beast around the corner and onto the final.

"CLUNK-CLUNK!" My copilot must have already started the wheels down, because I felt their drag immediately when I called for them.

"I've got a wheel!" he said.

Unable to look for my wheel, I replied, "I hope I've got one too. Give me *FULL FLAPS, COWL FLAPS* and stick your feet out." We needed all the drag we could get to slow us down, plus a bit of necessary lightheartedness.

"*FULL FLAPS and COWL FLAPS.*" came the echo. We've got green lights on *WHEELS DOWN and LOCKED.* I'll save my shoe leather, if you don't mind."

"Call me airspeed," I requested.

"You don't want to know," my copilot wisecracked. Okay! One-fifty…One-fifty!"

Shit! If I didn't get it slowed down, we'd have to go around and then we would be the very last to land and maybe we wouldn't even have enough fuel to make it.

I allowed us to coast past the line of approach and even cross-controlled some with top rudder in opposition to the left aileron to force a forward slip in the turn back to line up on the final approach.

"One-forty-five…One-forty…One-forty."

I held the slipping bank past the straight-in line of approach to bleed off a bit more speed and to get us closer to the threshold.

"One-thirty-five…One-thirty-five….One-thirty-five…"

Right where I wanted it.

We were straight and level as we hit the apron in a three-point landing at 90 mph.

Except, the ship in front of us was not rolling fast enough and we would chew up his tail feathers if I didn't brake hard!

The caution light came on in my head, because the instinct was to tromp on the brakes, but that was wrong. Moon had burned out three sets of tires under the same circumstances.

The fault was in the physics and the design of the B-17 and not in a pilot's instinct to stop by putting on the brakes. The problem was in the characteristics of a tail-dragger aircraft, which gave the wings more lift by an increased angle of attack of the wing when the tail was lowered onto the tailwheel. And with the wings lifting the weight of the plane off of the wheels, the brakes would lock and the tires abraded on the runway.

So as soon as we contacted the runway, I shoved forward on the control wheel to lift our tail up, reducing the angle of attack, the lift, and putting the weight of the ship onto the main wheels. Then I tended the brakes until we slowed and the tail plopped down ungracefully onto the tailwheel.

Corky was the first to greet me when I dropped out of the front hatch and hit the ground. He hugged me excitedly and just kept repeating, "Yes! Yes! Yes!"

Carmen congratulated me as the first of our original crew to have "graduated" from our tour of combat.

Moody dropped out of the hatch and added his praise. And as our "bookkeeper," he reported that the rest of the crew members still had one more mission to complete their tours; except poor Moon, who had dropped at least four missions behind, since he'd been grounded.

I was totally wrung out, so after debriefing I didn't even go to eat at the Combat Mess, but went straight to the billet and flopped down on top of my bunk.

According to my watch, I hit my bunk at 16:20 hours and awoke at 17:25, which meant that my nap had lasted from 4:20 to 5:25 in the afternoon: one hour and five minutes.

I felt like Hell. I ached and was stiff all over. The skin on my chest prickled like it was a filled pin cushion. The side of my face that had been against the wool blanket was numb. Even my skin had gone to sleep.

I heard voices mumbling and slowly I recognized them as those of the replacement crews.

"DAMNNN!" I groaned loudly to make my presence known, "That was some kind of a nap."

"Nap, my ass?" someone questioned. "You've been asleep since yesterday afternoon."

"What?" Not believing that my mental and bodily functions had shut down on me, I asked, "What is today, anyway?"

"Sunday."

Merseburg had been on Saturday. So if it really was Sunday, I had been asleep for twenty-five hours and five minutes…I'd never done that before.

Somebody else said, "Your copilot came by yesterday evening and left you some food, there on your chair."

Why would he do that? Nothing made much sense.

"He said that somebody was hunting for you in the chow-line yesterday after the mission, claiming you'd cut him out of the traffic pattern and that he was going to beat the shit out of you."

The way I hurt I felt like he must have found me, so I asked, "Did he find me?"

"Nope," the informant continued. "He stopped looking for you when your copilot told him that he didn't have to find you. That, as your copilot, he would settle any problem."

Hmmm? I must have misjudged my copilot…Strange, I thought, because I couldn't even recall his name.

"Carl Fisher." Captain Vance said.

"Can I have him tomorrow?" I asked.

"I didn't think you wanted him flying with you."

"I owe him one more flight," I explained.

Captain Cerrone had told me the Group had released one B-17 from combat operations and he wanted me to fly to Prestwick, Scotland, and take three Lieutenant Colonels up there who had to get back to Washington D.C. in a hurry; providing I could get a crew together.

Fisher had changed a great deal during the last three flights with me. "I owe him one more lesson," I repeated.

"You can have him," Vance said. "He hasn't been assigned to a crew yet…Are you sure you want him?"

"You bet," I answered with a smile and suggested, "You should give him another check ride. He's a better pilot now."

When the word got out that I was going to fly to Scotland, there was no problem getting a crew together. In fact I had two flight engineers. There were four Sergeants on pass who wanted to hitch a ride. Then there was the Orderly who tried to keep our billet in order. He was a PFC who had never been in an airplane.

In all there were more than a dozen guys aboard the next morning and we must have looked like a crowded school bus on the way to an outing. I didn't even know who all was on board.

Captain Cerrone had set the takeoff for 08:00. It was finally "playtime"– no combat, a flight to Scotland, everybody happy, early and eager to go.

A quarter before eight Captain Cerrone drove up in his Jeep, got out, waited around, looked at his watch and waved me a "Goodbye." So as happy campers, we left.

After landing in Scotland, almost everyone left before I even got out of my seat. The question was, would I have enough of a crew left to get the ship back to base?

There was Fisher, the Orderly, Burnell, Carmen, Hill and the one extra flight engineer. More than enough. We had lunch and departed.

It had been a great disappointment that my orders sending me back home were not waiting for me right after I'd finished my tour. I was homesick, anxious to see and be with my mother and brother and dad. Of course, dad wasn't home either. He was stationed in Omaha. Wars were famous for breaking up families, but at least we were all alive while so many others were not.

It was a further disappointment that my next duty assignment was not even in the States, where I could go home for a short leave. Some guys were lucky enough to be stationed near their homes, but all of my assignments for two years had been over a thousand miles from home. Yet, despite the homesickness, I was one lucky little boy. Yes, Sir…I was ALIVE!!! It was the end of July 1944, I had completed my tour of combat and I was ALIVE!

My next duty assignment was with the 482nd Bomb Group at Alconbury to fly airborne radar students around England. So having been given a couple of weeks leave to get there, I did take advantage of having a Seventeen at my disposal for the day to take three Colonels to Scotland. I took the opportunity to drop off my footlocker and belongings at Alconbury on the way back from Scotland to Great Ashfield. And what do you know?

Along the last leg of the trip was the fighter base at Bassingborne, near Cambridge, where Bud Bishop was stationed and I was sure that Bud and any hot shot fighter jocks around would like to see what a B-17 could do at low level. This would also be the delayed buzz-job that I owed Fisher – and myself.

The lower we got the more I focused my attention on where we were headed and did not glance at the spare flight engineer at my shoulder. I waved him closer and spoke with interruptions as I pulled and pushed the controls to clear the fences and other obstructions as they appeared.

"Put...Put a Yellow-Yellow flare...Put a Yellow-Yellow into the flare gun." I told the engineer over my shoulder, "And when – "

There was Bassingborne off to the left a few miles ahead. I would bisect it from the northwest to the southeast, not down the runway. I told everyone on the intercom to call out any air traffic they might see.

When I pulled up over Bud's billet, I would fire the Yellow-Yellow, non-distress flare.

I waved for the attention of the flight engineer. When I felt his head next to mine, I continued my instructions.

"When I go...When I go...When I go like THAT (Demonstrating by swinging my right arm) – you *fire the flare*."

BARHOOOM! I heaved back; jumped up over Bud's billet; flung my arm to cue the flare; spotted a flagpole just in time to avert it and pushed it back low to the deck and across the airfield and away – staying low and on the deck; not returning to give anyone a chance to read our numbers.

It was exciting; more so than running faster, jumping higher, scoring a touchdown – anything I could imagine. I was powerful and I was BIG! And like any good pilot, *I* was the plane. The span of my arms was 104 feet; one-third of a city block...Like a giant bird larger than any in nature...I was FREE! When I wished UP, I was UP: LEFT, RIGHT, DOWN! I was faster than a speeding train and I could jump over high buildings in a single leap. I was in reality – *Super-Boy!*

I was the luckiest kid on the block. I controlled the power of 6,000 *horses* in my right hand alone. In my left hand I managed a 30 ton "hot rod," even into the fourth dimension of Time.

While the size of my dream-machine might make it appear to be slow compared to a much smaller fighter plane, I was still jumping and buzzing around between 150 and 200 miles per hour. It was certainly more impressive than the Model "T" Ford I had owned when I was 14, or Bob Nichol's Model "A" when we were both in high school.

Yet, It was not a *dream*. It was *real*.

"Lieutenant?" the flight engineer asked for my attention.

I answered him and relaxed a bit as we climbed up to a respectable altitude, perhaps a hundred feet.

"When you told me to fire the flare when you went like *THAT*," he said, duplicating my arm movement and starting to stutter.,"Th-Th-THAT's when I f-f-fired the f-f-flare."

What's the problem? I thought. He was supposed to fire the flare when I went like *THAT* – but not when I was telling him when to fire it…Had he actually fired the flare when I was explaining it to him – before I gave him the signal?

"Smitty?" It was Hill in the tail.

"Go ahead, Herby."

"It looks like we just set a wheat field on fire back here."

Ohhh, SHIT!

I dropped the nose and we went back down onto the deck, so as not to be identified.

C aptain Cerrone was awaiting my return and I could tell that he was not pleased with me. He didn't come forward, but just waited at his Jeep for me to come to him. I took my time, wondering if those on board would chip in to help me pay for a wheatfield.

The Orderly shouted for me excitedly, "Lieutenant Smith!"

He came running toward me, stumbling and having trouble with his parachute to which he was unaccustomed. "Lieutenant, I've never experienced anything like that in my life!!!"

"Great," I said, "Keep your voice down."

"DOWN!" he bellowed. "Talk about DOWN! We were DOWN-DOWN. We were so low I could – ."

"Five-hundred feet," I interrupted.

"Nooo, Sir!" he exclaimed. "We were so low that I – ."

"Hold it!" I told him; looked at the serious Cerrone and wondered how much evidence he'd heard from this witness to my upcoming Court Martial. Then I looked at the smiling Fisher, who was obviously much pleased with the delayed buzz-job.

"Fisher," I said. "Would you take the Private aside and explain to him that we did not fly below five-hundred feet."

"FIVE HUNDRED FEET???" the Private persisted. "Sir, I was in the nose and I was looking UP at that flag on the pole! I would've saluted it, but it was gone as soon as I saw it! But I did read the "KEEP OFF THE GRASS" sign! I've gotta tell ya, Sir, *that* was some kinda flyin'! I've never seen anything like that in my life!"

Even though the cat was out of the bag, I waved my hand for Fisher to take him away some place, but darned if the kid didn't grab it and insisted on shaking it until Fisher pulled him away.

I strolled over to Captain Cerrone for him to readjust my ego.

"You had a fun trip today, Smith?" he asked.

"Yes, Sir," I replied, committing myself to the rule of Yes, Sir / No, Sir / No excuse, Sir.

"Do you recall what your assignment was, Smith?"

"Yes, Sir."

"You have no idea how much trouble we had in getting just one ship off of combat operations for a single day to fly three Colonels to Scotland who were on a very important mission to Washington D. C.. I did explain that to you, didn't I?"

"Yes, Sir."

"Did you know that a recommendation for your promotion to First Lieutenant has already gone forward for approval?"

"No, Sir."

"Did you know that tomorrow you have to be at Wing Headquarters for General Le May to award you the Distinguished Flying Cross?"

"No, Sir."

"Smith – ?"

My God. He was crucifying me, taking his time to drive in the nails before dropping my cross into the hole.

"Smith – do you have any idea where those three Colonels are at this moment?"

What? He threw me a curve. What a question. Weren't they in Scotland on their way to the States? I was confused and didn't answer. It would have been bad form to try and answer his question with a question."

"Smith. Do you know where those three Colonels are at this moment?" he repeated.

"No, Sir."

"Well, I'll tell you where they are…They are all three up at the Club right now – and they're *stinking drunk*! You left without them!"

"What?" I couldn't believe it.

"They weren't even on board when you took off for Scotland!"

"Yes, Sir." I spoke my defense quickly, "I left as soon as you signaled me to leave."

It was true. Captain Cerrone had waved me off.

So without any change of expression or saying another word, Captain Cerrone got into his Jeep and drove away...He didn't even offer me a ride to Flight Operations in his Jeep and I had to wait for the truck.

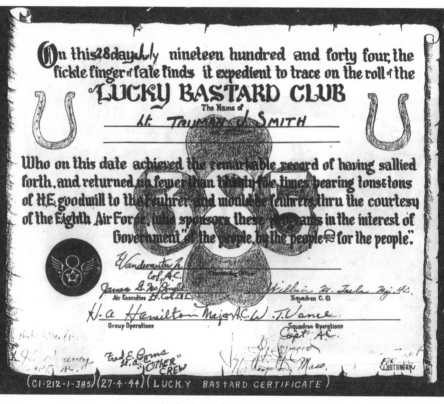

Lucky Bastard certificate.

SKUNK HOLLOW
CHAPTER 17

Having completed my tour of combat I felt like a trapped wild animal given its freedom. I didn't know what to do, nor did I feel the need nor an urge to do anything. I'd made no plans, because there had been no future. Everything had been in the present and I was still in the *NOW*; not moving, not going, just *HERE* and *NOW* in the *MOMENT*. I was not sad nor happy, just neutral. I simply *WAS*; confident that I could handle any crisis. For nothing could ever match the challenges I had faced – and survived. It had been a trial that should serve me well for the rest of my life, for however long that might be.

Regardless, there had been times of weakness and occasions of doubt, even envy. Like the copilot raping the nurse. He had been found guilty and sent to prison at Leavenworth, Kansas, which might have even saved his life.

But what kind of justice was that? He'd gotten laid and was safely in prison, while I had not done the crime and had been subjected to cruel and unusual punishment in front of the firing squads of the enemy. Surely there was a higher justice.

Within a couple of days I was overtaken by melancholy. But why should I be so depressed when I had so much to be thankful for? I had actually survived the worst and I was alive to celebrate.

Well, there were the others who were less fortunate: those I saw going out on their missions, those who didn't come back, the foot-soldiers fighting on the Continent, as well as those they fought. How many hundreds of thousands of people had we killed with our bombs? How many more would have to die?

While I expected to be sent to the States before going to the Pacific Theater of Operations, I received orders transferring me to the 482nd

Bomb Group at Alconbury, to fly radar navigation students around England.

It would be good to get away from the memory and the ghosts of acquaintances who had not returned from their missions. Yet, I didn't want to leave until I knew if the rest of our crew who remained would also "graduate" from combat.

I had kept others at a distance so as not to become emotionally involved. But the CREW was different, because we had become as one from our shared experiences.

So each in turn, having been assigned to fill in on other crews, had all finished, except Moon. Thus, he who had been first, as our leader, was last. And until all of us had gotten over the hurdle, we had a common worry. We didn't want to lose Moon.

The Squadron wisely chose Moon to be the Troubleshooter. The trouble being that a few pilots were aborting their mission too frequently. So it was Moon who was assigned to show them how *not* to abort. It went like this:

PILOT: "We've got a rough engine. I think we'd better feather it and abort."

MOON: "Think again. We don't abort!"

It seemed like such a simple solution, but it took a great deal of fortitude to help someone find their real strength and courage that is buried, if not lost, down deep in one's character.

Therefore, Moon was to them what Mullins had been to me. But Mullins got killed…Would Moon survive?

It is a fact that heroes venture their lives, and each day there were thousands more of them, giving their todays for the tomorrows of others. Was it that life was so worthless? Or was it that the hoped-for tomorrows might be worth more? Or was it that life was on autopilot and it was curiosity that kept you buckled in your seat?

Finally, Moon, like the rest of us, received his *"LUCKY BASTARD"* certificate after the completion of his combat tour and I said "goodbye" to the only ones that mattered to me: Moon and the crew. Our combat had ended, at least temporarily, and at Alconbury I would be out of harm's way…Or so I thought.

C aptain Jack Ford was a dashing, athletic and daring pilot with black wavy hair. He'd flown two tours of combat in B-24's, as well as being checked out on every plane in the inventory of the U.S. Army Air Force, as well as the Royal Air Force.

"Smilin' Jack," as he was thought of, smiled and introduced us to his bride at the Alconbury Officers Club. Her name was Mary and she was an American Women Auxiliary Service Pilot, a WASP, who had ferried a B-25 to England early in the war. She had married an RAF pilot and remained to ferry planes for the RAF after he was killed. She and Jack – both "Hot Pilots" – made a debonair couple.

By unkind, but honest, comparison, the rest of us randy and unsophisticated bachelor fly-boys, while envious and enchanted by the romance of such a blissful relationship, were cursed to live the hapless lifestyle of randy, unsophisticated bachelor fly-boys down in "Skunk Hollow."

"Skunk Hollow," named after a location in the Lil' Abner cartoon strip, was, as if to keep us from setting a bad example, isolated from the Base, across the highway and down a small road into a depressed area. It was indeed depressed and depressing.

However, as flak-happy ex-combatants we were, thanks to the normal abnormalities of weary warriors, a rather "happy" lot, which others considered eccentric.

No…To be honest, we were considered "crazy" and best avoided – banished to "Skunk Hollow." This perception was mainly based on a *wrong* impression by the Group Commander.

Early on, the Commander, who was a Colonel, decided to reinforce the pecking order by giving Captain Jack Ford a check-ride that would prove to all of us nonconformists who was the boss.

The highest rank does not always guarantee ability. Had the test been on Military Science, Jack would probably have failed. However, the check-ride was to test his piloting skills.

While the highest rank in "Skunk Hollow" was Captain, there was no one who had less than one Distinguished Flying Cross and an average of a dozen awards and decorations. This meant that everyone had not only passed the ultimate test in flying, but that they had the guts to get them through combat.

Well, the Colonel had the rank, but he was short on combat and flying experience. Therefore, it was ironic that he was going to test Jack.

It's easy to imagine that the Colonel became envious, if not intimidated, during the test, because Jack was on top and ahead of every trick the Colonel pulled on him: steep banks; stalls; engine out on the right; recovery from unusual positions; missed canyon approach and go-around to the left with left engine out – turning into the dead engine...It was the stuff that Jack relished. No matter what the Colonel threw at him, Jack overcame the challenge with precision and artistry...And then the Colonel went too far...

As they approached the base at the conclusion of the test – for whatever ungodly reason – the Colonel feathered *all four engines* and asked Jack, "What are you going to do now?"

Matter-of-factly, Jack lowered the nose of the sixteen ton bomber, with all four of its engines shut down, and headed for the runway, picking up speed in the dive.

DIVE?

It wasn't a gradual descent, conserving precious altitude to extend valuable flying time. It was a roller-coaster DIVE! The Colonel had pushed the over stressed former combat pilot over the edge. They were going way too fast to land and the only conclusion would be a crash at the near end of the runway. Or, so it seemed. The Colonel was dumbstruck by fear.

However, just before crashing into the ground, Jack hauled back on the controls and shot the bomber straight down the runway at red-line speed.

It was an unbelievable sight: A Flying Fortress buzzing the field at the speed of a fighter plane – with all four engines feathered!

Reaching the far end of the runway, Jack hauled back and they shot skyward. It was then that the Colonel spoke. Trying to unfeather all four engines all at once before they ran out of flying speed he yelled at Jack, "YOU CRAZY SONOVABITCH!!!"

"I'm a crazy son of a bitch?" Jack asked. "If the batteries are down and you can't start those engines, we'll know who's a crazy son of a bitch."

Well, the engines did start and the word got out to "Stay away from those 'Crazies' in 'Skunk Hollow,' because they're flak-happy."

The operative word was HAPPY. For as far as we were involved, the war was over and there was fun to be had. And while resources were limited, we did pretty well at inventing entertainment.

Our in-house inventor was Captain Charley Forth. His grandfather had invented the standard egg beater and Charley had a copy of the patent to prove it. He himself held a patent on a carburetor. However, what really mattered to us was his talent for inventing the games we played.

Condoms. The Air Force kept us well supplied with condoms. So it was Charley who came up with the hot air balloon competition. Blow up the condoms like balloons, heat the air inside of them from above the coal stove, race outside, release them in the cooler air and watch them soar until the air cooled and they descended – usually in the nearby village.

There were also the flare wars between barracks, which had started one night when we surprised some card players seated next to the stove in their billet. Colorful signal flares dropped down their stovepipe set off a memorable fireworks display in the blackout, which prompted them to retaliate.

On other occasions a drama, like Commedia del Arte, might invent itself from the unique cast of characters. For example, Frank Brown, a "happy" young pilot, had a flair for theatrics. He claimed to have played the part of Frankenstein's monster in the movie. It was not true of course, but we went along with it.

Now, Frank, in his early twenties, was bald. So to keep his head warm at night he wore his sheep-lined flight helmet. Okay, but he wore it inside out. So with his kinky white "fright wig" and wearing white long underwear he looked like an albino Little Liza, which might be the kick off for a scene of "Runnin' over the ice flow with the hound dogs snappin' at her ass."

Such folly was not restricted to off-duty-hours. I was even pranked one day by Francis J. Hartle while flying radar students around England. Compared to combat it was boring and begged for diversion.

Hartle and I alternated pilot/copilot duties. It was a day when he occupied the right seat and was, therefore, more bored than I. So, being creative, he decided to sit on his throat-mike. And being especially full of gas that day, he sent the amplified and unusual sounds of escaping gas into my earphones.

Well, I had never heard such overstated sounds and he made me crazy trying to figure out what they were and where they were coming from. He found a great deal of amusement in my reactions for about an hour; until I think he went too far and possibly hurt himself.

"Don't be depressed," Bill Usher would proclaim. "You've never had it so good."

Well, that was easy for him to say. At fourteen he'd run away from home during the Great Depression, ridden the rails and became a merchant seaman when he reached the west coast. His ship was sunk in the China Sea by the Japanese and after so long in the water that his flesh started separating from his bones, he'd been picked up by Chinese pirates. Grateful, he fought with the Chinese guerrillas until he was put in contact with the American Flying Tigers. From there he was gotten back to the States, went through flying school, flew combat in the Eighth Air Force and ended up in "Skunk Hollow" like the rest of us.

By comparison to Bill Usher, we realized deep down that "We really never had it so good," and that circumstances could be much worse.

Therefore, having it so good, I should have known better than to volunteer with Hartle to make a flight to a radar site on the Continent at the end of December in 1945.

The 482nd Bomb Group was responsible for navigational sites and there were supplies, mail and Christmas packages to be delivered to a Sergeant and a Corporal on detached service at a site in Belgium.

"You guys are nuts," Usher said. "There's a goddamned WAR going on over there!"

Richy Norris, our bombardier, said he wouldn't be needed, wasn't going and had a sure thing lined up with a couple of girls for the weekend in Peterborough. "Come with me Smitty and you'll get checked out on something real special."

Hartle countered with an offer to check me out as pilot on the B-24 that had been assigned to the mission. He'd done his tour in Twenty-Fours, knew I'd studied and passed my written test on the B-24 and that I was anxious to get rated in another four engine plane. It would come in handy and maybe help me get an assignment with the Ferry Command.

Usher urged me to go for the girls with Richy. However, my experience with Richy was that he only took me along as a decoy and a diversion, since it invariably worked out in his favor and not mine.

"Don't push your luck, Smitty. You've never had it so good." Usher insisted. "Just stay here and away from the WAR!"   What war? The last I'd heard we were on our way to Berlin.

"Nooo," Charley Forth interrupted. "There's been a delay. The Germans have launched a counter offensive."

Well, Charley ought to know. He stayed up on those things. He asked Hartle for the map he held, spread it out for us all to have a look and asked, "Now, where is it you're supposed to go?"

"Airfield 89, Hartle replied. "It's a captured German field that American P-47's were operating out of."

Usher broke in, "Nobody is operating out of any airfields on the Continent. Eveything's socked in. The only things moving over there are German tanks." He'd been listening to history being made over the radio and he laid it out for us.

The German Sixth Panzer Army is just outside of Liege, Belgium, and headed for fuel at the port of Antwerp, Belgium. To protect the flank of the Sixth Panzer, the Fifth Panzer Army had crossed the Meuse river near Namur, Belgium.

"Now, where is it you're supposed to go?" Usher asked.

"A-89," Hartle replied.

"Yeah," Charley said, pointing to the map. "A-89. That field just north of Namur a few miles."

"I'd say, that's piss-poor planning," Usher commented, "It looks like you and the Fifth Panzer Army will both being invading Belgium at Namur."

I looked at Hartle with that "Look what a fine mess you've gotten us into, Ollie." He simply reacted with a slight shrug of his shoulders and commented, "In for a penny, in for a Pound." Whatever that meant.

ANTWERP is a seaport just inland from the North Sea in the northern part of Belgium. This, according to Usher, was the objective of the Sixth German Panzer in a desperate spearhead drive to secure fuel for their tanks.

LIEGE, Belgium, approximately 65 miles southeast of Antwerp, was on the centerline of the German spearhead. Aachen, Germany was just about 20 miles northeast of Liege and held firmly by the Germans, representing the right barb of the arrowhead.

NAMUR, Belgium, was 30 miles southwest of Liege, as the left barb of the spearhead.

LOUVAIN, Belgium, is 15 miles east of Brussels. Only a few miles from Louvain was our destination: Airfield "89"!

"You know," Usher said, studying the map with us, "Nobody really knows right now exactly what's going on in that triangle. But, you can count on one thing for certain: there's a goddamned BATTLE going on there! It'll probably end up as the biggest battle of the entire war. You've gotta be nuts for even thinking about going into that mess."

Well, we all thought about it for awhile, then Usher continued. "But if you are able to find that field in the bad weather and you do land there in Belgium, be careful not to hit any of those German tanks that have probably recaptured the field."

"No big loss," Hartle tried joking. "We're taking old 'D' DOG."

No shit! That's how Hartle got in on this deal.

The old 'D' DOG was a war-weary B-24 that would have been a 'hangar queen,' if we'd had a hangar. I had never even seen it fly. In fact, I had assumed it was some kind of a war relic.

The 482nd Bomb Group was equipped with B-17's, but they had found Hartle, who knew how to fly B-24's, and offered him the job of flying the relic.

"Listen, Hartle," I reconsidered, "Just being next to you is as close as I ever want to get to a B-24."

"Aw, come on, Smitty," he said. "It'll be a good adventure. No guts, no glory."

I was about to learn that success is sometimes better achieved by saying, "No."

We took off from Alconbury on the 2nd of January 1945 in 'D' DOG and headed across the Channel, being careful to avoid Dunkirk. We had been briefed that a pocket of German antiaircraft was still trying to win the war at Dunkirk.

The speculation was that it was the Dunkirk Ack Ack that had shot down the band leader Glenn Miller just a few days before when he had departed Alconbury in a Nordun Norseman for a concert in Paris. However, the truth was that an RAF bomber returning to England with a bomb load had dumped its bombs into the Channel and accidentally dropped onto the Norseman.

According to our briefing, due to the extremely bad weather, there was no air traffic at our destination. It was unfortunate, because the U.S. Army was suffering from the German counter attack and could really have used air support.

The great advantage had been with the U.S. Army until bad weather set in and eliminated the support of the U.S. Air Force. The Germans, of course, had been forced to do battle with limited air cover, because we had paid a heavy price in destroying the Luftwaffe and other battle resources in the months prior.

Therefore, with both sides being denied air power, the Germans were proving to be an overwhelming fighting force in their counter attack against the Americans. It would be recorded in history as *THE BATTLE OF THE BULGE* – the most stunning, confused and costly single battle ever fought by Americans.

More than a million soldiers on both sides were fighting urgently for their lives in the unsolved jig-saw puzzle below us. It was the worst of man-against-man and man against-the-weather. American prisoners had their hands bound and were massacred at Malmedy. Many more, who were wounded, simply froze to death in the snow.

"You are to approach the radio beacon from the west," we had been instructed. "From any other direction, you will be fired upon by the Allies. When you reach the beacon, you will execute a ninety-degree standard turn to the left on a course of three-five for three minutes to the airfield. In case of a missed approach break left, because the Germans will fire at anything overflying their territory."

I figured that, under the circumstances, anyone on the ground would shoot at any airplane that flew over, because that's what I would do.

So we were lucky as hell when we bottomed out of the clouds at less than 200 feet without getting shot down or flying into any hills.

The field was straight ahead and we stuck ol' D-DOG into the snow and onto the ground. I really appreciated the fact that ol' D-DOG was a ground-lovin' '*Lead Sled.*'

The Non Commissioned Officer in Charge of the radar site was waiting for us with his 6x6 truck; which we loaded up from the plane with mail, Christmas presents, tires and other supplies. He dropped us at Flight Operations in a chateaux that also served as quarters for the P-47 fighter pilots. He had left a Corporal in charge of the radar site, which he would show us tomorrow.

Any tour of Belgium should include Brussels. So we headed for an evening in the big city. The music and wine were good. I couldn't recall very much, except that the hat-check in the ballroom of the hotel wouldn't return my cap and I left bare-headed.

The next morning at breakfast/lunch, as I was late getting started, the Jug pilots told me that some German was probably wearing my cap by now; explaining that a lot of Germans had been left behind and that they collected American uniforms to disguise themselves for escaping.

Well, that's right. There was a war going on. So I acquired a steel helmet as a head cover, which was really more appropriate for a war zone anyway.

Things were certainly different in this combat environment. Listening to the Jug pilots talk about a local girl having been executed by the Underground after they had shaved her head for fraternizing with the "Krauts," I was shocked at their reaction: "What a terrible waste of such a lovely piece of ass."

Man, oh man, oh man. Was that it? Was that the fundamental meaning and basic purpose of life? Sex? Was everything else just a sideline, a hobby? Sex meant life to overcome death. Therefore, death was the justification for sex and vice versa. It was the sparkplug that drove the entire system – that had kept it going for millions of years. The males killed while the females nurtured and resupplied the losses. So with all of the killing going on, well, sex had to be an important consideration. The outcome should prove interesting. Would the war produce a boom or a bust in population?

There had been a heavy snow during the night. By noon Hartle, T/Sgt. Hunton L. Morgan, our flight engineer, and S/Sgt. Bryant, our radio operator, the radar site Sergeant and I had all worked very hard and had pushed the snow off of D-DOG so we could return to England. However, the weather worsened to below absolute minimums with fog and we were stuck.

Bill Usher might have philosophized, "Be careful of what you wish for, because you might just get it…You wanted to go to the Continent for a little adventure? Well get ready, cause you're grounded and you'll have to play out whatever comes."

I don't know where the rest of the crew went, because I went with the Sergeant in charge of the radar site; I inspected the site and also met the Belgian farm family who had taken the "Sarge" in as one of their own.

It was a unique situation, since the Sergeant, his radar trailer and his Corporal had been put in place alongside a road at designated coordinates, been given a 6x6 truck and had been left alone. So he simply became a part of the farm village, helping out with the chores and, along with his Corporal, was adopted by the villagers and practically worshipped by the children.

It was the damndest thing. Every place we went we were accompanied by a half a dozen boys, ages six to ten.

The Sarge introduced me to his 'family' and 'Grandpa,' who insisted we join him in a drink of cognac. The boys then took us to the location of a recently crashed Focke-Wulf-190 in the woods, gleefully pointing out the scalp of the German pilot that was stuck on a tree.

As it got dark the Sergeant drove us into Namur and we were halted by an American G.I. at the pontoon bridge that crossed the Meuse river.

I felt sorry for the guard, because it was miserably cold and he was stomping in place in the snow trying to keep from freezing. There was no question that he took his work seriously, because he had his rifle aimed at us as we approached. So we stopped.

I opened the canvas flap on my door and gave him a friendly greeting.

Looking at me over the sights of his rifle, his response was unspoken, but unmistakably, "I'm in charge here. We'll do it my way or I'll kill you on the spot."

No problem. I was ready to do anything he asked.

"Trip ticket," he demanded.

I relayed the order to the Sergeant who was driving.

"They're in the glove compartment," was his nervous reply.

Motor Pools made out trip tickets, not the driver of a vehicle. And since the Sergeant didn't have a Motor Pool, he explained to me that he made out his own Trip Tickets, but had forgotten to do so.

"We don't have a trip ticket," I told the guard.

While I had taken him to be serious at first encounter, he became even more intent as he firmed his grip on his M-1 and made sure of his aim – between my eyes, and I didn't doubt that his weapon was loaded.

"Who won the World Series?" he asked sternly.

Ohhh, boy. Every muscle in my body tensed to the point of quivering. My instinct told me I was in grave DANGER! However, I prayed that his instincts were sending him the right signals, because I sure as hell didn't comprehend his question or what he was really after. Certainly there was more to it than a simple quiz on baseball. But unfortunately, I didn't even know the answer to his question.

"Who won the World Series?" he repeated, sounding impatient.

I glanced at the Sergeant who only looked straight ahead, gripping the steering wheel tightly.

"Wait! Just a minute." I pleaded with the guard, hoping my brain would give the right answer. "I don't know much about baseball. I really don't care for it."

No, that was wrong, wrong, wrong! I certainly didn't want to offend him.

"I mean – ," I continued, trying to dig myself out, "I've been in England for a year and I don't know who won the World Series."

"How much is an airmail stamp?" he asked promptly.

God, I was going nuts, because I couldn't make any sense out of the questions, or even why I was being asked. But maybe it wasn't me. It was probably the unfortunate freezing 'Dogface' G.I. who had gone crazy on his miserable post, because baseball and postage stamps didn't even fit together.

"How much?" he asked.

"A nickel," I said, having no choice but to play the game. I'd play it all the way and the best I could. "An airmail stamp costs a nickel – five cents." I repeated.

"Not anymore it don't," he mumbled.

"No, shit?" I responded in surprise and felt my chest tighten as fear gripped my heart, realizing that I was coming up loser in whatever kind of game we were playing.

The only thing I was sure of was that a rifle was pointed at my head – loaded – the safety off and his cold, and probably numb, finger on the trigger.

"It used to be a nickel," The voice at the trigger end of rifle spoke. "It's now six cents."

Was that it? Had I lost? Did I have to pay with my life, not even – and especially – not knowing the score, nor how much a goddamned airmail stamp cost?

"Who's Jiggs?" was the next and – I was certain – the very last question.

"What?" I asked…This was some kind of a nightmare and I couldn't get it organized. My life was in jeopardy, because I couldn't answer some disconnected questions from a freezing and crazy G.I. who had a rifle pointed at my head.

"Who's Jiggs?" he almost shouted.

"Sure. Sure," I replied. "The only Jiggs I know is in the funny papers and his wife is Maggie – Jiggs and Maggie."

That was the best I could come up with.

"Okay," the guard said. "Go ahead."

"And go?" I asked.

"GO AHEAD! Move it out!"

As we rumbled, rattled and rolled across the pontoon bridge I asked the Sergeant, "What in hell was that about?"

"Infiltrators," was his answer.

The Germans had put specially trained English speaking saboteurs in American uniforms and entered them behind American lines as an integral part of their counter offensive. Many of them drove armed American vehicles and they were very effective in their piracy. Complete with forged identification, they had been able to create a lot of havoc and there was no way to know who was or was not an Infiltrator – except one: ask them questions that only those who had actually lived in America could answer.

Well, I sure wished somebody had briefed me on that before I almost got my head blown off. And for a moment, I thought of Richy making out in Peterborough, wishing I'd gone with him instead of coming to the Continent.

When we drove up to the main gate of a military fortress that had been captured by the Americans, the guard asked the Sarge, "Who won the World Series?" He answered the sentry and we were allowed to drive inside.

The first stop was at a headquarters where the Sarge was known. I followed him inside.

With friendly greetings to everyone, the same as to the farmers in the village, the Sergeant went to a classified wall map, pulled the cover away from in front of it and briefed himself on the status of the battle. Satisfied, he put the cover back over the map and we left.

It was obviously a necessary routine, since he and the Corporal were on their own out in the boonies and the line of battle was so fluid.

"It's a good thing I turned right this time on the way down here," the Sergeant said. "Otherwise, we'd probably be eating sauerkraut for dinner – if we got lucky and they fed us."

I, of course, was totally out of my element and didn't even know enough to be as frightened as I should have been. I was completely at the Sergeant's mercy to get me safely back to the airfield – if it hadn't been retaken by the Germans.

We stopped in for a cup of coffee at the Canteena before heading for the airfield and the Sarge said, "It's getting late and I've really got to get those boys back home."

"What boys?" I choked on my coffee. "Where?"

"In the back of the truck," he said.

Ohhh, shit!!! I'd wondered what happened to those kids when they weren't around anymore, but I couldn't even imagine that the Sergeant had brought them along with us – right into the fortress – right past the guard at the pontoon bridge.

Jesus Christ! What if someone found out we'd 'smuggled' those kids into a military fortification?

"Let's get the hell outa here right now!" I ordered and thought, this is CRAZY!

"Well," the Sergeant hesitated, "I'd sure like to get some doughnuts for the boys."

"WHAT? You're thinking about getting doughnuts for the boys?" I asked. "We've got to get the Hell out of here. We've got to get back over that bridge with smuggled civilians – and you're thinking about getting doughnuts for the boys?"

"Well," the Sarge drawled, "they sure do like these doughnuts… You can wait for me in the truck, Sir. It'll only take a minute."

"I'll get the damned doughnuts!" I said. "You go get the truck started!"

"Yes, Sir," he said, and added, "The Corporal would sure appreciate a few doughnuts, Sir."

I turned away to get a few extra doughnuts and he said, "And, Sir, Grandpa. Don't forget – ."

"GO GET INTO THE GODDAMNED TRUCK RIGHT NOW, SERGEANT!"

"Yes, Sir."

"Sergeant!" I called after him.

"Yes, Sir?"

"Give me your helmet."

There was no question, except in his eyes, as he came to me offering his helmet.

"Well, I've gotta have something to carry 'em in." I explained.

"This isn't exactly a carry-out operation here."

"Yes, Sir," he said, staring at the helmet on my head, as if to ask, "How come you want my helmet when you've already got one on your head?"

I took off my helmet and said, "The guards on the bridge. We can't forget those guys out there in the cold, can we?"

"No, Sir!" he said, smiled, and turned to leave for the truck.

Author's Note:
Truman J. Smith and Francis J. Hartle are featured in the book FLYING THROUGH FIRE by Geoffrey Williams, 1995, Allan Sutton Publishing, ISBN 075090 8815.
The incident described in the book is about their night landing at the RAF Gravesly fog dispersal airfield.

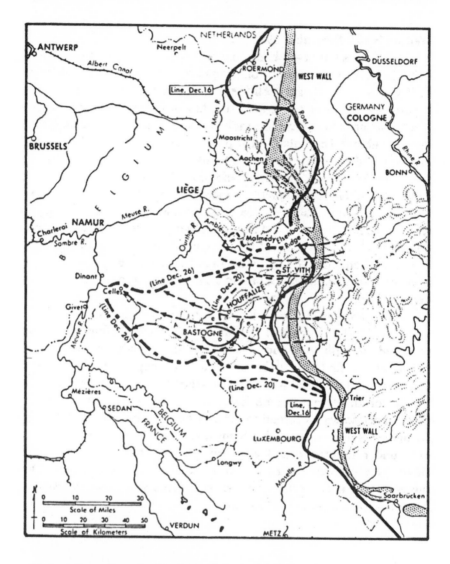

The battle line on December 16, 1944 is shown by the solid black line. Four days later, the Germans had extended their offensive push as indicated by the light dotted line. By December 26, the "bulge" extended to the Meuse River, where it was stopped.

THE BULGE
CHAPTER 18

H ISTORICAL NOTE: The *BATTLE OF THE BULGE*, starting 16 December 1944 until 21 January 1945, in the rugged Ardennes sector of Belgium, constituted the heaviest Allied battle toll of World War Two. Combined casualties of British and American troops were over 80,000 – 20 Americans to each British loss – the greatest in U.S. history. German losses were over 100,000 men, plus 1600 planes and 700 tanks.

At midnight between the 4th and 5th of January 1945, the hinges of hell were blown off by a barrage of V-1 Flying Bombs!

I was convinced they were flying in formation just above my head. Head???

I grabbed my steel helmet off the floor and pulled it tightly onto my head instinctively – as if that could have possibly done me any good.

I was on the top floor – naturally – in a small attic room of the tallest hotel in Liege, Belgium.

'Naturally,' because it seemed to be my nature to end up as close as possible to the threat of Buzz Bombs and other dangers.

What I had assumed was going to be an opportunity to tour the Continent actually turned out to hit some snags, because it was not really the tourist season, being in the middle of one of the worst winters in history. There was also a military battle going on. It would go down in history as *'THE BATTLE OF THE BULGE.'*

I was with the American Forces in Liege, Belgium. Just about 20 miles away was Aachen, Germany, which was occupied by the German Forces. It was not known by anyone exactly where the line of battle was located, because it was being fought back and forth along the highway that connected the two towns, like the 'line-of-scrimmage' in a closely matched and major football game.

While the Buzz Bombs I had witnessed in England usually flew at an altitude of 300 to 500 feet, the ones coming over Liege must have been launched from close by, because they had not yet reached their cruising altitude. In fact, some would never attain it, since they must have malfunctioned and were exploding back to earth under full power.

Therefore, it occurred to me to wonder what in hell I was doing in Liege, when I'd "never had it so good" back at Skunk Hollow, according to Bill Usher.

Well, there was an APO military post office in Liege and it was there that I hoped to locate Don Hatfield, Walt Harris, Jack Paris and other buddies from my hometown, surprise them with a visit and cheer them up.

Being grounded by the snow-covered runway and the bad weather, our departure had to be delayed. So I took off for a day or two for Liege, maybe 50 miles away, on foot, confident that I could hitch a ride.

However, my confidence was shaken after a couple of hours alone, standing in the snow alongside the highway watching the steady stream of supply trucks of the "Red Ball Express" headed for the front – and not stopping.

Oddly enough, a very small civilian European touring car finally came along and stopped, which was strange, since all other vehicles were American military.

A, presumably, Belgian civilian got out from the rear door of the little car and held it open for me to enter. I did so with caution.

I was wearing my helmet and a great and long olive drab trench coat with a woolen liner. Under the coat at my hip I had a Colt .45 automatic service pistol. Since my hands had been in my coat pockets for warmth, I slipped my right hand through the inside slit in the coat pocket, unsnapped the cover of the holster, unholstered the pistol, thumbed off the safety and held it in my hand inside of my coat.

There were two civilians in the front seat and I was invited to sit between the two guys in the back seat. If their intention was to kill me and to take my uniform, I was ready for them to try. They evidently didn't speak English, because they didn't speak to me, obviously an American. Nor did they speak to each other. Therefore, we just rode along in silence, because I couldn't speak French nor Flemish.

I did think I might try just a little German that I had learned from my German grandmother. But having already been assumed to be a

German Infiltrator at the pontoon bridge in Namur, I wisely decided against it and kept silent.

It seemed like an awfully long ride and many thoughts went through my mind, like: how come these men were the only civilians driving on the highway? With a war going on, they must have a permit and a purpose. So when they dropped me off safely in downtown Liege, I concluded that they were members of the Underground.

Well, one night in Liege was enough for me. I would hopefully see my buddies back home after the war, because it would not be easy for my family to understand how I, a bomber pilot stationed in England, had been killed on 'holiday' in the Battle of the Bulge.

So I had a good breakfast, because I assumed it might have to last me all day, and I walked to the outskirts of Liege, hoping to catch a ride back to Louvaine, near the Airfield 89, where I planned to remain until the weather cleared and we could return to the relative peace of England.

DAMN! It was COLD! There was no place I could go to get warm. It was almost noon. With the walk and the waiting, I had been out in the weather for four hours. My only consolation was the thought of the thousands of G.I.'s who had been living and dying in this SHIT for weeks!

Sure, I felt I'd paid my dues and I'd already had my share of cold temperatures, but that only made me more appreciative of the sacrifices being made by the foot-soldiers.

While stomping my feet to try to keep from freezing, a Jeep drove up and stopped. It was driven by a Military Policeman and another MP was riding in the back seat.

"Hop in Lieutenant," the driver said.

It was an open Jeep without heat, but at least it was a ride and it gave me a chance to sit down.

However, I was made uncomfortable by the guy in the back seat who had a sub-machinegun on his lap and – it was pointed at my head.

"Who won the World Series, Lieutenant?" the driver asked.

Ohhh, shit…Not again…It really irritated me; mainly because I should have remembered the Sergeant's answer to who won the World Series when asked in Namur, but for the life of me I couldn't recall it.

Goddamned baseball. I hated it! I hated myself for being so stupid. I hated the war. I hated this dumb game…Who ever heard of such nonsense in the middle of a war? I was even more angry than afraid.

The driver let the clutch out and we started down the road to – where? Either they were going to shoot me, or maybe take me to the

Provost Marshal. Either way, I wouldn't feel so cold. But if they took me back into Liege, there were those goddamned Buzz Bombs.

"I don't know who won the World Series," I answered.

"Why don't you ask me the one about "Jiggs." I know who Jiggs is. I even know how much an airmail stamp costs. Go ahead, ask me about Jiggs."

The driver pulled over, stopped and said with disgust, "You can go now, Lieutenant."

I got back out into the snow. They made a u-turn and headed back toward Liege.

I yelled after them. "Six cents!!! A goddamned airmail stamp costs *SIX CENTS!! IT'S INFLATION!!!*"

There I was, standing alone at the edge of the highway in the snow on a hilltop yelling to – NOBODY.

The Red Ball Express just kept rolling by on the way to the front without taking any notice. So I yelled profanities at them, too.

After I stopped shouting I noticed how quiet it had become. There was no more traffic on the highway. No sounds. No movements of any kind. It was as if I was the only living thing in this strange snowy-white crystalline world of wonderment.

At first it was a pleasant relief from the barrage of Buzz Bombs that had kept me awake all night and the roaring of the Red Ball Express on the highway. But then, as the silence and the cold soaked into my body and mind, I began to feel as if I wanted to, and was, drifting off toward sleep. I was very tired and weary. All I wanted to do was to lie down in the snow and go to sleep.

A t first it came to me as a gut feeling, beyond my five senses, that something enormous was happening, or was about to happen and – it was coming *my way*. What the hell was it anyway?

Only by some subliminal perception did I know that it was a feeling of – DANGER!

Even before my ears could hear it, my body detected a strangeness that communicated fear.

Hmmm?

As the force of it increased in intensity I began to recognize it as SOUND.

Yes, and as the volume grew it became directional. It was coming from the west, and it was from high in the sky.

I looked up and saw the source of the sound between the clouds that were starting to break up. Thankfully, it appeared that the weather would be improving.

This was a new experience for me, because I had never seen the entire Eighth Air Force from the ground. It was composed of both B-17 and B-24 bombers.

Each B-17 Flying Fortress had four 1200 horsepower engines with nine cylinders for each engine and two sparkplugs for each cylinder. The B-24s were similarly endowed.

The point is, the 144,000 sparkplugs in their engines were firing about a half-a-million explosions each second to drive almost *ten million* horsepower and there were also some 20,000 propeller blades slashing the air like oversized swords.

It sounded like the coming of hell itself! And while I had been in the midst of such an armada in the thin silent air so high above, I was unfamiliar with the effect of it on the ground.

To be underneath such a force passing overhead was *terrifying* and as I watched, the atmosphere itself seemed to chatter as if the air was crystal and the entire world was about to shatter.

Of course the illusion of the world about to break apart was really the effect of the impact of hundreds of millions of pulsations onto and through my physical being; real enough that I would have agreed at the moment with Henny Penny that the sky must truly be falling. That was the physical aspect of it.

Emotionally I was moved by a deep sorrow for all of those who were living on the targets of the day. Yet, I was also grateful that my homeland was being spared such holocaust.

Distracted by the awesome spectacle above, I didn't realize at first the opportunity for a ride. A small olive drab truck was parked just down the road from where I stood, so I jogged toward it. And like the ambulances, it too had a door on its backside.

However, I went forward to check with the driver first, noticing along the way a large Red Cross painted on its side. I didn't know exactly what it was, because I had never seen anything exactly like it before.

The driver, sitting behind the steering wheel on the right side, was dressed in olive drab and wearing an O.D. cap with a Red Cross patch. Her brunette hair was cut rather short. She had a fetching smile and waved for me to come inside.

"Ohhh, thank you, Ma'am," I said, feeling the warm air as I slid inside and onto the seat.

Starting to drive, she asked, "Are you going to Brussels?"

"I'm probably going just about any place you're willing to take me, Ma'am."

We introduced ourselves. Her name was Rose and her accent was understandable middle-English.

I, too, tried to be as friendly as she appeared to be and I asked, "What's a nice lady like you doing in a place like this?"

She pleased me again with her seductive smile and explained that, while her assignment was to give moral support to the British Forces, she had come to Liege to pick up supplies from the American Red Cross, offering that she *did* like Americans.

I guessed her to be about twenty-four. And since she was older than I, I addressed her respectfully as "Ma'am" as I had been brought up to do in Oklahoma.

However, taking no offense, she invited me to call her "Rose."

Ohh Boy, oh boy, oh boy! If only Richy could see me now.

After awhile Rose announced that she must get some "petrol" and stopped the little van toward the side of the road as best she could in the snow.

I followed her outside and to the rear, thinking she had a spare can of gasoline in the back and I could help her by putting it in for her.

She opened the door and invited me to join her inside, which I did.

Each wall was stacked with all kinds of goodies like candy, peanuts and cigarettes. These were obviously gifts from the Red Cross to lift the spirits of the fighting men. There was even a spring driven portable phonograph record player with Glenn Miller records stacked next to it.

Since there wasn't much room in the back of the little van, we were forced to stand closely together and her female fragrance was most disarming.

In a winsome way she asked me, "Is there anything in here that you'd like to have?"

"Yes, Ma'am," I answered without hesitation. "I'd sure like to have one of those big Hershey candy bars over there."

"It's not, Ma'am, remember?" she said provocatively, "And you're certainly welcome to have *anything* you want."

As I munched on the Hershey, not having had lunch, I looked about, but could not see anything that resembled a can of gasoline. There had not been a service station where we'd stopped. So what was her plan to get some "petrol," if that was her real intention?

Rose pulled out two fifths of Irish whiskey from a lower shelf and went out the door. I followed to see what she was going to do. Maybe there was gasoline in the whiskey bottles.

The Red Ball Express was speeding through the snow-slush in the opposite direction toward the front. I watched with curiosity and amazement as the little Red Cross gal, Rose, walked fearlessly onto the highway toward the unstoppable convoy of heavy trucks coming toward her under full power.

I got the idea that she knew exactly what she was doing. Rose took a straddle pose and extended her arms like a cheerleader holding a bottle of whiskey in each hand as if they were pom-poms.

It made no difference as to the priority of their mission, nor to the punishment for failing to carry out their orders. For when the drivers of the Red Ball Express saw a petite female with legs spread and holding up two fifths of whiskey in the middle of the highway, brakes growled and the war stopped!

I made myself scarce as I watched the exchange of goods and services. For less than a half-gallon of booze, the troops of the Red Ball filled Rose's van with twenty times as much gasoline, checked the oil, tires and coolant and even cleaned her windows.

With no disrespect to General Eisenhower; the war would have ended months earlier if a spirited woman as talented as Rose had been put in charge of 150,000 females. I could see this as a real possibility for future and smarter wars. There was definitely a place for women in the military. Not as combatants. They could suck up all kinds of men for those jobs. But if the contest was for dominance – which wars are – there was no greater power than Pussy-Power.

Practically all men, including presidents and generals, were under its influence. And I was no exception.

I followed closely behind Rose as she got back into the rear of the little van and I closed the door behind me to shut out the cold. She bent over away from me to pick up a few items that had come loose and had fallen into the narrow aisle and I moved in closer behind her.

She seemed to sense that I was there and deliberately took her time. Then slowly she straightened up turning to me. And for the first time, she took her time to really look into my face.

My eyes studied her face as hers searched mine.

"I think I've fallen in love," I told her.

"Well," she replied coyly. "We should be able to handle that."

"How?" I asked.

"Peanu-s?" she replied, a bit flustered; held up a can of peanuts she'd retrieved from the floor and repeated more clearly. "Peanuts?"

"Ohhh, " I said, "Peanuts." We're going to handle my love affair with peanuts?"

She smiled, totally unaware of any Freudian slip she'd made, cocked her head to the side flirtatiously and suggested we have some brandy with our peanuts.

I agreed to be refreshed and she knelt to the floor in front of me, leaned forward with her hands to the floor and started searching for the brandy that was kept on the bottom shelf in the liquor locker.

How can this possibly work out with any success, I wondered. It was so damned crowded inside of the little lorry it would be like a wrestling match on top of a man-hole cover. No. It would be more like the inside of a man-hole. There wasn't even enough room to take off my coat, at which I tugged.

"Be patient," she said.

For what? Was she going to wave a magic wand and turn the place into a paradise?

"If you'll step outside and get ready, I'll rearrange in here. Hurry along now. And when you're ready, give a rap on the door." She handed me the brandy bottled and I was outside.

God Damn it was cold! A strong wind was coming up and the sky had already gotten dark.

"…and get ready."

What did she mean by that? I was already ready when I was inside. Get ready?

The only thing in my way had been my clothes and no room to take them off inside.

Well, there was plenty of room outside. But surely, she didn't mean for me to take off my clothes outside! That would be suicide as cold as it was. She had to be out of her ever-lovin' mind to think that I would be crazy enough to get naked out in the snow.

But on the other hand, I reasoned, I wouldn't have to get entirely naked.

I rolled around to the lee side of the little van to get out of the biting wind, took a couple of generous swigs from the brandy bottle and thought about it.

There was no doubt, it was definitely an invitation. It was obvious that she wanted me. She needed me.

But I needed her, too. Yet, at what sacrifice? What would Richy do in a case like this?

I took another couple of swigs of brandy and thought of Richy.

Hell, he'd of already had his clothes off, been back inside and scored while I was still outside thinking about it and freezing off my balls. Damn, it was cold!

Another swig or two and I unbuttoned my great coat. I wasn't as cold as I had been. That brandy was pretty good. It seemed to thaw me out, because I had an urge to pee.

I couldn't unbutton my pants with my gloves on, so I took them off and I dropped them in the snow while I tried to hold the bottle and dig down through the fly of my pants and search for the slit in my long underwear.

It must be colder than I thought, because I had trouble finding myself, even with both hands.

I had to chuckle at the irony of such big expectations from a little thing that I could hardly get a hold of.

I took time out for another drink.

No problem. I found it. All I had to do was to get stretched out far enough so as not to wet on myself. I had just too many clothes on. That was the problem.

Well, the solution was simple. My clothes had to come off.

I thought, with enough brandy inside of me I could probably manage the affair.

Sucking on the brandy, instead of sniffing it, I decided on a compromise.

So I fortified myself with a few more nips and resolved that I would absolutely not strip down anymore than my long-johns until I got back inside. Not romantic, but necessary to survive.

Even so, I was still outside and had to gather up my clothes.

Oh shit! I discovered I had wet my gloves in the snow.

Maybe I'd better not have anymore to drink, even though I was starting to feel the cold again.

In fact, it occurred to me while I was getting ready that it would be a good idea to get one of the condoms out of my billfold and put it on. That way I would be ready-ready.

Then I remembered, for some unknown reason, that I had been carrying three condoms in my billfold for months. It was probably a carryover from having optimistically always carried at least one condom in my billfold since high school.

So the idea came to me that, as cold as it was, it might even help some if I put on all three condoms. After all, it was terribly cold, three had to be warmer than one, and they were Government Issue and free.

I had another drink and thought about it.

No. It was better to forget about it and to take care of such details inside. I'd better concentrate on getting stripped down to my long underwear and combat boots.

Damn boots! I had to take 'em off to get my pants off and they were hard to manage. All of which caused me to stagger around in the icy snow in an effort to keep my balance, which of course was not possible.

I not only got my feet wet, but I was wet all over before I got my pants off and my boots back on. So I rewarded myself with a little drink.

Now, I wasn't drunk, because I was thinking clearly. Of course I was. And the main thought in my mind as I walked around in long underwear and unlaced combat boots picking up my belongings out of the snow was, what if those MP's happened to drive up and ask me who won that goddamned baseball game. And even worse, some Kraut might catch me out of uniform.

So I rapped on the door – and the back – and the sides of the little van as I collected my pants, my great coat – and decided to leave my frozen gloves – so there wouldn't be any delay in my getting back inside.

However, like every date I'd had in my life, she wasn't yet ready and I had to wait.

Jesus! Even praying wouldn't change the fact that at the very moment I was standing in the snow, freezing, somewhere in the midst of a great battle zone and hoping to get laid.

If I did make it back, I would report to Usher that he had been right. I had never had it so good back at the base.

Rose had to come outside and help me inside, because I was almost a cake of ice and I was a little fuzzy in the head.

Things were not too clear to me and I must have even blacked out for a bit.

My first awareness was that something good was happening to me. It was a warm gentle massage. I opened my eyes and was looking at the ceiling of the van, which was illuminated by candlelight, and Glenn Miller was playing STRING OF PEARLS – until the needle stuck on the phonograph record.

It could have been a dream, except for the reality of my luck with the needle sticking on the phonograph record. But it wasn't all that bad.

I finally saw Rose as she stood up in the narrow passageway without any clothes on and stepped over me lying on the pallet on the floor. She balanced herself, straddled above me, as she unstuck the needle and took her time to select another record that would hopefully not get stuck.

Then I completely relaxed as Glenn Miller started playing *IN THE MOOD* and Rose stood up there wiggling and winding up the spring on the phonograph player. I was no longer cold and my senses melted into sheer pleasure. My life, despite the nightmares, felt worth living.

By the 17th of January 1945 I was back in Skunk Hollow for my twenty-first birthday. My war was over and I finally qualified officially as a MAN.

Author's Note:
Experiences of Truman Smith's encounters with the German pilotless bombs are detailed in the book V-1 / V-2, HITLER'S VENGEANCE ON LONDON, by David Johnson, 1982, Stein and Day Publishers, New York, ISBN 0 8128 2858 5.

WAR DEPARTMENT
AAF FORM NO. 1
APPROVED DEC. 7, 1942

DIVIDUAL FLIGHT RECC¯D

(1) SERIAL NO. 0-756341   (2) NAME Smith,   Truman   J.   (3) RANK 2nd Lt.   (4) AGE 1924
LAST FIRST MIDDLE

(5) PERS. CLASS 1B   (6) BRANCH Air Corps   (7) STATION APO 559, USAAF 155

(8) ORGANIZATION ASSIGNED 8th 8th Bomber 4th 385th 550th none RED FOR FLYING
AIR FORCE COMMAND WING GROUP SQUADRON DETACHMENT

(9) ORGANIZATION ATTACHED none
AIR FORCE COMMAND WING GROUP SQUADRON DETACHMENT

(10) PRESENT RATING & DATE Pilot 10-1-48   (11) ORIGINAL RATING & DATE Same

(12) TRANSFERRED FROM   (13) FLIGHT RESTRICTIONS none

(15) TRANSFERRED TO   (14) TRANSFER DATE

(16) DO NOT WRITE IN THIS SPACE

PERS CLASS	RANK	RTG.	A. F.	COMMAND	WING	GROUP NO.	TYPE	SQUADRON NO.	TYPE	STATION	MO.	YR.	(17) MONTH May 19 44
:		:	: :	: :	: :	: :	: :	: :	: :	: :	:	:	

DAY	AIRCRAFT TYPE, MODEL & SERIES	NO. LANDINGS	FLYING INST. (INCL. IN 1ST PIL TIME) S	COMMD. PILOT C CA	CO-PILOT CP	QUALI-FIED PILOT DUAL QD	FIRST PILOT DAY P	FIRST PILOT NIGHT P N OR NI	RATED PERS. NON-PILOT	NON-RATED OTHER ARMS & SERVICES	NON-RATED OTHER CREW & PASS'GR	INSTRU-MENT I	NIGHT N	SPECIAL INFORMATION INSTRU-MENT TRAINER	PILOT-NON-MIL AIRCRAFT OVER 400 H.P.	UNDER 400 H.P.
18	19	20	21	22	23	24	25	26	27 28 29	30	31	32	33	34	35	36
1	B-17G	1			6:30		*		LeGaosseillien					2:00		
3	B-17G	1			4:10						2:00					
2	Link Tr.													1:00		
6	Link Tr.													1:00		
8	B-17G	1			5:00		4:00	*	Berlin, Germ.							
9	B-17G	1			2:25		3:00	*	Leon Couvran, France							
10	B-17G	4				1:00										
11	B-17G	1			3:00		3:00	*	Brussels, Belgium.							
12	B-17G	1			4:45		4:30	*	Zwickoy, Germany							
13	B-17G	1			6:35			*	Osnabruch, Germany				2:15			
19	B-17G	3														
20	B-17G	1			5:40			*	Aachen, Germ.					1:00		
25	B-17G	1			7:00			*	Liege, Belium							
26	B-17G	1				3:30										
27	B-17F	4				2:10								1:00		
28	B-17G	1			8:30			*	Konnigsbonn, Germ.							
29	B-17G	1			8:00			*	Leipzig, Germ. nov mock on							
30	B-17G	1			4:45			*	Watten Stracourt							
31	B-17G	1			7:00			*	Hamm.							

* Denotes Combat Missions.

CERTIFIED CORRECT:

[signature]

WARREN E. CERRONE,
Capt. Air Corps,
Operations Officer.

COLUMN TOTALS			74:20	6:40	14:30						2:15	2:00	2:00	4:00	
			(42) TOTAL STUDENT PILOT TIME			(43) TOTAL FIRST PILOT TIME			(44) TOTAL PILOT TIME						
(37) THIS MONTH						14:30			95:30						
(38) PREVIOUS MONTHS THIS F. Y.			74:20			7:55			321:20						
(39) THIS FISCAL YEAR			143:25			22:25			416:50						
(40) PREVIOUS FISCAL YEARS			217:15			5:00 Jan			143:25						
(41) TO DATE						22:25			560:15						

AIRCRAFT	NL	CARD NO. 1							CARD NO. 2				CARD NO. 3			
19	20	21	22	23	24	25	26	27	28	29	30	31	32	33	34	35	36
DO NOT WRITE IN THIS SPACE																

Flight Record from April 1944

BACKWORDS

Hat's it all about anyway? It's been a half century now that I look backward in an attempt to determine the consequences and perhaps learn a few things from some rather extraordinary experiences that might be distilled into some wisdom that could serve humanity. However, for each question answered, the mystery seems to become even greater.

God certainly didn't have to worry that man was going to "be like God" from the Tree of Knowledge in the Garden of Eden, since God's system was set up so that the more we learn, the less we really know.

For example, the war left me with many questions. Some I was able to solve. But I found it strange how an even greater question sometimes accompanies an answer.

I wondered for 50 years what happened to Bill Shannon, whom I'd buddied with. When writing the book I mentioned how he'd been wounded over Paris. Nevertheless I was unable to answer what had actually happened to him.

Therefore, there was really no point in writing about it if I didn't provide the reader with the outcome of the incident. So I thought about it for several days, unable to proceed, because Bill Shannon was gone from my life and I didn't know how to bring him back.

Finally I decided I would have to drop the event from the book and to stop worrying about it, when the telephone rang.

"This is Bill Shannon in North Carolina...Do you remember me?"

"I do, if you were a navigator and were wounded over Paris?"

It had been a half-century before on the 22nd of June 1944 over Paris that I had looked down on his ship, the nose of which had been riddled with flak. He'd told me before it happened that he wanted to get every medal possible, including the Purple Heart, and his wish came true that day. But what exactly had happened?

AAF FORM NO. 5
APPROVED DEC. 7, 1942

INDIVIDUAL FLIGHT RECORD

(1) SERIAL NO. O-756341 (2) NAME Smith, Truman J. (3) RANK 2nd Lt. (4) AGE 1924
(5) PERS. CLASS 18 (6) BRANCH Air Corps (7) STATION APO 559 USAAF 155
(8) ORGANIZATION ASSIGNED 8th 8th Bomber 4th 385th 550th none
(9) ORGANIZATION ATTACHED none
(10) PRESENT RATING & DATE Pilot 10-1-43 (11) ORIGINAL RATING & DATE Same
(12) TRANSFERRED FROM _____ (13) FLIGHT RESTRICTIONS none
(15) TRANSFERRED TO _____ (14) TRANSFER DATE _____

(17) MONTH April 1944

DAY (18)	AIRCRAFT TYPE, MODEL & SERIES (19)	NO LANDINGS (20)	FLYING INST (INCL IN 1ST PIL TIME) (21)	COMMD PILOT C CA (22)	CO-PILOT CP (23)	QUALIFIED PILOT DUAL QD (24)	FIRST PILOT DAY P (25)	FIRST PILOT NIGHT P N OR NI (26)	NON-PILOT (27)	(28)	(29)	OTHER ARMS & SERVICES (30)	OTHER CREW PASS'GR (31)	INSTRUMENT (32)	NIGHT N (33)	INSTRUMENT TRAINER (34)	PILOT NON-MIL AIRCRAFT OVER 400 H.P. (35)	UNDER 400 H.P. (36)
5	B-17G	1			1:00									1:30				
4	Link															1:00		
6	B-17G	1			4:00													
7	Link															1:00		
8	B-17G	1			5:30	•			Quakenbrück (Munster)	Germany								
9	B-17G	1			:55													
10	B-17F	1			5:15				Diest/Schaffen									
11	B-17G	1			5:30		5:30	•	Politz									
12	B-17G	1			2:20	1:00												
17	B-17G	1			1:00	1:25												
18	B-17G	1			9:15	•			Berlin	Germany								
16	Link															1:00		
20	B-17F	1			5:15	•			French (No Ball)									
21	B-17G	1			3:00								1:00					
23	B-17G	1	3:40															
26	B-17G	1			1:05													
25	Link															1:00		
28	B-17G	1			2:30													
29	B-17G	1			8:20	•			Berlin	Germany								
30	B-17G	1			3:20													

• Denotes Combat Missions

CERTIFIED CORRECT:

WARREN E. CERRONE,
Capt., Air Corps,
Operations Officer.

COLUMN TOTALS 3:40 | 64:15 | 7:55 | 1:30 | 4:00

(42) TOTAL STUDENT PILOT TIME
(43) TOTAL FIRST PILOT TIME
(44) TOTAL PILOT TIME

(37) THIS MONTH			72:10
(38) PREVIOUS MONTHS THIS F.Y.		7:55	392:35
(39) THIS FISCAL YEAR		7:55	464:45
(40) PREVIOUS FISCAL YEARS	217:45		
(41) TO DATE	217:45	7:55	464:45

Flight Record from May 1944

WAR DEPARTMENT
AAF FORM NO. 5
APPROVED DEC. 7, 1942

IDIVIDUAL FLIGHT RECORD

(1) SERIAL NO. **O-756341**   (2) NAME **Smith,** LAST   **Truman** FIRST   **J.** MIDDLE   (3) RANK **2nd Lt.**   (4) AGE **1924**

(5) PERS. CLASS **18**   (6) BRANCH **Air Corps**   (7) STATION **APO 559, USAAF 155** ATTACHED FOR FLYING

(8) ORGANIZATION ASSIGNED **8th** AIR FORCE **8th Bomber** COMMAND **4th** WING **385th** GROUP **550th** SQUADRON **none** DETACHMENT

(9) ORGANIZATION ATTACHED **none** AIR FORCE ___ COMMAND ___ WING ___ GROUP ___ SQUADRON ___ DETACHMENT

(10) PRESENT RATING & DATE **Pilot 10-1-43**   (11) ORIGINAL RATING & DATE **Same**

(12) TRANSFERRED FROM ___   (13) FLIGHT RESTRICTIONS **none**

(15) TRANSFERRED TO ___   (14) TRANSFER DATE ___

PERS. CLASS	RANK	RTG.	A.F.	COMMAND	WING	GROUP NO.	TYPE	SQUADRON NO.	TYPE	STATION	MQ.	YR.	(17) MONTH **June 1944**
:	:	:	:	: :	: :	: :	: :	: :	: :	: :			

DAY	AIRCRAFT TYPE, MODEL & SERIES	NO. LANDINGS	FLYING INST. (INCL. IN 1ST PIL. TIME)	COMMD. PILOT C CA	CO-PILOT CP	QUALIFIED PILOT DUAL QD	FIRST PILOT DAY P	FIRST PILOT NIGHT P N OR NI	RATED PERS. NON-PILOT DAY P	RATED PERS. NON-PILOT NIGHT	NON-RATED OTHER ARMS & SERVICES	NON-RATED OTHER CREW & PASS'GR	INSTRUMENT 1	NIGHT N	INSTRUMENT TRAINER	PILOT NON-MIL. AIRCRAFT OVER 400 H.P.	PILOT NON-MIL. AIRCRAFT UNDER 400 H.P.
18	19	20	21	22	23	24	25	26	27	28	29	30	31	32	33	34	35 36
2	B-17G	1			5:00	*	Equihen-Wimereux										
7	B-17G	1			9:00	*	Niorte, France.								2:00		
14	B-17G	1			6:15	*	Florenness, Jurzine										
15	B-17G	1			8:30	*	Hannover, Germany										
18	B-17G	1			6:45	*	" "						3:00				
20	B-17G	1			8:00	*	Fallersleben, Konnigsborg, Ger.				4:00						
21	B-17G	1			9:30	*	Berlin, Germ.				3:00						
22	B-17G	1			6:25	*	Paris, France				2:00						
24	B-17G	1			7:15	*	Wesermunde,										
25	B-17G	1			9:00	*	French Special.										
26	B-17G	4			1:00										1:00		
		* Denotes Combat Missions.															

CERTIFIED CORRECT:

[signature]

WARREN E. CERRONE,
Capt. Air Corps,
Operations Officer.

| COLUMN TOTALS | | | | | 75:40 | 1:00 | | | | | | | 12:00 | 2:00 | 1:00 | | |

	(42) TOTAL STUDENT PILOT TIME	(43) TOTAL FIRST PILOT TIME	(44) TOTAL PILOT TIME
(37) THIS MONTH		1:00	76:40
(38) PREVIOUS MONTHS THIS F.Y.		22:25	416:50
(39) THIS FISCAL YEAR	74:20	23:25	493:30
(40) PREVIOUS FISCAL YEARS	143:25		143:25
(41) TO DATE	217:45	23:25	636:55

AIRCRAFT	NL	CARD NO. 1						CARD NO. 2				CARD NO. 3			
19	20	21	22	23	24	25	26	27	28	29	30	31	32	33	34	35	36

Flight Record from June 1944

INDIVIDUAL FLIGHT RECORD

(1) SERIAL NO. O-756341 (2) NAME Smith, Truman J. (3) RANK 2nd Lt. (4) AGE 1924
(5) PERS. CLASS 18 (6) BRANCH Air Corps (7) STATION APO 559, USAAF 155
(8) ORGANIZATION ASSIGNED 8th 8th Bomber 4th 385th 550th none
(9) ORGANIZATION ATTACHED none
(10) PRESENT RATING & DATE Pilot 10-1-43 (11) ORIGINAL RATING & DATE Same
(12) TRANSFERRED FROM (13) FLIGHT RESTRICTIONS none
(15) TRANSFERRED TO (14) TRANSFER DATE

(16)

(17) MONTH July 1944

DAY	AIRCRAFT TYPE, MODEL & SERIES	NO. LANDINGS	FLYING INST. (INCL. IN 1ST PIL. TIME) S	COMMD. PILOT C CA	CO-PILOT CP	QUALI-FIED PILOT DUAL QD	FIRST PILOT DAY P N OR NI	NIGHT P	NON-PILOT P-AI	RP	PCO	OTHER ARMS & SERVICES	OTHER CREW OP & GR RI	INSTRU-MENT I	NIGHT N	INSTRU-MENT TRAINER	PILOT NON-MIL AIRCRAFT OVER 400 H.P.	UNDER 400 H.P.
18	19	20	21	22	23	24	25	26	27	28	29	30	31	32	33	34	35	36
6	B-17G	1		4:30		*	Sautrecquat, France (Aia Drome)											
7	B-17G	1			1:30						:45							
8	B-17G	1		6:00		*	Conches (AuDrme)					2:00						
10	B-17F	1				2:45		1:30				XXXX						
11	B-17F	1		3:00														
12	B-17G	1		9:30		*	Munich, Germ.					3:00						
13	B-17G	1		4:30								4:00						
14	B-17G	1		10:35		*	"Caddilac (French Special)					2:35						
15	B-17G	10		:45	:45						:45							
16	B-17G	1			4:15							3:00						
17	B-17G	1		1:00														
20	B-17F	2		3:00								:30						
21	B-17F	1			1:30													
21	B-17F	8		1:00	1:00													
22	B-17G	1				4:40												
23	B-17G	1				3:30		:30										
24	B-17G	1		5:00		*	St. Lo - Nabombing = Weather weather											
25	B-17G	1		2:15		①	1:15 Started For Brussels P.M. (Recalld 30,000'											
25	B-17G	1		5:45		① *	:45 St. Lo. France											
28	B-17G	1		9:00		*	:30 Merseberg Germ											

* Denotes Combat Missions.

CERTIFIED CORRECT:

WILLIAM T. VANCE,
Capt. Air Corps,
Operations Officer.

COLUMN TOTALS			40:50	12:00	32:55	4:30	:45				15:50					
			(42) TOTAL STUDENT PILOT TIME		(43) TOTAL FIRST PILOT TIME				(44) TOTAL PILOT TIME CP & QD-AI							

	CF N QD-AI
(37) THIS MONTH	32:55 4:30 85:45 15:50
(38) PREVIOUS MONTHS THIS F. Y.	
(39) THIS FISCAL YEAR	32:55 4:30 85:45 15:50
(40) PREVIOUS FISCAL YEARS	217:45 23:25 1:20 636:55 23:05
(41) TO DATE	217:45 56:20 5:50 722:40 38:55

AIRCRAFT	NL	CARD NO. 1							CARD NO. 2					CARD NO. 3			
19	20	21	22	23	24	25	26	27	28	29	30	31	32	33	34	35	36

Flight Record from July 1944

When Bill called I asked him to bring me up to date and – how and why he'd called me when he did.

He said his wife had insisted he call me after he mentioned to her several months prior that he'd seen my name in a newsletter of the 385th Bomb Group Memorial Association and that he knew me. So at her urging, he had searched me out in the months following and finally made the call. But why it happened exactly when it did remains a mystery.

So what had happened to Bill Shannon?

A piece of aluminum speared him in the left eye over Paris, and was stuck there. To remove it would cause a loss of fluid in his eyeball and he would become blind.

"Take it out!" he demanded on his return to base and was transported to a specialist in London where the metal was removed.

Bill Shannon's recovery was so fast and complete that he was accepted into pilot training and assigned to fly B-26's. After the war he became a race car driver.

When I commented on his good luck, he agreed and said that he'd had the Last Rites on three separate occasions. On one auto crash he almost lost his other eye, but recovered 20/20 eyesight, bought an airplane and flew privately.

Shannon confessed that he'd had a great life, gotten married and had four children. However, he regretted the necessity of selling his airplane along the way, because he truly loved to fly.

So he told his wife that when she dies, he's going to take the insurance money and buy his airplane back. Her plan, he said, was that when he dies that she is going to replace him with a good husband.

Then laughing – which I assumed he had been doing for fifty years – Bill Shannon told me "goodbye," with his intention to see me sometime in the future.

Thus, the question of what had happened to Bill Shannon was answered, but it left an even greater question: Why did he call me when he did – after fifty years?

All I can figure is that something is going on beyond my comprehension. My wife, Margot, said, "Don't worry about it. Just accept it."

A friend asked how I was able to recall such detail after fifty years. It reminded him of Matthew writing about the life of Christ fifty years after Christ had died. "How did you do it?"

Well, I certainly can't speak for Matthew, but I feel that an event is impressed on us in proportion to its magnitude. And as for my combat flying, I had made a conscious effort (Which must have slipped into my unconscious) that I should never forget the ordeal, because it just might help in some way to prevent it from happening to others and I would be awarded the Nobel Peace Prize…Yet, I was puzzled in the recalling of the war.

Before writing anything down I referred to my log book and notes to refresh my memory. Then spending time alone – call it meditation – I was mentally back in the event.

Yet, in many instances, it was more vivid than mere memory. And as strange as it seems, during the replay, my viewpoint often shifted from subjective first-person to an objective perspective outside of myself, as if watching from a different camera angle. It was as if I were my own "angel" observing the event from behind my left shoulder…It astonished me.

Thus, it is that I am both compelled and impelled to acknowledge and give credit to something that I don't understand in my effort to try and know the results of my combat experiences.

I'm sorry to say that I still don't know some things. Like, Turner flying out of formation and around the flak-bursts one day as casual as if passing another car on the highway…He was saved. Yet, on another trip he was shot down. Why? What happened to Turner and his crew anyway?

The question was answered by Weisgerber, his bombardier. As former billet mates we were happy to accidentally meet in Oklahoma City a year after they had been shot down on that Munich raid, the 13th of July, 1944. He told me they had made it safely into Switzerland, from where they escaped and the underground had gotten them back to England.

Okay, but in finding the answer to what had happened to them, another one of those questions, which may or may not have something to do with anything, was raised.

Weisgerber handed me a ring of metal, one-half inch thick and an inch-and-a-half in diameter, while he completed his story about returning to England.

They had been sent back to the States for recuperation and also to prevent them from being shot down again and interrogated by the Germans for information about the underground. But in time, he did return to combat and had been wounded.

The piece of flak he had handed me had hit him under his right arm, spun and slid its way under his skin and around his chest to his left side, where it had been excised.

"Do you see those numbers on that shell?" he asked.

I examined the piece, recalling from my training in Field Artillery as a kid, that it was the arming ring from a shell, on which the numbers of the shell were imprinted. I acknowledged seeing the numbers.

"Now look at this," he said as he pulled his dog tags through the front of his shirt...

Discarding the first three numbers on the shell, the last seven numbers on the shell matched his serial number on the dog tags EXACTLY!

The odds of a match seemed inconceivable. But what did such a coincidence mean? It was another unsolved mystery.

I returned the shrapnel to him and he said he was going to take good care of it, because it had his number on it.

Why? Did he think caring for it would keep him from getting killed? Surely he didn't expect to live forever.

Something was certainly WRONG, because the order and the pieces of a great mystery were being presented to me, but I just couldn't put them together to make any sense. It wasn't natural. In fact, in trying to unravel the secrets of my experiences the answers seemed to be somewhere in the supernatural.

Things were skewed in the direction of Aristotle's pursuits in metaphysics and ontology; concerned with the nature of being, or different kinds of existence. He was trying to work a solution to my problem – 300 years B.C. ; over 2,000 years before airplanes and before I came along.

Even so, questions remained. Like, what happened to my other billet mates: McDonald's crew, as well as Captain White's crew with whom they had collided on the 12th of July 1944 mission to Munich?

Well, part of that question was answered in 1990 when Mike Pappas, driving from California, stopped in Oklahoma for a visit.

Mike and I had been in the same squadron, but we hadn't known each other in 1944. However, we'd met in 1950 in Hollywood, where I had become a television director and he became a production assistant for me. However, we didn't discuss the war; probably trying to forget it and to make new lives in the battles of the post war era.

It wasn't until 1990 when Mike spent a few days at my home that we got back into the war and he was talking about getting shot down over Berlin, and how the citizens captured him and tried to beat him to death – one old man clubbing him with a bicycle – until the German military showed up and saved his life.

Mike ended up in a POW camp, where he met another gunner from our squadron. It was a Sergeant Atiyeh who had been a waist gunner on McDonald's crew…He was the only survivor of the 20 crew members on the two ships in the midair collision.

Atiyeh recalled that a great shadow (White's ship) overtook them. The next he knew he was falling through space, because his ship had broken in two. As he fell he looked to his chest for his parachute. It was there, but it was clipped to the harness at his chest by only one of the two "D" rings. So while falling, he secured the chute by the second "D" ring, opened it and floated down to earth where he was captured and taken prisoner.

While I had not seen any, three chutes had been reported. However, Atiyeh was the only survivor. Had the other two landed safely and then been killed by civilians? It was another unsolved mystery.

At the end of 1995, I read in the HARDLIFE HERALD, Newsletter of the 385th Bomb Group, that Andrew L. Ryan had joined the Memorial Association in the hope of learning what had happened to his older brother Steve Ryan, who had been McDonald's copilot.

I called him in Virginia, telling him that I had known his brother and had witnessed the collision.

He was very grateful and sent a letter to thank me:

"Truman, there are so many things I would like to know, but just don't know the right questions to ask."

Well, hopefully that's what I was trying to do in writing the book; providing some questions and possibly some answers, which seemed to provoke more questions.

Along the way in writing the book I called the Air Force Historical Research Agency at Maxwell Air Force Base, Montgomery Alabama. I spoke with Archie Di Fante who was in charge and enthusiastically cooperative, obviously devoted to his work. He invited me to come and use the facilities of the Agency.

According to Archie there appears to be a want – a need – for wives, children, grandchildren, former combatants, friends, historians and the many who are just plain curious.

The number of us former combatants grows smaller, but time multiplies the wonderment of what took place in the now peaceful skies of Europe.

Perhaps the basic question is why anyone would volunteer to participate in such insanity.

I met a young pilot who flew corporate jets and he lamented the fact that he'd been born 30 years too late, because he would like to have been a combat pilot in World War Two. "Except," he said, "I don't know if I could handle somebody shooting at me... Tell me, did you ever get any holes in your airplane?"

Could you believe over 200 in one day? What did he think combat flying was about?

Well, he didn't really know, but he'd seen a lot of movies.

Then somebody asked me what I thought about the feature film *MEMPHIS BELLE*...Well, I had to confess, "It was a MOVIE. And the really nice thing about a movie is: You don't have to defy gravity; your life is not at risk; you aren't in a hostile environment doing battle in sub-freezing temperatures where a lack of oxygen is lethal; and you don't have to sit there held in suspense for an average of eight hours a day, month after month."

So why would anyone volunteer for such torture?

It was at the national meeting of the Combat Pilots Association in 1972 that I sat next to an older pilot who had volunteered prior to 1941 to fly with the American Eagle Squadron in the Royal Air Force, where he had become an Ace. He had an arm missing that he'd lost in a crash near Munich, Germany. So I cut his steak and prepared his baked potato as we visited.

Our president of the Combat Pilots Association, Steve Ritchie, had become an Ace in Vietnam. He concluded his keynote address praying for everlasting peace, so that nobody would ever again have to fly combat.

My dinner companion surprised me by mumbling, "Bull-shit!"

I asked him for an explanation.

"The world has been at war longer than at peace. It's always been that way and it won't change. We are training the pilots of the world – Israel, Iran, Germany – in the most sophisticated aircraft ever developed. The Russians are doing the same. These airplanes are on the cutting edge of technology and the pilots who fly them want their day in the sun. They want to test themselves in the ultimate trial of combat."

Years later I listened to the interview of a Top Gun pilot who verified this premise when he said, "I've proven myself to be the best pilot in competition with my peers, and I'm proud of that. However, I will never really know how good I am until I am actually tested in combat."

Well, I had taken the test and passed – so far. I might even deceive myself into thinking that the older I get, the better I was. But, that's what combat flying is about; challenging the odds in testing one's self for the reward of accomplishment.

So what's so *WRONG* with that?

What's the lesson?

If Moses received instructions from a burning bush, then burning bombers, or bombed and burning cities must also contain some instructions.

Therefore, it seems to be that fulfillment is in direct proportion to the effort made with one's abilities and the risks taken. Thus, FULFILLMENT equals EFFORT and ABILITIES in proportion to the RISK taken: F = E A R

However, this does not make combat essential to achievement.

Perhaps the greatest challenge and success in life comes from developing an affectionate family. Or lacking love, for a youngster to overcome such hardship and still become a reliable and caring adult. This of course requires GIVING and not TAKING.

Didn't someone once say, "It is more blessed to give than to receive."

So the lesson to "Do unto others" has been there all along. Too bad it takes a war to remind us.

Remember Jake McNiece, when we'd met in the London blackout, intent on jumping behind enemy lines and doing unto the Germans; and my worrying if he had survived?

Jake not only survived the odds of dropping behind enemy lines at Normandy in June, 1944, but he also jumped into Holland on a rescue mission in September when British Field Marshall Montgomery tried to go to *A Bridge Too Far*. Then in December, Jake jumped into *The Battle of the Bulge* on another rescue mission. And if that wasn't enough, on Friday the 13th, in February 1945, Jake jumped into the Siegfried Line on the German border.

Statistically it was not possible to survive two jumps. Yet Jake McNiece had managed to accomplish four parachute landings behind enemy lines in the fulfillment of his duties as a paratrooper in the 101st Airborne Division.

Actually, Jake returned home to Ponca City, Oklahoma before I did, where he is fulfilling his life in serving others as a lay minister in his church. He and his wife, Martha, take care of the aged and infirm,sometimes treating the entire church to a fish fry.

I haven't asked, but I assume that Jake McNiece no longer uses hand grenades when he goes fishing.

Rain fell from the low gray clouds. Black smoke belched from the exhaust of the first of four Wright Cyclone engines as it slowly came to life.

It was a typical 1944 early English morning. The brakes squealed and the hydraulic pumps honked as the B-17 was positioned at the end of the wet runway. Then slowly, but so powerfully, the four engines, rumbling and growling at first, grew to a crescendo that brought pain to the ears. The brakes were released and the giant lurched forward. Circular white contrails were drawn from the moisture laden air like huge stretched springs as the World War Two bomber accelerated down the runway – on and on until, as if in slow motion, it took to the air and disappeared into the cheerless overcast.

What was happening was that I was going through a time-warp, because it was not 1944 in England, but 1990 in Ponca City, Oklahoma, and I was on board.

This time warp was an ENCORE in flying a B-17 Flying Fortress for the last time in my life, 46 years after the war.

The war was ancient history for me in 1954. It had been nine years since I had participated, and no reason to think of it anymore, because I'd gotten on with my life: flying in the Amazon; retraining into Drama (because a few people had told me I told good air stories); directing television in Hollywood and being recalled into the Air Force to help develop TV for the military during the Korean "Flap."

Then one day I received orders to go to the Headquarters of the United States Air Force Europe, in Wiesbaden, Germany, to help establish a television station. It was an encore to return to Germany.

On the way the engines on the C-124 transport droned for ten hours and I was hypnotically transported back in time to the hundreds of hours of listening to the deep humming sound of the engines of a B-17. So when I landed that night at Rhein Main Air Base in Frankfurt, Germany, I was bewildered – and a bit frightened.

This was the first time, after having struggled so hard to avoid landing in Germany, that I was actually on German soil and I was overtaken by deep depression.

Few German cities had escaped the bombings. Five-thousand American and British bombers hammered Hamburg into fire-storms that depleted the oxygen. One Hamburg woman watching corpses being stacked into trucks like cord-wood said, "If there were a God, He would have shown them some mercy." An elderly man replied, "Leave God out of this. Men make war, not God."

Margot
(Photo courtesy of Carlton F. Weber)

ENCORE

I n Medieval Times the civilians were spared, as the armies
confronted each other on the field of battle. Such conduct was
changed in the American (un)Civil War by the burnings and
sieges of mainly Southern cities. And by World War Two, total
warfare reached its zenith.

Therefore, my depression was not caused by personal remorse, but
more from frustration. As an American I had done what had been
necessary, like hundreds of thousands of others. Otherwise, our country
would surely have suffered what Hitler had inflicted on all of Europe.

Then too, the Japanese had actually attacked us without a
declaration of war in an effort to benefit themselves by taking over our
economic advantage...One Japanese combatant stated, "Germany had
tried to develop the atomic bomb, as we had. And if we had gotten it
first, WE would have used it!"

There was no question that we Americans had to defend ourselves.
There was no guilt in that. But the consequences of it all??? My God,
even without the atomic bomb, over six-and-a-half million Germans,
themselves, had been killed and more than one-an-a-half million
Germans were missing. It was unimaginable.

On the 13th of February 1945 Dresden was destroyed by British
and American bombers. Over 135,000 Germans were killed within 24
hours; and Dresden was only one German City. So how must the
Germans feel about me, an American bomber pilot? How did I feel
about myself?

Well I was pretty screwed up. Nobody had briefed me for this
ENCORE. One day I had been in Orlando, Florida, and then I was
walking down the streets alone at night in Frankfurt, Germany, trying
to sort out my thoughts.

Across the street an old man limped along. I wondered if I had whatever it would take to overpower him and disguise myself in his clothes and try to escape back to England. In the lamp light two SS troopers surprised me when they came around the corner. I tensed for action and one of them greeted me in a friendly manner. "Guten Abend."

They were not SS troopers, but policemen.

Strange, I thought. Even in an American uniform I was not considered an enemy. Things had obviously changed, but I had not.

Inadvertently I felt I had put myself in jeopardy while trying to adapt to my new environment.

I needed a shave and stopped in a barber shop that was still open.

With my face lathered I was laying back in the barber's chair as he stropped his razor. He knew I was an American. Did he also know from the wings and the ribbons on my chest that I was the one who had bombed his homeland?

I was extremely uneasy as he slid the razor over my throat, and I tried to think what it had to be like to have been a German during the war...

Even so, before I realized it, I fell in love with Germany. My duties took me to North Africa, Saudi Arabia, Greece and France, but it was in Germany that I fell in love. So I was disappointed when my temporary duty was finished and I had to return to the States.

Within a year, however, good fortune smiled and I was sent back to Germany in a permanent change of station for three years as a motion picture officer.

It was the greatest assignment of my career and the start of the best part of my life, because I met Margot who would marry me and we would raise two wonderful children and live happily ever after. Yet, such a romantic outcome was not conceivable at the start.

There was a problem. Margot did not care for Americans. So, being a bomber pilot put me right at the top of her list.

Margot Licht had been born in Berlin the month and year that Adolf Hitler was named Chancellor of the Third Reich. In 1943, when ten years old, she and her parents and six older brothers and sisters lost their wonderful three story home during an air raid.

All hell broke loose in 1943! The British and American Air Forces began retaliating against Germany for the havoc it had created in Europe, and its continued bombing of England. So, Herr Goebbles, Minister of Propaganda for the Third Reich, directed all children be evacuated to Eastern Germany.

Frau Licht, Margot's mother, responsible for her seven children, disagreed. She took the three youngest of her flock in the opposite direction to the west near Bad Hersfeld, from where her husband, Herr Hans Licht, had originally come.

Approaching the train station the train stopped, because American P-51 fighter aircraft, "Tiefbombers," were strafing the station. Momma Licht abandoned the train with her brood and took to the woods for safety. Eventually they would walk ten miles to the village of Herr Licht's nephew – where they were not welcome, because Hans Licht had been arrested by the Gestapo.

Herr Licht was in a prison near Kassel; put there on testimony of a sixteen year-old Hitler Youth. Not because he had helped Jews escape the country. That they didn't know about. His crime was for swearing at a large photograph of Hitler in the local tavern.

Hans Licht would be allowed out of prison only if his oldest son, Gunther, who was 16, would volunteer for the S.S.. So, not telling his mother, Gunther volunteered. Even so, Hans Licht was not released from prison.

There followed a very rough time of inadequate housing, shortage of clothing and many times no food at all. Frau Licht performed miracles, cooking common weeds and making soup from stinging nettles. The children were allowed to help the farmers dig potatoes for a very small share of the produce. At harvest time they were allowed to glean the field for grains of wheat left over from the harvest.

Easter 1945: the Lichts would finally have meat for a special meal. Although, Margot was saddened that it was her pet rabbit. However, she didn't eat her rabbit. None of the Lichts ate the rabbit, because the "Amies" came through the village and plundered the cooked rabbit.

Frau Licht had met the Americans, offering a worn, but clean, towel and a bowl of water to refresh themselves. When finished they tore the towel into shreds and threw it back at her.

There was so much WRONGNESS that needed correcting.

When I met Margot in 1955 I was immediately attracted to her, even before I knew of her special qualities. I had been invited to dinner by Major Bill Cadmus, Head of Dentistry for USAFE Headquarters. I met his wife, Gloria, their three boys and Margot, who was the nanny for the boys.

Margot was a real prize. She was a much sought after nanny and had been highly recommended by a neurosurgeon who had returned to the States. Dr. Bill Cadmus had driven over five hours one night to find Margot living with her parents near Bad Hersfeld and to convince her that she was badly needed, because his wife was about to have their third child.

Well, I too felt a need when I watched and admired her at dinner. However, she did not respond in kind. In fact, she also didn't favor me after dinner. By her actions I could tell that she regarded me as a non-person.

The next week Bill suggested that I might stop by and possibly babysit and per chance "Americanize" Margot, who would be babysitting the boys, while he and Gloria went out for the evening.

Bill needn't have worried about keeping Margot company when they left us for the evening. An American Sergeant showed up and was invited to join me seated on the sofa, while Margot went to the door to visit with a young and handsome German Doctor who stopped by to say hello. There was also some fellow from Holland who happened to be "in the neighborhood" and a Lieutenant called on the phone. No, Margot was not short of company.

That evening the Sergeant and I sat on the sofa visiting with each other, both enthralled by the sheer beauty and grace of Margot's movements; fantastic ankles and neat feet in high heels; long sensuous legs and a firm buttocks; high cheekbones, sexy eyebrows and lips – .

I could hardly stand it and felt that I had to leave or go crazy, but I wasn't about to leave her alone with the Sergeant and – God only knew – whoever else might show up.

My tenacity was finally rewarded when the Sergeant decided to leave and the suitors stopped calling for the evening. However, there was an obvious chill in the room until Margot let me know that she really didn't care for Americans.

"Well, I'm fortunate, then," I announced, "because I am a German."

My response surprised me as much as it did Margot and I wondered how much difference there was between a line and a lie.

If I was a German, why couldn't I speak the language any better than I did?

I heard myself telling Margot how I'd been born in Darmstadt, and how my parents had taken me to the States when I was only three years old…Darmstadt, because the name came to mind. That's where my grandmother Schneider had come from in the 1800's… It seemed to work.

However, there was the problem of my having been a bomber pilot.

"And did you bomb Berlin?" Margot asked, explaining that her family had lost their home there.

Yes, I had bombed Berlin, but asked when had they been bombed out?

It had been a night raid in 1943.

Then that wasn't me. "It had to have been the British," I said, and I've stuck with that statement ever since.

That's the way it had started forty years ago – with a *line*, but never a falsehood afterward. Actually it wasn't the *line* that confirmed me as worthy, but Margot's older brother Gunther, captured and abused by Americans.

"It makes no difference that he is an American," he told her. "If you love each other, you should marry."

So the encore of returning to Germany nine years after bombing it was resolved in a happy ending to some terrible experiences. Marrying Margot was the best thing that ever happened to me and we've had a wonderful life together, despite the irony of being former enemies.

After a dozen years of marriage, Margot gave me a membership in the Confederate Air Force as an anniversary present.

It was at an Armed Forces Day at Tinker Air Force Base in the late sixties that I sat in the cockpit of a B-17 to answer questions from those touring the old bomber.

However, my own wonderment was how it had turned out that I was in the cockpit while – standing beneath the chin turret taking contributions to help maintain the historical bomber – was Margot; she having survived the Allied bombings; having married an American bomber pilot; having become a loyal American citizen and an advocate of U. S. Air power.

John Wayne leaned toward me, looked me square in the eyes and asked, "Did you bomb your wife?"

It was March 1979 and we were seated on the veranda of his home overlooking the harbor of Newport Beach, California. Burt Kennedy, a longtime friend of mine who had worked for Wayne as a writer and director, had arranged for us to spend a day with The Duke.

I had brought along two books about John Wayne and asked if he would autograph one for my children and one for my wife, Margot.

Sure. He asked about Margot to get an idea about what to write to her. I started off by saying that she had been born in Berlin, and Burt interjected, "Truman was a bomber pilot. He bombed Berlin."

John Wayne – just like I'd seen him do in many movies – stopped as if he'd been shot at. His expression became very serious. He looked up from the book in front of him, turned in my direction, leaned toward me very slowly, looked me square in the eyes and asked, "Did you bomb your wife?"

Oh, mercy…Thank you, Burt…I was innocent, but the story was too complicated to explain…My silence convicted me and Wayne said, "You bastard, you!" then he signed the book for Margot:

"Margot – Be happy. John Wayne."

In the book THE FILMS OF JOHN WAYNE he wrote to our children:

"A lot of hard work and FUN. John Wayne."

"HAPPY" and "FUN" evidently meant a great deal to John Wayne. And why not? There can be no greater triumph in life than to be happy and to have fun. After all, that's really what it's about.

"Smitty" and the "Duke"

"I've been here before."

DEJA VU

The members of the Ponca City Air Museum thought it would be FUN to have an air show in 1990, but several things went wrong: Iraq invaded Kuwait and all military aircraft scheduled for our show were canceled; Our top act was to be Tom Jones, a leading aerobatics pilot, but he was killed in an air crash.

There was no other choice but to downgrade the event from an air show to a fly-in. So, as the founding president of the Ponca City Air Museum and a Colonel in the Confederate Air Force, I was able to get the CAF's B-17, Texas Raiders, to come to the fly-in.

When the Seventeen first arrived in Ponca City I had taken the liberty to go inside of it.

I sat in the cockpit alone. Time stopped. Then it ran backward and I left the present. I was not in a specific time. It was as if I were in a vacuum; eyes open, but not seeing; mind spinning, but not thinking. I did not focus on anything.

A lot of things had happened in the cockpit of a B-17, but there was not a specific incident. Rather, the force of all events impacted on me altogether and my emotions were over-loaded. Tears came to my eyes and I wept uncontrollably. I asked myself, "Why am I doing this?"

The more I struggled to overcome such sensitivity the weaker I became until I finally relaxed and let it take me – wherever it wanted to take me. I didn't really care. For as weak as I was in total surrender, I actually felt cleansed and relieved of all tensions in my life. I was overflowing with both happiness and sorrow. I was not confined, but open. I was somehow everywhere, having gone nowhere. It was a total experience of all times and all places at a single intersection.

The experience wiped me out and I went home. Margot asked me how the fly-in was shaping up. The only thing I told her was, "I will never again, get into the cockpit of a B-17."

"Ohhh, yes you will," she said.

The Confederate Air Force crew, who traveled with and tended the ancient war-bird, had the opportunity to witness the reaction of those who came to pay their respects to the old "memory machine."

According to them, some people just stared in silence. Others would talk to their wives, children, grandchildren or – total strangers, expressing themselves about the memories that came. Then there were some who would gently touch the big bird: a tire, a wing, or the tail. In silence, tears would come to their eyes.

As the fly-in came to a close I was asked if I wanted to go with the crew to their next stop in Gainesville, Texas. "You could even get a little stick-time."

Not meaning to be unappreciative of an opportunity that thousands of pilots would have grabbed without hesitation, I asked for time to think about it and told the crew chief what I'd told Margot, that I could never return to the cockpit of a B-17.

The crew chief, a Confederate Air Force Colonel, said, "I understand. I saw you when you came out of the cockpit the other day and I knew that you'd had a pretty rough flight."

The Seventeen felt much heavier on the controls than I had remembered. Even so, when I thought about making a few turns, the Seventeen read my mind and performed them flawlessly. That part of it had not left me.

As we hummed along, I paid a silent tribute to the wonderful B-17; the men who had flown her and who had been wounded and who had died inside of her; the designers who had worked out the bugs and were able to put so much airplane into the sky; the men and women in the factories that produced it; the American citizens who paid for it and the wisdom and courage of the military and the congressmen who committed their reputations to the defense of the United States.

"How long has it been since you've flown a B-17?" the pilot in the right seat asked me. He was an airline Captain who volunteered his time to ferry the Seventeen from location to location.

After thinking a moment, I replied that the last time I flew a B-17 was in 1945.

The airline Captain smiled at me and confessed, "I'm not even that old."

The truth was that, on that day in 1990, when I was back on the controls and flying a B-17, I wasn't that old either. I felt as if I were twenty years old, back when I was wondering what it would be like to be twenty-one – so many years ago.

After landing at our destination the engines coughed and belched in protest to being shut down. I dropped to the ground from the old bird, walked away and turned back for one final look at the distinguished silhouette of the famous B-17. I felt more than good. It had been FUN and I was – HAPPY.

So??? What's WRONG with that?

SKYWAR

The sky is a world in which men died,
In giving the best of their hopes and pride,
"For what?" you ask, "Was it suicide?"
Normal people would avoid such a ride,
For if God had intended for men to fly,
He'd of given 'em wings to soar in the sky,
Instead o' legs and feet to grovel around,
As lesser creatures who stay on the ground,
But the trouble with Man, as God found out,
Was that Man, above others, is a gadabout,
And he never stayed where he was supposed to be,
Even leaving the earth in his desire to be free.
And Man, it turns out, is really the worst,
When it comes to wars, with which he's cursed,
It's not enough to fight on the earth,
The SKY is the place to prove your worth,
Since it's hostile enough just to be up there,
In that treacherous world, Of what? Thin Air,
Where the temperature is measured in minus degrees,
Who's fate for man and machine is to freeze,
Yes, the air gets so thin that everything dies,
Such are the hazards for those in the sky,
And if that's not enough to discourqage the weak,
There's the miracle of flight that makes it unique
For how can it fly when it weighs so damn much?
With metal, n-fuel, n-engines, n'such,
Then add the guns, n-bombs and also the men,
"Please make it *fly*!" "Do I hear an 'Amen'?"
And if it happens we can rise up from the ground,
The name of the game is The Lost and the Found,
Cause the weather is *stinko*. It's really perverse,
And as bad as things are, they always get worse,
Since what was up turns out to be down,
Even left and right get turned all around,
And if that's not enough to make you sweat,
You aint seen nuthin', At least not yet,
If it's not ice on the wings to kill your lift,

It'll be something else to get you miffed,
Like the warning of Proverbs, where wisdom is found,
"Keep thine airspeed up, lest a stall smyte thee down..."
Or an engine that sounds like it's coming apart,
Just one more flaw in your Fortress rampart,
From which you must fight on your way to Berlin,
Can it really hold up? Will you make it till then?
And should you get back, you'll do it again,
And again, and again, and again, and again,
Almost three dozen times of flying again,
To finish your tour, if you make it till then,
Sometimes people ask, "What was it like to be up there,
To penetrate deep into Hitler's lair?"
"What's it like to see men die,
In that world of air, that battleground-sky?"
Well, you really can't say and do it right,
How awesome it is, Yet a magnificent sight,
Of men and machines in the ultimate test,
Of life's spectrum from the worst to the best,
Just how much can you take? How well can you fight?
When you're numbed by fear, until you ignite,
With a strength you've never known before,
Such is the magic brought forth in war,
Have you ever seen a sky jam-packed full of planes?
I don't mean a dozen or so, Let me try to explain,
Not even a hundred, or two, but *TEN TIMES MORE*,
High above England, from shore – to shore,
Over TWO-THOUSAND ships amassed for attack,
But not as many as had *never* come back,
An impending storm from a metallic sky,
Who's mission and purpose is to rectify,
But at a cost so high to those on both sides,
The result of ideals when they fail and collide,
Yes, the sky *is* a world in which men died,
But never again, *PLEASE*, Let peace abide.

Truman J. Smith,
Lt. Colonel, U. S. Air Force, Retired

POST SCRIPTUM

Just as THE WRONG STUFF was going to press I received a large photograph and a blessing from Pope Albert the IVth.

No. The photograph and blessing were from my mentor in flying the B-17 during the war 52 years ago, Earnest "Moon" Baumann.

"Moon," the rounder, when I knew him back then, became an actor and in 1996 he was playing the part of the Pope in a theater in San Antonio, Texas, so he sent me his picture in costume.

Considering his lack of restraint and the contrast of his character with any religious figure, I was really surprised by the idea of "Moon" as a "Pope."

But then, when Moon and I were flying combat in the skies of Europe in 1944, there was a guy, 24 years old, the same as Moon, who was fighting with the Polish resistance down below us. His name was Karol Wojtyla. He was a poet. And like Moon would eventually become, he was an actor.

Well, Karol's life took a change. He became a Roman Catholic priest in 1946. By 1967, Wojtyla became the Cardinal of Krakow, Poland. And within eleven years, he changed his name when he became Pope John Paul II.

So when I got the photograph of "Moon" as the "Pope," a question came to mind: was Pope John Paul II anything like Moon was 52 years ago when they were both free-spirited youths?

Since I couldn't very easily ask him, I asked Margot, my wife, "Do you suppose that the Pope could have been anything like Moon was fifty-two years ago?"

Margot smiled her reply, saying, "If the Pope hadn't been like Moon and the rest of you would-be rogues, why else would he always be wearing the self-contented Mona Lisa smile of his?"

MISSIONS

Page	Mission#	Day		Destination	Flying Time
21	1.	Sa.	4/8/44	Quakenbruck, Germany	5:30
43	2.	Mo.	4/10/44	Diest Schaffen, Germany	5:15
55	3.	Tu.	4/11/44	Stettin, Poliz (Poland)	11:00
70	4.	Tu.	4/18/44	(Berlin) Barnewitz, Germany	9:25
79	5.	Th.	4/20/44	Fruges, France	5:15
83	6.	Sa.	4/29/44	(Berlin) Magdeburg, Germany	8:20
95	7.	Mo.	5/1/44	Le Grosseiller, France	6:30
100	8.	Mo.	5/8/44	Berlin, Germany	9:00
103	9.	Tu.	5/9/44	Laon Couvrais, France	5:25
104	10.	Th.	5/11/44	Brussels, Belgium	6:00
106	11.	Fr.	5/12/44	Zwickau, Germany	9:15
118	12.	Sa.	5/13/44	Osnabruck, Germany	6:35
136	13.	Sa.	5/20/44	Aachen, Germany	5:40
147	14.	Th.	5/25/44	Liege, Belgium	7:00
155	15.	Su.	5/28/44	Konigsborn, Germany	8:00
155	16.	Mo.	5/29/44	Leipzig, Germany	8:00
156	17.	Tu.	5/30/44	Watten-Stracourt, France	4:45
156	18.	We.	5/31/44	Hamm, Germany	7:00
157	19.	Th.	6/2/44	Equihen-Wimereux, France	5:00
162	20.	Tu.	6/7/44	Niorte, France	9:00
172	21.	We.	6/14/44	Florennes / Juzaine, France	6:15
173	22.	Th.	6/15/44	Hannover, Germany	8:30
175	23.	Su.	6/18/44	Hannover, Germany	6:45
177	24.	Tu.	6/20/44	Fallersleben, Germany	8:00
180	25.	We.	6/21/44	Berlin, Germany	9:30

Page	Mission#	Day		Destination	Flying Time
189	26.	Th.	6/22/44	Paris, France	6:25
199	27.	Sa.	6/24/44	Wesermunde, Germany	7:15
208	28.	Su.	6/25/44	Special: Grenoble, France	9:00
243	29.	Th.	7/6/44	Sautres Court, France	4:30
248	30.	Sa.	7/8/44	Conches, France	6:00
254	31.	We.	7/12/44	Munich, Germany	9:30
264	32.	Fr.	7/14/44	Special: Alps, France	10:35
273	33.	Mo.	7/24/44	St. Lo, France	5:00
274	34.	Tu.	7/25/44	St. Lo, France	5:45
285	35.	Fr.	7/28/44	Merseburg, Germany	9:00

INDEX

LET DOWN? HELL, I DON'T EVEN KNOW WHERE I AM!!!